RICHARD YOUNGS is a senior fellow at Carnegie Europe and a professor of international relations at the University of Warwick. He has authored eleven previous books, including, most recently, *Europe's Eastern Crisis: The Geopolitics of Asymmetry* (2017), *The Puzzle of Non-Western Democracy* (2015) and *Europe in the New Middle East* (2014).

Since the economic recession of 2008, the EU has been hit by a series of crises, most recently the UK's decision to leave the union following the Brexit referendum. In light of this, questions have been raised about the need to reform the whole model of European integration, with the aim of making the union more flexible and more accountable.

In this book, Richard Youngs proposes an alternative vision of European cooperation and shows how the EU must reinvent itself if it is to survive. He argues that citizens should play a greater role in European decision-making, that there should be radically more flexibility in the process of integration and that Europe needs to take a new, more coherent, approach to questions of defence and security. In proposing this model for a 'reset' version of Europe, Youngs reinvigorates the debate around the future of Europe and puts forward a new agenda for the future of the EU.

'An original and provocative contribution to the continuing debate about the future of Europe. The EU at the time of writing seems to be recovering from the succession of problems created by the financial crisis and its impact on the euro. As Richard Youngs stresses, much more is needed. "Output democracy" is not enough – reform must be driven by citizenship engagement and activism, and on a wide scale.'

Lord Anthony Giddens

'The European Union has muddled through many crises in recent years. If it is to survive in the age of populism, and indeed to thrive, it must urgently rethink its purpose and methods. EU leaders would do well to read Richard Youngs's book. He is surely right in arguing that the EU needs much more flexibility in what it does, and much greater democratic legitimacy for it.'

Anton La Guardia, Deputy Foreign Editor at
The Economist* and co-author of *Unhappy Union

'In a bold attempt to jumpstart new thinking on the future of the EU, Richard Youngs is not afraid to challenge conventions. He rightly encourages leaders to base Europe's future course on European citizens' own compasses. Let us hope his book leads to more creative solutions to the EU's democracy challenge.'

Marietje Schaake, MEP

'While their governments struggle with multiple crises, European citizens feel they run into the wall of Brussels consensus. In this stimulating book, Richard Youngs rightly diagnoses the need to reconnect democratic civic energies with innovative policy-making – for a continent that is ready for a new politics.'

Luuk van Middelaar, author of *The Passage to Europe*

NEW DIRECTIONS FOR THE EU

EUROPE
RESET

RICHARD YOUNGS

I.B. TAURIS
LONDON · NEW YORK

Published in 2018 by
I.B.Tauris & Co. Ltd
London • New York
www.ibtauris.com

ISBN: 978 1 78831 057 4
eISBN: 978 1 78672 320 8
ePDF: 978 1 78673 320 7

A full CIP record for this book is available from the British Library
A full CIP record is available from the Library of Congress

Library of Congress Catalog Card Number: available

Text design and typesetting by Tetragon, London
Printed and bound by CPI Group (UK) Ltd, Croydon, CRO 4YY

Contents

Preface

In recent years the European Union (EU) has often given the impression that it is coming apart at the seams. Problems have piled up, revealing discord, policy failure and public exasperation. Economic recession has been followed by terrorist attacks, a refugee surge, the Brexit vote and a wave of nationalist populism. In 2017, the mood has shifted towards a sense of optimism that the EU is finally moving beyond these multiple crises. Yet the Union is still in fragile health. In his inauguration speech in May 2017, French president Emmanuel Macron acknowledged that the EU must now be 'reformed and relaunched'. Few would disagree with him. The EU has been bombarded with so many problems during the last decade that the need for change appears self-evident. But what type of reform is really needed? And is a major overhaul of the EU actually possible? If European leaders believe an era of renewed unity and momentum is now beginning, will they take the opportunity for such root-and-branch reform?

Governments and EU institutions have been talking about and promising reform ever since the economic crisis began in 2008, and indeed even before that. In practice, they have declined to support any radical change to the existing model of EU integration. At a supposedly crucial summit in Bratislava in September 2016, billed as a meeting where a new course for European integration would be plotted, leaders spent a weekend talking earnestly about their desire to reconnect with ordinary people – yet they did so locked inside a castle, on a hilltop, cordoned off from the city and its inhabitants. They then posed on a Danube cruise ship, ostensibly to symbolise that they were all together in the same boat. Apocryphally, the boat had to return to shore prematurely: low water levels meant it could not make its journey. And indeed, six months later, at their March 2017 summit celebrating the sixtieth anniversary of the Treaty of Rome, governments categorically failed to deliver on the promised EU relaunch.

In this book, I propose an ambitious reform agenda that would change the core model of EU integration. I stake out a position that is hopeful and empowering, but also realistically cautionary. On the one hand, I adopt a positive stance in suggesting that European integration can prosper. I do this in very deliberately counter-intuitive contrast with the widespread fatalism stoked by Europe's crisis years. I explore how the EU can pick up the pieces from a calamitous decade of successive difficulties, and also how it can adjust to a less benign, more atavistic world order.

On the other hand, I stress that the magnitude of change required is considerable. The spirit of European cooperation and solidarity can only be replenished if EU governments and institutions are willing to contemplate fundamentally new ideas. The book's broadly constructive stance is offset by a warning that complacency is as serious a danger as self-destructive gloom. My contention is that if the EU is to thrive it must be radically rethought. A redesigned integration project must be based on Europe as it is, not on Europe as we might wish it to be – and this requires profound adjustment of the 'European project'.

The book tries to break through the standard pro-European versus anti-European debate. In this sense, I suggest there are twin dangers: if putative disintegration is one, governments' lack of adaptability in how they pursue European cooperation is another. While European leaders have been forced into short-term crisis management by the succession of emergencies they have faced in recent years, these crises actually intensify the need for structural adaptation of the integration model – the kind of change that is still nowhere near being realised.

Indeed, one of the main concerns underpinning the book is that governments' reform impulse may if anything be fading. As the EU apparently moves into a more positive phase, the greater danger may be the inaction of 'frog in slowly boiling water' syndrome – a risk that elites believe they have now navigated the worst of the EU's various problems and so there is no need to rethink the European project. After the failure of Marine Le Pen and Geert Wilders to win power in France and the Netherlands, respectively, in the first half of 2017, and as the Franco-German motor shows new signs of dynamism, a sense of optimism is welcome. It would be wrong to conclude from the reassuring change of mood, however, that the EU has addressed the root causes of its crises and can now simply return to business as usual.

This book adopts a perspective that is different from that of other accounts of the EU's recent travails. When the eurozone crisis began in 2008, books and articles appeared in which financial and economic matters predominated. Since then, the EU's crisis has deepened and extended into other areas of concern. Nearly a decade on, my aims in this book are to offer an updated assessment of the latest phases of the crisis and to add to current work by analysing its multiple components – the euro's struggle for survival, the surge of populist nativism, the refugee influx, Brexit and new international threats – within a single conceptual framework. The book's rationale is to provide the reader with a fully composite picture of the EU's various layers of crisis.

My core proposition is straightforward. I argue against old recipes for EU reform and in favour of fresher ideas – ideas that are more practical and realistic because they harness change emerging from within European societies. I do not propose a great leap forward to more centralised integration or, conversely, an unwound 'Europe of nation states'. Nor do I favour the kind of two-speed integration that many now tout as the best route forward for the Union. I reject both airy idealism and the fatalism of resurgent nationalism; my suggestions for a new approach to European integration more feasibly develop out of social change that is already happening across the continent.

Ever-onward integration is the foundational assumption that has made up the very air the EU breathes; today it needs another source of oxygen. The central thread of this book is the contention that this new source of integrative fuel must and can be found in empowering European citizens to map a new future for EU cooperation. Crucially, it shows that there are feasible pathways towards an alternative Europe by drawing on the views and activities of citizens' groups across the continent.

The EU's declared aim to reconnect with citizens is apparently widely supported but is also the hardest of long-standing reforms to pin down with precision – meaning that year after year nothing is done to address it. Indeed, the more I have followed EU reform efforts the more it seems to me that they amplify rather than soften the EU's shortcomings. This is what motivated me to write a book that does not simply advocate EU reform but highlights how many current changes move in the wrong direction.

Indeed, in many aspects of its response to today's crises, the EU resembles Charles Dickens's famous Circumlocution Office – an office ostensibly working for the people, but from whose labyrinth citizens always emerge further away from obtaining any clear, helpful decisions. Reflecting this unresponsiveness, the core narrative in Europe has become one of popular frustration and anger. In 2016, statues of ostriches with their heads buried in the sand were put up in the park next to the European Parliament; while the figures were apparently not designed to make a political point, the symbolism could not have been more eye-wateringly unfortunate – or apt.

And this leads into another core rationale for my writing this book. While many opinion essays and articles call for a renewed sense of European idealism and unity, it is surely not enough simply to assert this desire without any kind of grounded, analytical explanation of how this is feasible. Grand injunctions that are not backed up by a realisable theory of change are unlikely to serve the European project well. This book attempts to map out just such an alternative process of change.

Iconic Spanish philosopher José Ortega y Gasset seemed to pre-empt much of the EU philosophy in his often-cited aphorism that 'Spain is the problem; Europe is the solution.' The quip applies to the mindset of many other member states beyond the Iberian Peninsula; indeed, its spirit was emblematic for a whole generation of southern, central and Eastern European politicians coming out of democratic transition. Yet it no longer quite captures the essence of the continent's integration challenge. In essence, in this book I argue that an updated version of the famous line would read: 'Existing EU templates are the problem; new types of European democracy, the solution.'

I do not argue this in a way that over-idealises European citizens or envisages them magically converging on harmonious unity. The EU needs to be designed as a way of managing differences and diversity; the trouble begins when it is used as a vehicle to obliterate such differences. If we cannot expect divergences across Europe to disappear, nor can we expect them to be well managed if citizens do not have a better and stronger say in how this is done. My focus on bottom-up participative processes is meant as a complement to and not a substitute for top-down reforms; good leadership and strong institutional capacities are undoubtedly important, and nothing in my argument should be read as implying otherwise. Yet elite-led change is surely insufficient in itself and still too much of the focus in EU debates.

I am conscious that it is difficult to make a citizen-centred argument today because those wishing the European project ill have sought to appropriate the discourse of democratic participation and flexibility. Indeed, one common view holds that there has been rather *too much* popular influence over EU decisions in the last two years. One of my core concerns here is to urge Europhiles not to accept this: citizen influence and avenues for diversity should be seen as tenets for revitalising European integration and not as its defeat.

In recent years, articles about populism have become ubiquitous. Analysts and journalists have habitually seen the EU's crisis as one of rising populism. My take is different: populism in itself is not the crisis; rather, the crisis's essence is the malfunctioning structure of European cooperation, of which populism is one expression. The lesson I take from the catalogue of political shocks that have rocked European and international politics in the last two years is that liberal internationalism needs to find a way to speak to those rooted in national and local identities. While illiberal nativists clearly bring many ills, mainstream elites have also been disingenuous in using the populist label to disqualify views that reflect legitimate grievances with their own performance and with current EU policies – furthermore, some of their assertions in 2017 that nativist populism has now been defeated may also prove to be premature.

When Adolfo Suárez adroitly led Spain's democratic transition 40 years ago, he rebutted the criticisms of those who suggested that the country faced too many immediate challenges to worry about a far-reaching political redesign; he did so by saying that Spain had to 'change the plumbing without cutting off the water'. Spain's current rising centrist political star, Albert Rivera, has sometimes used this Suárez quote in the context of Spain's post-2010 crisis.[1] The phrase indeed captures exactly what the EU must do now, and it stands as a riposte to those who think that reforming the model of integration can be repeatedly postponed as governments deal with the immediate effects of the crisis.

This is the spirit in which I have couched this book: trying to maintain a focus on the positive potential of European cooperation, but also stressing the scale of qualitative change needed if the EU is to move forward. I try to chart a course between the position that says 'the EU is doomed' and the one that says 'the EU model is fine'. Even if readers think that the book does not get everything right in this sense, I hope at least to convince them that some kind of analytical recalibration is necessary and overdue – and that those who care about Europe's future now need to engage much more seriously in this endeavour.

I have also written the book as a form of exploratory atonement or self-criticism. As an analyst, I am part of a community that has tended to stick to a particular EU script and as a result sometimes looks increasingly out of touch with deeper social change. This is a modest attempt to acknowledge this failing and move the debate forward to new ground. Moreover, I write the book as a UK citizen who has lived for many years on the continent and is thus directly touched by *both* overzealous British Euro-negativity and the inverse tendency elsewhere passively to accept the integration status quo – the very polar opposites whose coexistence poses the book's central puzzle.

Several experts provided extremely helpful and extensive comments and input on the text, including Cornelius Adebahr, Chris Bickerton, Claudia Chwalisz, Michael Emerson, Stefan Lehne, Pol Morillas, Kalypso Nicolaïdis, Vivien Pertusot, Charles Powell and Jan Zielonka. I am also grateful to colleagues at Carnegie Europe and the Department for Politics and International Studies at the University of Warwick for vital research support, and to Joanna Godfrey and her team at I.B.Tauris for their expert guidance.

Introduction

A many-layered crisis has plagued the European Union (EU) for a decade. European governments have struggled to keep the euro currency area together, as harsh recession has swept across the continent. Recriminations over an unprecedented influx of refugees and migrants have unleashed further tensions between the EU's member states. A series of tragic terror attacks in Europe has intensified citizens' feelings of insecurity and raised questions about the EU's relevance as a provider of stability. The rise of anti-establishment populist parties seems to threaten a wholesale, nativist counter-reformation against the EU's liberal foundations. And the UK's vote to leave the Union has left a sense of foreboding within Britain itself and throughout Europe. Often in recent years, the pillars of European integration seem to have been besieged simultaneously from within and from without.

As the EU has grappled with this series of epoch-defining crises, an expanding chorus of voices has come to call for fundamental change to European integration. For 60 years, the EU has functioned as a project of reconciliation, fusing peace building with liberal-market integration. After the strains and turmoil of recent times, many believe that a fundamental shift in rationale is overdue. Politicians and commentators have constantly stressed that the EU confronts an unprecedented range and depth of problems. Even if many believe the gravest moments of crisis may now have passed, there is widespread agreement that new forms of cooperation are required and that the EU must reinvent itself if it is to survive.

MULTIPLE CRISES

With the EU facing a multifaceted set of ongoing challenges, some circles in Brussels aptly refer to this as a 'poly-crisis'. Given the breadth and magnitude of Europe's troubles, it seems increasingly self-evident that things cannot continue as they are. Politicians and diplomats assert that new and innovative ways of rebuilding European cooperation are needed after this long period of adversity. In the last several years, few days have gone by without opinion pieces being published insisting that fundamental reform is needed to prevent the whole European project from dissolving in acrimony. In 2017, Emmanuel Macron's election has engendered a renewed sense of optimism; Angela Merkel's re-election in September 2017 was less than fully convincing, but also offers reassurance. But both these leaders have frequently warned that European integration needs to be rethought if further crises are to be averted.

Britain's exit will have profound ramifications not just for the UK but for the broader process of European integration; it is the most dramatic wake-up call to date that the prevailing model of integration has left many people feeling alienated from the EU's complex and distant decision-making. The broader, much dissected populist surge now rubs uneasily against the EU project's core tenets. While Marine Le Pen and Geert Wilders did not win power in spring 2017, the factors feeding populism are still present across Europe.

Meanwhile, the eurozone crisis is far from definitively resolved. The euro has suffered numerous near-death experiences since 2008. The protracted and unedifying negotiations over Greece's third bail-out package in July 2015 took the EU closer to the precipice of self-destruction than ever before. While successive deals have been cobbled together between Greece and its creditors, the vitriol traded between governments has left a bitter aftertaste. The prospect of another bail-out crisis hovers constantly on the horizon and unresolved tensions still haunt policy debates in the eurozone.

The EU's international challenges are no less serious than these internal travails. The surge of refugees into Europe has combined with terror attacks to leave many citizens feeling acutely exposed. Security troubles have increasingly placed a strain on the EU's integration model. The international context is today not a self-contained domain of remote diplomacy, but an integral part of the EU's own crisis – it is an additional factor that enjoins deliberation on new modes of integration. Concerns over insecurity have spurred new commitments to deepen integration, but on occasion seem to be loosening rather than tightening the bearings that hold together current forms of European cooperation. In addition, for the first time Europe now faces a US president explicitly critical of the EU project. Donald Trump's erratic foreign policy more broadly exacerbates Europe's vulnerabilities to global threats.

Even as a sense of reborn potential grows in EU circles, these varied challenges remain unresolved. In its next phase of development, the EU requires an alternative approach to cooperation between European governments and citizens. Many politicians have made this point, and have done so over many years. Thinkers, writers, diplomats and journalists have argued that the EU cannot simply carry on in piecemeal, muddling-through mode. While Brexit would seem to make a change of approach almost unavoidable, the case for rethinking European integration was a strong one long before the UK held its epoch-making referendum. Now a new model must deal with the design problems of the euro, populism, security challenges and differences between member states over refugees and migrants, while also finding a way of keeping the UK constructively involved in continental cooperation. And it must do all this against a background narrative of uncertainty about the global order.

A RADICAL SHIFT

Clearly, this poly-crisis poses searching questions about the way the EU is designed. And yet extensive and radical change to European cooperation is nowhere near being given serious consideration. The common narrative of recent years – across the spectrum from Europhiles to Eurosceptics, from writers to politicians, from engaged activists to worldly diplomats – has been that things cannot go on as before.

Yet despite the seismic shock of Britain's exit, the basic forms of EU cooperation continue largely unchanged and reform efforts remain anaemic.

Meeting in Rome in March 2017 to celebrate the European Communities' sixtieth anniversary, leaders promised to work up ideas for a fresh start. However, they failed to identify what this might entail. The anniversary sparked a positive burst of renewed commitments to European unity, but no concrete plan for recalibrating the EU. It fostered a stirring sense of defiance against Euro-detractors and against Brexit – and this took precedence over any enquiring spirit of reinvention. Deflating months of anticipation and high expectation, the Rome Declaration agreed at the anniversary summit reads like standard Euro-speak – an awkward collection of each member state's particular concerns and a well-worn list of generic policy aims, bereft of radically new ideas.[1]

Existing routes to cooperation may have crumbled, but governments have done little proactively or enthusiastically to explore possible new paths to solidarity between states and between citizens. On the one hand, pro-Europeans now push with renewed confidence for 'more Europe', wanting powers to be centralised at the European level in line with integration templates that have dominated discussions for 60 years. On the other hand, doubters insist on 'less Europe'. Although many politicians and officials recognise the need to move beyond the 'more versus less' dichotomy, in practice they have not yet advanced anything very concrete or immediately operational as a different template for EU integration. Moreover, to the extent that many believe the EU has now turned the corner into a more positive phase, the clamour for qualitatively new ideas may once again be ebbing.

This backdrop shapes the most pressing questions facing Europe today. Is it really the case that many core tenets of EU integration need to be rethought, or is business as usual in fact a perfectly viable option? If the so-called 'European project' of integration and cooperation really does need to be reinvented, how is this to be done? With so much febrile discord in recent years, what is needed to rebuild solidarity between Europe's citizens and between its different governments? Is this at all possible? Can the EU bend, so as not to break? Does the ailing patient simply need a stronger dose of the integration medicine, or does it need a different curative regime altogether?

While calls are heard for far-reaching change to and within the EU, such change fails to materialise. Many talk of the need for more flexible and looser approaches to European integration, and yet agreement remains elusive on what these might look like. Even those who claim to be putting forward extensive reform plans are not going nearly far enough in the scale of change they envision. For a decade, the EU has been hit by successive waves of crisis – economic, political and security- and identity-related – and yet the ideas for change that are on policy-makers' tables today largely tinker around the edges of the prevailing model of integration.

Under this standard model, integration is defined as the pursuit of an ever-wider range of centralised EU policy competences, governed by firm legal rules and embedded decision-making processes involving the European Commission, the European Parliament and other supra-national bodies; combined with increasingly powerful roles for national governments in select issue areas; all applied with uniformity except where states negotiate otherwise; and run with only relatively weak channels of bottom-up democratic input. The model stands relatively unchanged after many years and appears to be immutable against the raging storm of crisis. In its resistance to far-reaching change, the EU sometimes seems akin to a church, in which the sermons may respond to evolving concerns but the liturgy brooks no change.

This raises the uncomfortable possibility that the EU is in fact beyond any major degree of qualitative reform. Given that calls for reform have been heard for a long time and yet very little has been done in response, some argue that there are only two options: either the EU ploughs ahead towards full political union and deeper integration based on the existing model of integration, or governments decide it is time to disband the Union. The tendency to frame the debate in terms of such a binary choice helps explain why the EU has not morphed into something different – and why European leaders muddle along trying to avoid fundamental change.

Taking a different approach, in this book I argue that qualitatively different forms of European cooperation are both possible and necessary. I explain why existing ideas for EU reform fall short of what is required to salvage and revive the spirit of solidarity. And I try to think through what a truly radical change would look like. Many articles and books call for an EU that is more democratic and gives citizens a stronger say in decisions – indeed, this has become an almost default line of advocacy. I attempt to go further than existing accounts by laying out concrete ideas for how very general conceptual thinking on a flexible, less uniform and more participative process of European integration could be translated into reality. I also go further than standard analysis by examining emerging citizens' initiatives.

The book elaborates both a different kind of analytical explanation of the poly-crisis and a series of concrete policy ideas. It proposes a genuinely new beginning for European integration. It explores the means of restoring solidarity from a kind of ground zero for EU cooperation. This is a path that rejects standard ideas for deeper integration but also eschews sceptics' doubts over the viability of the whole European project. It is also different from proposals for a minimalist 'Europe of nations' based on the restoration of traditional governmental sovereignty.

My notion of an alternative Europe is one driven by bottom-up citizen participation. It is likely to house a degree of both deeper cen-tralised integration and reinforced nation-state policies. But it will be neither a United States of Europe nor a Europe of nation states; nor will it be a two-speed Europe. Rather, it will incorporate an eclectic mix of policy dynamics, and a balance of cooperation and diversity – a balance that will be more directly determined by citizens as lead protagonists.

To these ends, I advocate three levels of policy initiatives. First, I map out a 'Compact of European Citizens'. Second, I offer a template for radical flexibility in European integration. And third, I propose novel means of pursuing European security. I explain in detail what each of these would entail and how each policy idea differs from the existing and well-worn integration script.

Of course, venturing concrete options for change will open the book up to objections that talk of 'bringing citizens back in' is far too starry-eyed, as today's fractious European populations are unlikely to agree on crucial issues. It seems to me that this response misunderstands the case for democracy. Deeper democracy is needed precisely because differences are so marked, not as a means of magically conjuring pan-European harmony but as a process necessary for managing diversity and divergence. Far from advocating a vapid 'people power', I argue that more meaningful citizen participation could help reinforce the formal, institutional power that is needed to deal with Europe's contemporary challenges.

In a similar vein, many insist either that far-reaching change is not possible or that radical reordering would traduce the founding ethos of the European project. I believe the very opposite. The ethos of the European dream is more likely to flounder if novel, out-of-the-box options are *not* considered. Governments, EU institutions, analysts, civil society organisations (CSOs) and other actors will look increasingly false in their frequent rhetorical calls for new ideas if in practice they then baulk at any radical change to existing integration processes and policies.

EXISTENTIAL ISSUES

Of course, many books and articles have been written on one or another dimension of the EU crisis. My contribution adds to these accounts by linking together the different aspects, drawing on updated empirical information and reflecting on the future of European integration through the prism of participative citizenship. Within this general framework, and against the perturbed backdrop of multiple crises, I focus on three specific strands of possible reform. These strands reflect the standard narrative that the future EU must be more democratic, more flexible and more secure.

> *Participative Europe.* I ask how the EU can be democratised, after different elements of the poly-crisis have made the Union's notorious democratic deficit far more acute. How can we actually 'bring the citizens back in'? Can a sense of solidarity and

European identity be rescued from the bottom up? How can European politicians engage with sectors of the population that have begun to turn against the EU?

Flexible Europe. There is a general feeling that the EU needs to become looser and more flexible. But what does this mean in practice, beyond minor tinkering with the current institutional set-up? What policies can be developed that take on board the widening diversity between member states that the crisis has revealed? How do we rebuild a core and basic sense of European solidarity that allows simultaneously for a healthy expression of diversity? How far can such flexibility prove itself valuable to the challenges related to Brexit?

Secure Europe. I explore how security imperatives now raise questions for external strategy, for internal policies and for the general design of the EU project. This is because I believe that this is an integral part of the EU crisis, and not simply a tangential add-on. What kind of new thinking is needed to address European citizens' concerns over security? How must the traditional model of integration adapt to make the EU more secure within a changing global order? What can be done in EU foreign policy to help rebuild intra-EU solidarity and the legitimacy of the overall European project?

The EU's overarching challenge is to combine these different strands of reform – participation, flexibility and security – and address possible tensions and trade-offs between them. Is it really possible to hand back ownership and direction to citizens without cooperation collapsing and reactionary isolationism prevailing? And is it really possible to have a more flexible, less centralised, less heavily bureaucratic and less constraining model of integration that does not simply entail *less* cooperation between states and between citizens?

Europe is caught in an impasse: most agree that cooperation is needed to deal with the battery of serious challenges that the Union

finds itself obliged to tackle, and yet citizens now say they want accountability brought back closer to home. Is there any way this circle can be
squared? Can pathways to effective cooperation be mapped out that
also address people's apparent desire to recover local identities and
democratic control? Again, seeking to move beyond the somewhat
idealised menus of reform routinely served up, I explore these tensions
and look for ways in which an alternative Europe can embrace rather
than breezily wish away such trade-offs.

A CIVIC ETHOS

In order to address these questions, the book develops its argument in
a number of steps. It explains the structural nature of the EU's crisis,
and then suggests why existing reform options are misdirected, before
moving on to lay out ideas for change based on a European civic ethos.
After this introduction, Chapter 1 disaggregates the different dimensions of the EU's poly-crisis. It explains why, underlying each specific
area of policy turmoil, the crisis denotes a set of challenges to the basic
structure of European integration. I contend that, even if care is needed
not to exaggerate the extent of the crisis, this structural dimension
cannot be dismissed.

Chapter 2 examines the ideas most commonly advocated to overcome the current crisis. It laments that most debates replay long-standing
ways of analysing the EU, rather than seeking a qualitatively different
prism through which integration can be assessed and revised. Pressing
ahead with deeper integration is unlikely to address the roots of the
EU crisis. Conversely, if governments start to unwind integration, or in
some cases choose to detach themselves from the European project – as
the UK is now doing – the autonomy they gain is unlikely to help them
solve today's problems. The standard 'more versus less' dichotomy is a
deeply unsatisfactory framework for thinking about the future of EU
cooperation.

Having mapped out the nature of the poly-crisis and the challenge
it represents, the book explores alternative ways forward. Chapter 3

unpacks the EU's growing democracy problem. It examines the lack of effective democratic accountability and legitimacy that cuts across the different dimensions of the EU's predicament. Talk of the Union's democracy shortfall has been prominent during the crises of the last decade. The chapter argues, however, that it is important to distinguish between what are in fact quite different components of this snowballing problem.

Based on this diagnostic, Chapters 4 and 5 map out a different route to democratising the integration project, based on open-ended and more critical civic engagement. European cooperation needs to move beyond a focus on union between states to a notion of partnership between citizens. The EU must above all be an amplifier for citizens' voices. This will entail combined processes of direct and indirect democratic participation. I detail the civic initiatives that have either emerged or gathered momentum in the wake of the crisis, and explain how these need to be extended in more ambitious directions. To this end, I propose the aforementioned 'Compact of European Citizens'. Crucially, this flows from a bottom-up framework of political change and power contestation – a framework that offers a more promising route forward than existing EU reform options because it works with the grain of unfolding social development.

Chapter 6 contends that an overriding feature of today's Europe is diversity: a growing divergence in policy preferences, aims and values between countries and between societies. In a more divergent Europe it is unlikely that any single solution to given problems can be acceptable or appropriate to all. The EU's challenge today is not so much to find single, optimal policy templates, but to allow different parts of the European population different ways of expressing broadly common goals. The chapter argues against the notions of a two-speed or multiple-speed Europe that have been prominent in recent debates. Rather, it advocates a more radical form of flexible integration based around practically oriented policy communities; flexibility *within* and not merely between member states; and a concept of 'democratic flexibility' that is very different from the forms of EU-variable geometry that experts and politicians have traditionally advocated.

Chapter 7 examines the security and international dimensions of the crisis. While Europe needs more commonly and more effectively managed borders, the EU risks relying too heavily on an assumption that such controls are the primary way to guarantee European security and thus save the integration project. The chapter proposes new forms of interaction with the outside world that could do more to revive the spirit of European cooperation – novel forms that go beyond the simple and standard injunction that the EU needs 'a more common foreign and security policy'. It also suggests ways to give international policy a citizens' dimension. All this invites new perspectives, to the extent that analysis of EU institutional redesigns invariably omits the security aspect. Today, this aspect is as much a part of the poly-crisis as internal institutional questions, and a better fusion is required between external and internal European challenges.

SOLIDARITY FROM SCRATCH

My central concern through the book is to turn the debate about democratic reform in a more positive direction. When political elites and many analysts acknowledge that a new, more inclusive and flexible Union is required, they tend to couch this as a grudging tactical adjustment to citizens' disgruntlement. At most they see wider civic participation as an unavoidable expedient – as damage limitation to placate a restless populace. In contrast, I conceive a reform impulse led by civic empowerment as a positive opportunity that might open up the possibility of a better form of European cooperation and make EU institutional capacities more effective.

The European enigma is that a more malleable integration mould is needed to salvage the Union's core spirit. The EU should be reimagined as an umbrella framework that safeguards citizens' different policy and ideational choices – and allows these choices both to coexist benignly and to be fashioned through local and national, as well as European participative channels. Citizens need reasons to see the Union as empowering, rather than forbidding and didactic. Solidarity should mean defending the right to make different choices within a common web of mutual support. When convergence around a certain set of policy prescriptions takes place, it must come about from a gradual and bottom-up process of local demand and conviction, not through the diktats of a supposedly enlightened and well-meaning elite.

The future model of integration must build a balance of productive roles for citizens, sub-national actors, nation states and European rules. And it must ensure that these different levels of cooperation fuse together far more harmoniously than has been the case so far – recognising that top-down and bottom-up dynamics are equally important and need to be more evenly balanced. Participation is needed at multiple levels – local, national and European. To the extent that much effective participation will be structured at the national level this would accord the arena of the nation state more of a role than most templates for deeper integration allow for. Yet this is not a role that privileges the traditional notion of national sovereignty, but rather one that conceives and harnesses the national democratic sphere as one vital component of a new process of participative integration.

Some will feel it is not at all possible to enhance flexibility and solidarity at the same time, and that there is a zero-sum choice to be made between national or local leeway and deeper cooperation between member states. This book takes a different line. The combination of popular self-determination with effective policy coordination will certainly not be easy. But the trajectory of the EU's crisis suggests these are far from being mutually exclusive, incompatible options.

There is certainly a problem with sceptics now calling for more direct popular participation simply as a means to undermine European integration. However, this disingenuous ploy should not blind us to the ways in which more participative and direct accountability can serve the European project positively. The tendency to conflate calls for direct popular input with Eurosceptic nativism is erroneous. I certainly do not contend that citizen participation is capable of dissolving the tensions that currently beset European integration or is a substitute for more effective formal institutional power – far from it. Yet giving citizens more control and more ability to influence decisions is surely one potential way to mollify their current introspection, soften their distrust of the EU and help repair today's badly damaged solidarity between nations. Such participation can be the much-needed yeast to Europe's unleavened integration project.

The climb to an alternative Europe will clearly be a steep one. My overarching contention is that that the EU's rethink must include new voices and involve a fully participative process of consultation. A reset European project must at its core be about people-based democracy and, through this, about finding effective ways to build a new spirit of mutualism between citizens. To avert a wholesale meltdown of the European dream, the EU's whole *raison d'être* must evolve, from reconciliation between nations to democracy among citizens.

CHAPTER ONE

Confusion's Masterpiece
The European Poly-Crisis

The EU's crisis has been multifaceted. Vitriolic invective has at times reached unprecedented levels between national governments in some areas of policy; economic strains persist; barriers and controls are reappearing at borders between member states; and the unsettling possibility of a populist-driven turn to more insular and intolerant identities discolours politics across the continent. The existence of so many different elements of crisis together suggests that there is something *structurally* amiss with European integration.

This chapter outlines the different strands of the poly-crisis. It assesses how far the crisis represents a *systemic* challenge to the current template of European integration. My aim here is not to delve deeply into each individual area of policy, but rather to explain how each dimension of the crisis reveals common, structural faults in the process of European integration – and to show that these systemic failings persist, even now that governments and EU institutions feel that the worst is over. This is the chronicle of the EU's near-death – if not precisely foretold, then certainly a long time in visible gestation.

THE BREXIT EFFECT

There has, of course, been exhaustive commentary on the UK's vote to leave the EU. What is relevant to this book is not the detail of the Brexit campaign per se or internal post-referendum debates in the UK, but how Britain's decision rebounds on the broader process of European integration.

Many EU leaders and officials insist that Brexit both requires and enables the Union to accelerate towards deeper integration. Since the summer of 2016, a number of proposals have been forthcoming for a rapid move to political union. The French and German foreign ministers released such a plan in July 2016. Commission president Jean-Claude Juncker and party leaders in the European Parliament have forwarded this line of argument many times. Some experts are also convinced that the only solution after the UK's decision is to move ahead with political union, against public opposition if necessary, and leaving aside more flexible integration templates.[1]

The increasingly acrimonious politics of Brexit have made many EU elites dig in their heels ever more firmly against flexible adjustments to the integration model. Key players such as Juncker, Council president Donald Tusk, chief Brexit negotiator Michel Barnier and European Parliament party leaders have all explicitly insisted that the scope for à la carte, pick-and-choose flexibility must be drastically limited as a result of the UK vote. Their logic is that the European project must now be shored up by ensuring that Brexit does not open the way for any broader questioning of the EU's existing cornerstone structures.

The positive line of thinking is that Brexit represents an opportunity for the EU, removing the most contrarian member state and clearing the way for deeper and more effective integration. Optimists note that polls carried out since the referendum suggest that citizens in other countries look at the chaos in Britain and now reject any idea that leaving the Union could be good for their country.[2]

Behind the official views, however, Brexit has also widened differences between member states over the EU's future. Some politicians have put forward a contrasting line, namely that integration needs to slow down and be rethought while the EU acts as flexibly as possible in constructing a positive relationship with the UK. Central and Eastern European countries have been vocal in pressing for a repatriation of powers to national governments and insisting that France and Germany be prevented from using Brexit as a platform from which to accelerate moves to political union.

Brexit forces European leaders to decide more clearly whether the European project requires more or less flexibility. Given that the UK already had several opt-outs, some say that Brexit shows that so-called differentiated integration ultimately cannot work because of the tensions that flow from having different memberships and decision-making arrangements across policy areas. Others say it makes such flexible arrangements even more necessary. Many feel that if the EU had shown the British government greater flexibility in the months prior to the referendum then the UK would have voted to remain – a sobering lesson of possible relevance to other member states.

In a sense, Brexit forces differences between other states over the EU's future direction into the open. The UK is no longer the protective scapegoat for other doubters to hide behind, and this reveals more clearly that in nearly all policy areas there are one or more member states that object to deeper integration. An ethos of difference and divergence has dominated debates since the referendum, militating against a clear new momentum towards any refounding of European integration.

Notwithstanding the rhetoric about Brexit being harnessed as a catalyst for deeper integration, governments' debates are for now still embryonic. German chancellor Angela Merkel seems to have gradually backed away from firm commitments to political union since the referendum. Far from leading a clear EU-reform agenda, Germany and France have, at least until mid-2017, been in 'wait and see' mode, unsure about how to adjust their own partnership in light of post-Brexit uncertainty.[3] As we will see later in the book, French and German ambitions may be set to rise in the latter months of 2017. But for now, most member states are eager to find ways for Brexit to proceed without a general process of treaty change, as any such revision would open a Pandora's box of governments adding different demands to the necessary process of reform.

Cutting across such differences, the UK's decision certainly puts aspects of the European project on the defensive. While the referendum's outcome was the result of peculiarly British concerns and the idiosyncrasies of UK domestic politics, it raises questions applicable to other countries too. To many, Brexit symbolises the dysfunctional nature of the EU system of governance and how this was unable to react in a flexible way to allow a member state narratives and institutional arrangements more tailored to its particular needs. Even if one believes that British voters simply made a terrible decision, Brexit has shone a harsh spotlight on the aspects of European integration that have become problematic in a more general sense across the continent. Some writers argue that it reveals the EU's broad failure to grasp and deal with the social adjustments required by EU policies.[4]

No clear line has taken shape on how to address such challenges. The UK's June 2017 election failed to clarify the likely parameters of Brexit. As the Conservative government hung on without an overall majority, these questions about the relationship between Brexit and the general shape of future EU integration were even further from being broached. The apparently dire situation into which Britain has now dug itself renders this failing increasingly and painfully apparent.

The significant point in the context of this book's subject matter is that the UK referendum could have helped usher in a new incarnation of European integration, but in practice has had almost the opposite effect. With most of the focus on the nitty-gritty of trade and migration rules, so far neither the UK nor any other European government has forwarded ideas for how Brexit might ignite a new vision of cooperation involving a full range of different institutional possibilities.[5] British politicians are somewhat parochially immersed in the details of the UK's own future relationship with the Union – the balance between so-called 'hard' and 'soft' Brexit in the matters of trade and free movement. And for their part, EU leaders appear to be more nervous about any fundamental rethink and indeed more confident that this is now less necessary. Much European commentary now takes the form of harshly berating the UK for its follies and asserting that the EU is in much better shape than Britain, with much less critical self-reflection on how European integration itself needs to change.

THE REFUGEE EFFECT

Prior to the Brexit referendum, the EU was already reeling from the challenge of absorbing an unprecedented wave of refugees and migrants. In 2015, more than 1 million refugees and migrants came into Europe, mainly from Syria, Iraq and Afghanistan, and high numbers continued to arrive throughout 2016 and into 2017. This influx has further eroded the foundations of EU solidarity and cooperation, unleashing bitter recriminations between member states. The *Financial Times* called the refugee and migrant surge 'the most serious emergency in the EU's history'.[6]

The crisis overwhelmed the EU's so-called Dublin asylum system, under which refugees are supposed to register in the member state where they first arrive. As this became impossible for Greece and Italy to manage, interior ministers adopted an alternative package to relocate 160,000 refugees across member states. However, most governments have declined to implement this agreement, which was passed by majority vote, not unanimity. Central and Eastern European countries, in particular, have objected to the way that the larger member states imposed the deal on them. Most states have refused to support a longer-term comprehensive mechanism for distributing refugees and migrants within Europe; they blocked the Commission's latest proposals for a quota-based system in summer 2017.

In the midst of the influx, many member states rushed to find a way of controlling their borders – the very antithesis of the EU's core ethos. Hungary, Austria and Slovenia have built fences; Hungary has extended its fence significantly in 2017. Eight Schengen countries – Austria, Belgium, Denmark, Germany, Hungary, Norway, Slovenia and Sweden – either reintroduced or strengthened border controls (some external, some internal to the Schengen area). After extending these measures several times beyond their initial time limit, Austria, Denmark, Germany, Sweden and Norway still have the controls in place in 2017. In May 2017, the Commission said the five states could extend their border controls for another six months; while this was set to be the last such renewal, Denmark said it would keep controls indefinitely.[7]

Angela Merkel won plaudits by initially opening Germany's borders to refugees, but other countries then closed off the so-called Balkan route to make sure that in practice refugees could no longer get through to Germany – a move that caused chaos in states further south.

Even the EU's most open and liberal states have implemented curbs. All Nordic governments tightened asylum rules over the course of 2016. Sweden introduced checks at its border with Denmark, and Denmark imposed controls at its border with Germany. Sweden, Finland and Denmark placed severe limits on their intake of asylum seekers. Driven by concerns over migration and refugees, in December 2015 the Danish people voted against their country joining the EU's justice and home affairs policies, in a referendum whose result was widely interpreted as another blow to the wider European project.

A chain reaction spread south. As northern member states introduced border controls, this caused bottlenecks of refugees in central Europe that in turn restricted crossings from southern member states, who became angry that the responsibility for managing the refugee surge was being pushed onto them. Several EU states threatened to eject Greece from Schengen to stop refugees moving northwards. Some accused southern member states of simply pushing people into northern Europe.

Much of the challenge of dealing with the influx has fallen on the EU's most broken state. The Commission proposed 700 million euros of aid to help Greece manage the refugees. However, when Greece asked for flexibility on its crisis-related bail-out conditions in order to have more funds available to manage the inflow of refugees, Germany refused to grant this. The Commission was harshly critical of Greece for its record in managing arrivals, just when Greece itself was overwhelmed and appealing for help.[8]

In early 2016, Austria organised a ministerial meeting with all Balkan states, pointedly without either Greece or Germany, insisting that unilateral measures were necessary due to the lack of an EU policy. In a move of unprecedented symbolism for how far the Europe project had fractured, Greece recalled its ambassador from Vienna. In February 2017, 15 central European and Balkan states met again to draw up plans to strengthen further measures against border crossings.[9] Germany tightened up its rules dramatically, granting only a quarter of Syrian refugees the right to remain in 2016, down from 99 per cent in 2015.[10]

Citizens in the member states most affected by the refugee flows today say they attach more priority to the control of their national borders than to the principles of European solidarity, believing that the latter have failed them in this crisis.[11] More broadly, polls show that a large majority of French (72 per cent), Germans (66 per cent) and Italians (60 per cent) support the re-establishment of border checkpoints.[12] Citizens have reacted highly critically to the EU losing control over refugee and migrant inflows.[13]

Italy has proposed a common EU migration bond to help spread the costs of managing such large numbers of arrivals; other states have not agreed to put funds into such an initiative to help southern states. Italian prime minister Matteo Renzi threatened to veto the whole EU budget in protest at member states' lack of solidarity with his country. In preparation for the March 2017 sixtieth-anniversary summit in Rome, which was supposedly aimed at reviving the EU, the Austrian government threatened to stop financial contributions to member states like Hungary and Poland that refused to accept their migrant quotas. And indeed, in June 2017, the Commission moved to impose sanctions on the Czech Republic, Hungary and Poland for refusing to take their share of arrivals. As of summer 2017, only 18,000 of the promised 160,000 refugees had been relocated.

In February 2017, more than 200,000 people demonstrated in Barcelona because the Spanish government had accepted only 700 refugees out of its 17,000 quota. Showing how internal debates have come unhelpfully to mix up questions of free movement, migrants and refugees, Eastern European states feel angry that they are being pushed into accepting refugees by the same northern countries that refused access to Eastern European workers for a decade after accession. Northern states insist that the hypocrisy runs the other way: while the likes of Poland and Hungary celebrate free movement for their own workers, they refuse to apply a similar logic of hospitality to migrants coming into *their* economies. When French politicians have been especially critical of the Visegrád states (the Czech Republic, Hungary, Poland and Slovakia), the latter have responded angrily that they are paying the price for reckless and unilateral French policies in Syria and Libya that have contributed to the wave of migrants coming through central and Eastern Europe.

The inflow of refugees eased after mid-2016, largely due to the EU striking a deal with Turkey. This accord allows the EU to return refugees to Turkey, in return for accepting asylum seekers through legal routes and a hefty 3-billion-euro aid package (with another 3 billion promised to Turkey for a second stage of cooperation). However, the crisis is far from solved. One year on from the deal, in March 2017, fewer than 1,000 people had been returned to Turkey and more than 60,000 were still trapped in Greece. Migrants moved towards central Mediterranean routes in 2016 and the early months of 2017. Far from helping Italy with this, France and Austria tightened border controls to prevent refugees leaving Italian territory. As Italy, in turn, has tightened controls and brought down the numbers arriving on its shores by September 2017, arrivals into Spain through west Mediterranean routes have begun to increase. Pierre Vimont, who led preparations for a key migration summit in November 2015, acknowledges that even if new controls have brought inflows down from their peak, they have not stemmed the mounting antipathy between member states.[14]

Many politicians, policy-makers and commentators have suggested that all this reveals fault lines in European integration that extend well beyond the refugee issue itself. Jean-Claude Juncker warned that if the principle of free movement collapsed, other areas of EU cooperation would fail too. The EU's foreign policy chief, Federica Mogherini, ventured that the refugee crisis posed 'a risk of disintegration' and of the EU committing 'suicide'.[15] Angela Merkel argued that the impact of the refugee crisis would be felt on the whole process of EU integration.[16] Some polls showed that by 2016, citizens saw the refugee influx as by far the most serious challenge to EU cooperation.[17] Prominent writers on EU affairs concur that the refugee issue has weakened some core pillars of the whole integration process.[18]

THE SECURITY EFFECT

The refugee challenge has gone hand in hand with heightened concern about security. Terrorist attacks shook Paris in January and November 2015, killing nearly 150 people. Attacks in Brussels in March 2016 killed more than 30. An attack in Nice in July 2016 was followed by a series of smaller incidents in Germany and France over the summer. Attacks of a somewhat different nature then took place in Berlin at the end of 2016, London in March and June 2017, Stockholm in April 2017, Manchester in May 2017 and Barcelona in August 2017. Radicals linked to Islamic State (IS) were responsible for all of these attacks, and the organisation regularly threatens a wave of further violence.

The EU agreed a new European Agenda for Security in 2015 and by 2017 had introduced six implementation packages to take this forward. It appointed a commissioner to oversee a new concept of 'Security Union', designed to catalyse security coordination. Europol detailed what was a peak in terrorism attacks in Europe in 2015 and 2016 (although overall terrorist-related deaths were still lower than in the 1970s). Polls regularly show that security and terrorism are now citizens' main worries, especially in France.[19]

Security challenges are deeply interwoven with other aspects of the poly-crisis. Terrorist experts point out that causes of European Islamist radicalisation overlap with the wider sense of alienation among parts of the European population that has been a driving force of the EU crisis.[20] In addition, polls indicate that most citizens see insecurity and terrorism as inextricably bound up with the migration and refugee challenge – albeit on questionable grounds, as we will see later.[21] After the Paris attacks, the French government explicitly redefined the refugee influx as a security threat.[22] Central and Eastern European states protest that Germany has offered temporary protection status to migrants and refugees without undertaking security checks.

Security services across Europe say they have disrupted dozens of planned attacks. French politicians fear that thousands of French citizens are at risk of radicalisation. The then French prime minister Manuel Valls warned: 'The European project can die, not in decades or years but very fast, if we are unable to face up to the security challenge.'[23] Europe is importing insecurity from elsewhere, while the number of EU citizens going to fight for IS has also continued to rise. Not only has the existing EU model failed to stem the instability encroaching from outside, but in addition Europe seems to be contributing to the underlying drivers of radicalisation and terrorism – a huge dent in the credibility of what is always presented and celebrated first and foremost as a project of peace and security.

The terrorist attacks have raised doubts about some of the core premises of European cooperation. The attacks suggest that the EU has failed to provide basic security to European citizens. The Commission admitted in a March 2017 report that free movement rules allowed the perpetrators of terror attacks in France, Belgium and Germany to cross borders without detection.[24] Europol's remit does not cover law enforcement or core counter-terrorism work; it cannot stop suspects coming into Europe or detain them, but merely facilitate information exchanges on known radicals. EU terrorism legislation in 2016 included a new, sweeping definition of terrorism.

After the Paris attacks, the French government imposed a state of emergency, tightened terror laws and temporarily reinstated security checks at the country's borders. In June 2017, President Macron indicated that he would lift the state of emergency but make its counter-terrorism provisions permanent. The Polish government said it was the security context that prevented it from accepting its allocated quota of refugees. The Investigatory Powers Act passed into law in the UK in November 2016 dramatically extends the British government's powers of surveillance. The three attacks in the UK in the first half of 2017 led Theresa May's government to promise an intensification of security measures. In June 2017 France and the UK agreed new counter-terrorism cooperation, especially to clamp down on the problem of online radicalism. Member states are focusing increasingly tightly on the imperatives of national security.

Fears have intensified of a so-called 'third generation' of terrorism, with IS morphing into a more decentralised grouping focused on attacking Europe.[25] Even if the perception of danger may exceed its actuality, in some parts of Europe radicalism has intensified a new psychology of fear, mistrust and protective introversion, a new cognitive or identity insecurity. While the EU has always been about the renunciation of security-based 'bordering', many now argue that European coopera-tion needs to change dramatically in order to take on board just such a security logic. Eurosceptics have increasingly used the argument that today the EU project is making citizens less rather than more secure. In a confused way, the EU has become a target for those pushing back against the general notion of multiculturalism.

In addition to terrorism, other security challenges have also inten-sified and placed strains on European cooperation. Many European diplomats fear that Russia is intent on undermining the core tenets of the whole European security order, well beyond its actions in eastern Ukraine and Crimea. Differences exist within the EU over what Russia's ultimate intentions are, as it builds up its military arsenal, threatens Baltic states with military over-flights and engages more aggressively through propaganda and misinformation in the politics of European states. But there is a general agreement that Russia's current truculence towards the West constitutes another security dilemma and another strand of the EU's poly-crisis that governments have struggled to contain in the last four or five years.

Security challenges may provide a powerful fillip to deeper inte-gration. The new EU 'Global Strategy for Foreign and Security Policy', agreed in June 2016, acknowledges how insecurity and vulnerability now impinge upon EU integration. This strategy aims to build a stronger interface between the health of the Union and the way in which the EU addresses external threats. This is very different in tone to the pre-vious European Security Strategy in 2003, which was all about the EU projecting its transformative experiences abroad. The 2016 strategy is more focused on the need for a core defence of the EU itself, through a foreign policy tightly oriented towards ensuring tangible security gains for EU citizens.

When French president François Hollande, Merkel and Renzi met for a mini-summit in August 2016, they homed in on security as the most important area for upgraded cooperation. At the September

2016 summit in Bratislava, leaders promoted a new leitmotif of 'protection' as the guiding principle for EU reform.[26] Seven Mediterranean member states gathered for their first summit in September 2016 and declared security, the control of borders and counter-terrorism to be the Union's new top priorities.[27] Council president Donald Tusk has been especially adamant that a more effective ability to provide citizens with security must be the leading edge of an EU relaunch.[28] Crucially, Donald Trump's actions have intensified this EU security dynamic. In June 2017, the EU launched major new proposals for a Defence Fund and mechanisms for military missions (these are explained in the next chapter).

THE EURO EFFECT

With Brexit, insecurity and refugees dominating the headlines, the spark that lit the poly-crisis has receded into the background. The quest to keep the single currency intact has for now succeeded and the EU has clawed itself back from the depths of economic recession. But the euro's core imbalances and design flaws persist. And the broader implications of the euro saga are relevant to understanding the apparent exhaustion of traditional approaches to European integration. The structural legacy of the eurozone crisis is one of distrust, unaccountable decision-making and a wider divergence of policy preferences.

While the eurozone crisis has certainly prompted national governments to adopt some additional cooperation, it has not (yet) led to definitive breakthroughs in economic integration. Germany has reluctantly agreed to transfer funds to Greece and other debtor member states. New EU financial regulations have reduced the risks of future banking-sector meltdowns. However, most member states lament that the eurozone crisis has demolished any sense of pan-European solidarity. Southern states see the process of economic adjustment as unfairly asymmetrical, relying entirely on their efforts to cut deficits rather than also on creditor states stimulating demand. Debtor states insist the crisis was driven by German surpluses as much as by deficits in the south – and yet the EU has imposed no constraints at all on Germany's economic model.[29]

All states have sought to push the costs of managing interdependence onto other member states, either through racking up debts or by competitive deflation of wage and other costs. Each state has been out for itself, and behind much principled rhetoric few have acted primarily with a common European interest in mind. One of the most extensive accounts of the eurozone crisis compares the way it has been managed to an interstate conflict that has left in its wake deep antipathies.[30] Former Greek finance minister Yanis Varoufakis's insider account of the crisis reveals an eye-watering degree of vitriol and enmity between governments (albeit not from a neutral perspective, of course). If governments have pulled the euro back from the abyss they have done so through extremely grudging trade-offs.[31]

Populations across Europe have different reasons for feeling aggrieved by the politics of the eurozone crisis. Debtor states express little gratitude because EU rescue funds have gone to bail out French and German banks and have simply shifted private-sector losses onto taxpayers' shoulders. EU help has been given in a way that entails a further redistribution of wealth away from poorer states to the rich, surplus states. Rather than a celebration of European unity, each rescue package has deepened the sense of hostility. The evaporation of solidarity has led to some ironic inconsistencies: the Spanish government pleads for flexibility on its own deficit overruns but has often adopted a hard line against Greece.

Conversely, Baltic states feel that Greece and other debtors have been shown too much leniency. They point out that they are much poorer than the Mediterranean member states and yet have got on with implementing structural reforms without fanfare or assistance. Despite public misgivings and feelings of unfairness, Estonia supported Greece's bail-out – only to find the Greek government showing no reciprocal solidarity with Estonia's main concern, namely the need for robust EU unity against Russia. Central European states feel that they get less preferential support than the 'core' member states and are still treated as second-class members. In Cyprus, the effect of the crisis was very tangible; after citizens lost a part of their savings, the EU is now associated with unjust financial power and a lack of solidarity.

The European Court of Auditors has criticised the opaque nature of Commission decisions over financial assistance to countries hit hard by the economic crisis.[32] Offering money in return for very detailed and unpopular policies has bred discontent among both those lending the money and those forced to adopt the prescribed policies. The crisis has ended the era of depoliticised monetary policy, with long-term and profound implications for the way that European economic strategy is devised.

While the single currency was undoubtedly saved by skilful crisis management at several crunch moments between 2010 and 2015, second-order risks remain. Tensions persist, with governments in Greece, Portugal, Spain and Italy still resisting many reforms and bitterly resenting intrusive Commission and European Central Bank diktats about how they must cut pensions, health services and education. When Matteo Renzi resigned as Italian prime minister in December 2016 after losing a referendum on constitutional reform, the sense of uncertainty over the euro's future returned. With the populist Five Star Movement riding high in the polls, a caretaker government has held on in Rome with little power to implement reforms (although it did agree to 3 billion euros of cuts in April 2017). Meanwhile, Portugal's left-wing coalition government has brought down the country's deficit by expressly rejecting and reversing EU austerity strictures.

In May 2017, the Greek government reluctantly accepted further spending cuts worth 2 per cent of GDP to unlock its next tranche of support. This agreement came only after a tense, months-long stand-off during which Germany resisted IMF pressure for Greece to be granted large-scale debt relief and finance minister Wolfgang Schäuble suggested Greece might be better leaving the euro. Including a hefty 18 per cent cut in already-lowered pensions, the deal was met by protests involving more than 10,000 people in Athens. With the Syriza-led government resting on a wafer-thin majority and a general strike called against the new cuts, the deal's implementation was far from guaranteed.

Frustration has grown over apparently politicised decision-making. In summer 2016, the EU decided not to impose sanctions against Spain and Portugal despite deficit overruns in these two states. While this suggested a welcome degree of new flexibility, Greeks asked angrily why they had not been offered such clemency. Wolfgang Schäuble was reportedly instrumental in this move, keen to help his fellow conservative, Spanish premier Mariano Rajoy. Spain's deficit rose because Rajoy had made a deliberate choice to increase spending to improve his chances of electoral success in a December 2015 vote – exactly the kind of opportunism that EU rules were supposed to stop. Economist Daniel Gros concluded that the decision not to impose the fines made any talk of completing economic and monetary union 'meaningless' as it was 'now clearer than ever that EU member states prioritise domestic political imperatives over common rules'.[33]

The euro's governance structures are still largely those that existed before the crisis and are unlikely to prevent the next one.[34] While important new rules oblige creditors to accept write-offs when banks hit serious problems, neither full banking union nor fiscal union has advanced. The so-called Five Presidents' Report on completing economic and monetary union – a template published by the presidents of the Council, Commission, European Central Bank, European Parliament and Eurogroup – gathers dust.[35] At the end of May 2017, the Commission published a paper setting out the series of steps still needed to complete a banking and financial union.[36] While President Macron has revived calls for deeper economic union, member states' positions are yet to converge in a way that would enable such an agenda to advance. (This dilemma is explored in the next chapter.) More broadly, the crisis has increased some member states' resistance to deepening and extending the EU internal market.[37] France has sought to use the so-called 'Posted Workers Directive' to place restrictive conditions on companies moving workers between EU member states.

The pain of austerity does not appear to have resulted in significant structural gain. The Commission noted in early 2017 that, even after three years of economic recovery, Spain had levels of poverty and inequality higher than when the crisis started and youth unemployment was still above 40 per cent.[38] The overall level of indebtedness across the EU is now higher than at the outbreak of the crisis.[39] Banks' balance sheets are more, not less, exposed and the regulations on capital requirements introduced after 2008 have been rowed back. European Central Bank intervention may have saved the euro, but many people see its role as protecting large banks, not European citizens.

The euro is held together partly by the fear of how costly a break-up would be – not a healthy launch pad for future economic cooperation.[40] One particularly thorough academic study concludes that governments and EU institutions have 'done little to resolve the core issues and imbalances at the heart of the crisis'.[41] Noted economists argue that the crisis has left Europe more fragmented and divided, and less well equipped to meet long-term economic challenges.[42] The debate has been about more versus less austerity, not one centred on the underlying changes needed to reverse the continent's declining competitiveness. Short-term crisis management has pushed Europe away from designing a better model of political economy.[43]

THE POPULISM EFFECT

These different dimensions of crisis have together unleashed a wave of so-called populism across Europe. Even after Emmanuel Macron's victory in the French presidential elections, this remains a potent and unsettling legacy of the poly-crisis. This is not a book about populism per se, a topic on which numerous works have appeared in the last two years; but it is concerned more specifically with the relationship between the populist surge and debates about the model of European integration.

Populism is in part a result of the poly-crisis, and in part driven by its own dynamic, which itself aggravates the crisis. Parties commonly defined as populist are situated on both the right and the left, with both poles of Europe's ideological spectrum now asking more demanding questions of EU integration. Crucially for this book's subject matter, different populists react against different parts of the European project and their proposed remedies differ accordingly – the prevailing tendency to hold populism as synonymous with a blanket, uniform anti-Europeanism is inaccurate.[44] Many leftist populists want an EU that protects vulnerable communities from economic globalism; many rightist populists want one that helps protect a sense of local community, place and order.

Radical right-wing populist parties have risen to wield notable degrees of influence and political representation in Austria, Denmark, Finland, France, Germany, Greece, Hungary, the Netherlands, Poland, Sweden and the UK. The victory of the Law and Justice party (known by the abbreviation PiS) in Poland's October 2015 elections provides one of the starkest illustrations of the drift in public concerns – as will be explained further in the next chapter. In Germany, Alternative für Deutschland made dramatic gains in regional elections in 2016 on an anti-refugee and anti-euro message. The 2016 Austrian presidential elections very nearly handed victory to the far-right Freedom Party. The Croatian Democratic Union government took power in Croatia in 2016 on a deeply illiberal platform. So-called 'identitarian' groups have appeared in a clutch of member states, even more militant than rightist populists. Unsurprisingly, conservative populists felt emboldened by Donald Trump's election victory.

What are conventionally labelled as populist parties follow a range of stances on Europe. The UK Independence Party played a significant role in pushing Britain out of the EU. Nordic populists expound a slightly different narrative of preserving the traditional Scandinavian welfare and state–society model against change associated with the EU.[45] The Danish People's Party wants a looser and more limited EU model, based on sovereign states and select areas of pragmatic cooperation. The Sweden Democrats want to renegotiate membership. In Belgium, Vlaams Belang (Flemish Interest) wants EU policies to be based on more democratic engagement of regional entities and a more limited range of policy competences. While not victorious in the Dutch election of March 2017, Geert Wilders's Freedom Party finished second on a commitment to take the country out of the EU; the less well-known Forum for Democracy also attracted support for its more limited pledge to take the Netherlands out of the euro.

The radically illiberal Jobbik for many years pushed to get Hungary out of the EU but has recently re-evaluated its position on the grounds that EU politics are now moving in its direction. The country's ruling Fidesz party is highly critical of the EU but more accepting of Hungary's membership. In Bulgaria, Attack advocates a similar agenda of social conservatism and pushback against neo-liberalism but is more une-quivocal in wanting Bulgaria out of the EU. In contrast, the 'outsider' victor in Bulgaria's 2016 presidential elections, Rumen Radev, advocates a more pro-Russian policy but is not in favour of an EU exit. Several populist Czech parties want to leave the EU, while others seek a looser union. The Conservative People's Party of Estonia wants deeper security cooperation, in particular to stand up to Russia.

In France, all eyes have been on the National Front, as Marine Le Pen competed for the presidency in 2017 on a strongly anti-euro and anti-EU platform. Alternative für Deutschland wants Germany to leave the euro, but remain in a more streamlined EU based on cooperation between sovereign states and more citizen influence. The Austrian Freedom Party wants more subsidiarity and an end to assistance for southern member states and freedom of movement. In contrast, Italy's Liga Nord (Northern League) calls for deeper political and economic union with a bigger centralised EU budget, and a more formalised role for regions.[46]

While left-wing populists tend not to be so explicitly anti-European, scepticism is rising on the left, for example from within the Dutch Socialist Party, former communist parties in Eastern Europe and Die Linke (the Left) in Germany. Communists and the Left Bloc, born from anti-austerity protests, were brought into a minority Socialist govern-ment in Portugal, giving leverage to many anti-EU voices within these two parties. In Slovakia, prime minister Robert Fico has developed an anti-Brussels, anti-Muslim, illiberal agenda, all from a nominally centre-left, social-democratic perspective.

Podemos has assured voters in Spain that it would reverse austerity, increase public spending and ditch labour-market reforms, going against EU rules to do so. While formally Europhile, the party ran its 2015 and 2016 electoral campaigns around 'sovereigntist' slogans widely seen as having a somewhat EU-critical tone. The party's momentous internal elections in February 2017 pushed an anti-capitalist wing to the fore, with an agenda incompatible with the most basic of EU commitments. Italy's Five Star Movement is hard to pin down ideologically, combining elements from both leftist and right-wing populist parties; while opposition to Italy's membership of the euro is at the forefront of its manifesto, at the end of 2016 it softened some of its anti-EU stances and sought to join the Liberal group in the European Parliament. The Nuit Debout protests that spread across France in 2016 were aimed against labour-law reforms, but gradually took on a more anti-EU line.

While leftist populists may reject the illiberal identity politics of rightist populists, they question some of the EU's foundational tenets of economic openness. Research shows that in the European Parliament opposition to neo-liberal austerity has gradually become more closely associated with Eurosceptic positions – and this trend is evident on both left and right.[47] A June 2016 Pew Research Center survey shows that in some member states voters on the left have a more favourable view of the EU than those on the right, while in others (including Sweden, Greece and Spain) it is the other way around, with people on the left defining themselves as more anti-EU than those on the right. In other states (like France, Hungary and Poland) there is virtually no difference, with hostility to the Union rising among those on both left and right.[48]

Despite the differences between populists, there is some convergence among rightist and leftist ends of the spectrum and a shared disappointment in the European dream. For example, politicians at both ends of the populist spectrum tend to be economic nationalists, whose economic programmes sit uneasily with the rules of an open European market. Of course, rightist populism places more emphasis on racial and nationalist identity and tends to be more overtly and uncompromisingly anti-EU; it posits a three-way split between nationals, elites and foreigners, whereas left-wing populism rests on a more binary division of the people against the elites. Yet rightist and leftist populism make many similar charges against the prevailing model of European integration.

A broad consensus has taken root that populism now represents another layer of threat to the European project. Despite the relief felt when Emmanuel Macron won the 2017 French election, in the first round of this contest more than 40 per cent of the French people voted for candidates who fundamentally questioned the country's place in the European project (Le Pen and, on the far left, Jean-Luc Mélenchon). Alternative für Deutschland's third-place finish grabbed headlines in Germany's September 2017 election and the Five Star Movement has been set to do well in Italy's election, due in 2018. Populist movements have built transnational alliances that have shaped public discourse across Europe. Populism unsettles national political systems, but is even more damaging to the EU because it puts in doubt the Union's whole rationale for existing.[49] A rise in illiberalism goes hand in hand with rising Euroscepticism, with the two phenomena feeding off each other.

If populism is a new spoiler for European integration, however, it also holds a mirror up to the underlying causes of the EU crisis. Populists may be simplistic in dividing society into the 'good people' versus the 'bad elite', but they have hit a nerve in emphasising the extent to which citizens seem to have lost influence over EU and national elites. When EU elites talk about 'defeating' this phenomenon to protect the European project, they merely reinforce widespread anger at how unresponsive those elites have become to the democratic will.

Populism has put down roots in countries that are doing well economically as well as in those that are doing badly, those with high levels of immigration and those with very little immigration, in big, powerful member states and small, newer ones – a ubiquity that suggests a profoundly structural problem. Statistical testing shows that the rise in populism is more strongly correlated with a cultural backlash against liberal and internationalist norms than simply with economic problems (far-right parties have not emerged in some of the states hit hardest by austerity, such as Spain, Portugal and Ireland).[50] Experts stress that Europe's populism is rooted in decades-long social changes, reinforcing the point that some fundamental rethinking will be needed to dissolve the phenomenon.[51]

A STRUCTURAL CHALLENGE

The summary of these different policy domains and political trends reveals deep-cut structural shortcomings to the current model of European integration. These include citizens' lack of voice, a growing divergence of policy preferences, spiralling mistrust and a creeping feeling that the EU now functions in a way that deepens all kinds of vulnerabilities rather than insulating citizens from them.

Combine the different trends together and they present a profound challenge to the very foundations of the European project, a general political crisis extending well beyond a few areas of difficult policy decisions. Certainly, there is widespread agreement among politicians and experts that the poly-crisis has been deep enough to raise profound questions. Jean-Claude Juncker took office as Commission president saying this was a 'last chance', make-or-break moment for the European project. The then president of the European Parliament, Martin Schulz, warned: 'No one can say whether the EU will still exist in this form in ten years.'[52]

In the depths of the poly-crisis, barely a day went by without a media article predicting the EU's disintegration. Academics also agree that the whole European project has at moments come close to unravelling. Loukas Tsoukalis writes that member states are less united than ever before, leaving the EU project 'as fragile as a glasshouse'.[53] Historian Mark Mazower is of the opinion that 'Stepping back and thinking about the EU's long-term evolution is now almost impossible [...] the EU is living on borrowed time.'[54] Some believe that the EU must pull itself back from a wholesale crisis of 'constitutional disorder'.[55] Pol Morillas suggests that the so-called Monnet method of incremental progress in integration almost went into reverse: a step-by-step deconstruction of the EU that threatened to take on a self-sustaining and inexorable momentum.[56]

The effect is played out within the two biggest member states. One German analyst warns of a watershed change in German aims: 'European unity for Berlin seems no longer to be an objective in and of itself [...] Germany's *Europapolitik* has become *Realpolitik*.'[57] This trend is deepening as other member states increasingly challenge German policy preferences. France has long been the most enigmatically contradictory player, being the member state most representative of the standard, establishment model of integration but also an increasingly strong bulwark of the nation state against the myriad failings of the European project. The poly-crisis has accentuated the contradiction and pulled France in both directions simultaneously. Emmanuel Macron's stirring victory does not in itself resolve this. And while Marine Le Pen was defeated, France's election revealed deep unease with the whole design of the integration model, to the extent that the role of one extremist party in one election in one member state could easily have put the whole EU at risk.

Polling evidence confirms how steep a climb the EU faces to recover citizens' trust. Eurobarometer polling shows that for many years more citizens trusted than distrusted EU institutions until the crisis started; by 2013 the share of people saying they did not trust EU institutions shot up to 60 per cent, double the 30 per cent who said they still trusted EU institutions.[58] There has been a significant shift away from citizens feeling they have both a national and a European identity and towards their laying claim only to a national identity.[59] Citizens' faith in European institutions has fallen dramatically and continually from 2004 – albeit recovering slightly from late 2016.[60] And none of this can be blamed on simple popular ignorance: polls show that citizens' satisfaction with the EU has decreased as their knowledge and understanding of its policies has increased.[61]

In a 2016 survey of ten EU countries, 42 per cent of respondents said they want power returned to national governments against only 19 per cent who want more powers transferred to the EU level. Benign views of the EU have plummeted: 69 per cent of French citizens had a favourable view of the EU in 2004; by 2016 this figure was only 38 per cent. In 2006, 80 per cent of Spaniards had a favourable view of the EU; this has declined to only 47 per cent.[62] A November 2016 Demos–YouGov poll confirmed that support for 'reducing EU powers' is now far stronger than support for the opposite or for creating a single European government.[63]

Even as the general context has begun to stabilise, a potent residue of dissatisfaction remains. On the eve of the sixtieth anniversary summit in March 2017, one poll found that only a quarter of European citizens thought the EU was moving in the right direction.[64] Another survey, published after that summit, revealed an ever-widening division between elites and citizens on key issues such as migrant flows, the democratic deficit and whether the EU should have more or fewer powers.[65] Confirming these trends, a June 2017 Pew Research Center survey showed a (Brexit-induced) rise in support for EU membership, but also majorities unhappy with the EU's handling of specific issues like migration, economic policy and trade, and wanting more powers moved from Brussels to governments in these areas; the poll also revealed that more than half of those surveyed wanted national referendums on the EU, due to a persistent feeling that citizens' voices are not being heard in European debates.[66]

The key structural change is that doubts have grown that European integration is capable of being a win–win phenomenon rather than one that necessarily involves ever-wider differences between powerful winners and ingrained losers.[67] Historian Luuk van Middelaar writes that the rise of identity politics 'has come as an existential shock', leaving the EU uncertain over how to switch focus from the positive-sum expansion of freedoms to 'protecting citizens'.[68]

Positive trade-offs have given way to a revengeful mistrust that drives negative issue linkages – with disunity in one area generating disunity in another policy sphere. In the eurozone economic crisis, southern member states asked Germany for generous solidarity and felt they did not get it; in the refugee crisis, Germany in turn asked southern states for solidarity and felt it was let down. The Visegrád states used the migration crisis as a means of trying to reassert their general power at the EU level, feeling a structural inability to get their concerns onto the Union's agenda.[69] The amount of zero-sum bargaining on show within EU deliberations has patently increased.

This in turn feeds into the pivotal structural predicament that the EU can apparently move neither forwards nor backwards. Governments are simply muddling along, with ad hoc policy initiatives addressing popular disaffection at the margins but bereft of ideas for really getting to grips with the EU's malaise.[70] Structurally, this is not like previous crises, which gave a positive prompt to EU integration. Political scientist Jan Zielonka notes that this is because the crisis has undermined the basis of the EU's 'modernist credentials' of shared progress.[71]

Many experts have in recent years focused on the issue of disintegration – this has become a topic of enquiry in EU debates in a way that would have been unthinkable a decade ago. Public intellectual Ivan Krastev senses that 'the disintegration train has left Brussels's station' and that 'Europe' has definitively lost its allure as an ideal, against the backdrop of a fundamental shift to more parochial notions of political community. As the whole notion of interdependence is increasingly seen as bringing insecurity rather than security, European identity formation seems to have gone into reverse. From the vantage point of 2017, Krastev cautions against the EU adopting overly ambitious post-crisis plans, when simply surviving will be difficult enough.[72]

Historians tell us that these trends are more than ephemeral inconveniences to an onward-marching European project. A repeat pattern has conditioned European geopolitics for more than 500 years. Various centralising or unifying projects have often gained traction in Europe for a period of time – the Catholic Church, the Holy Roman Empire, the Habsburgs, Louis XIV, Napoleon, Nazism, communism – but they have always been pushed back eventually. The doubts and tensions that are returning today are less of an anomaly than a reversion to the historical norm.[73]

THE MEASURE OF CRISIS – AND REFORM

Many writers and politicians protest that the EU's crises have not been as dramatically threatening as widely reported and that if there were potential breaking points these have now been successfully overcome. The EU is still standing after years of experts predicting its collapse. Previous crises have, optimists stress, been just as serious and were overcome with relatively little drama or extensive change. Anti-EU populists have not swept to power across the continent; indeed, after the 2017 Dutch and French elections a common view is that European populism has peaked. Emmanuel Macron's victory in particular has produced an avalanche of commentary that an EU revival is now well under way – even if Angela Merkel's weakened post-electoral position may have a more mixed impact. The European economy is reviving and still scores relatively well on global competitiveness rankings; by spring 2017, EU unemployment had fallen to its lowest level since 2009. The refugee crisis may have brought a few passport controls back, but has not torn the whole EU project apart.

Some EU leaders insist that the Union has contained its problems so well and is so favourably positioned that 'the next ten years can be the European decade'.[74] In August 2017, Jean-Claude Juncker declared the crisis over and asserted that there is now 'really nothing to complain about' in the Union.[75] Many reason that the visible ills that Brexit is visiting upon the UK will bind other states together in tighter harmony. EU politicians and leaders now raise the UK's unenviable situation to justify and close ranks behind the existing model of integration, which is now much more unconditionally celebrated as providing the stability and economic predictability that Britain appears to have relinquished.

Optimists insist that beneath the dramatic press headlines and febrile summits, a common European identity is quietly taking shape. Many insist that there is no need to revisit any core principles of European integration and that to do so would play into a disingenuous and already-retreating Eurosceptic agenda. Given that radical change is anyway unrealistic, it is better for the EU to stick to minor adjustments to the existing integration model and simply ensure that citizens are better informed about the Union's achievements.[76]

To a point, these warnings against hyperbole are well made. Tensions have clearly been worse at previous points in European history. And the change in atmospherics in 2017 is undoubtedly reassuring and significant. We certainly need to take proper measure of the EU's poly-crisis. However, while it is important not to exaggerate its effects, this poly-crisis has had more pervasively troubling ramifications than previous cycles of disintegration. The current upturn in the economic cycle does not solve the structural drivers of the crisis. Undoubtedly, modest forms of adaptation and low-level coordination have helped sustain European cooperation through the most turbulent moments. But, as one pillar after another has trembled menacingly in the EU temple, so the integrity of the whole edifice of integration has begun to look increasingly shaky. Confusion has weaved such a masterpiece through years of multiple European crises as to make an instantaneous turnaround unlikely.[77]

Europe's bleeding may have ceased, but its wounds still need to be healed. A few well-packaged policy changes will not suffice to maintain the EU's health and well-being over the long term. Many articles urge important policy innovations – for example, in the area of economic support to debtor states or new security and border provisions. My concern in this book is different. There are, of course, many *policy* responses that European leaders need to take; but I want to probe more deeply into what the crisis means for the broader *structure* of EU integration. Flowing from this chapter's discussion of the structural pathologies of the poly-crisis, my aim is to assess the need for a different *model* of integration – for a new polity, not just new policies.

If the EU really is now on the verge of a reawakening, then it becomes even more important that it qualitatively changes the way it structures integration, rather than simply dusting off previous cooperation plans. While 2017's more benign context might enable governments to adopt such long-present ideas for deeper integration, these would risk storing up repeat crisis cycles for the future. If, as many now contend, the EU is indeed moving from a dynamic of disintegration towards one of renewed integration, the question is how it will use this opportunity: to advance select areas of cooperation along familiar lines or to rethink the whole notion of integration? Surely politicians need not merely to celebrate the current upswing but to get ahead of the curve and prepare the EU for the next downswing or crisis.

On this score, the EU's paralysis is quite staggering. It is now over a decade since French and Dutch citizens rejected the text of a proposed EU constitution. This shock unleashed much talk of changing the model of integration and 'bringing in the citizens'. Yet nothing effective has been done to this end in all the subsequent years. For governments that are unsure how to reform the EU, the business-as-usual option is a dangerously seductive temptation. When times are bad, leaders say it is not possible to introduce ambitious and innovative change; when times improve, they feel it is not necessary. In the periodic moments of peak tension, European governments, leaders and citizens clamour for far-reaching change. When the panic subsides, such change appears less urgent. The root causes of the EU's malaise remain unresolved and calls for radical reform are ignored. Many might empathise with the deadpan humour of the prime minister's spin doctor in Danish political saga *Borgen* when he bridles at such unresponsiveness: 'In Brussels, no one can hear you scream.'

CHAPTER TWO

False Solutions

What solutions have politicians, diplomats and analysts proposed to the EU's multifaceted crisis? Debates have traditionally focused on two familiar paths. One option is to take a leap forward towards far deeper integration, to 'complete' the integration project by putting in place the final pieces of a full 'political union'. The other option is to take a step back, accept that post-crisis European economies, societies and political systems are simply not ready for significant convergence, and give back greater autonomy to EU nation states. Some experts insist there is no halfway option: either the EU opts for full federation or its national economies must unhook themselves from each other.[1]

Most policy-makers have come to adopt a more subtle position, talking of the need to overcome such sharp divisions. Yet, in practice, their debates still focus on *degrees* of integration, more than on qualitatively new ideas for reshaping the European project. Even if they claim in principle to be open to novel types and permutations of policy cooperation, politicians and officials retain a preference for very traditional approaches to integration. And as the poly-crisis appears to flatten out, innovative concepts of integration have received little airing in recent policy documents.

New approaches are needed because both sides of the 'more versus less' debate present an overly narrow diagnosis of the EU's problems and envisage solutions that are one-dimensional. Both fail to home in on the most potent sources of the EU's woes. In the absence of deeper democratic quality, a leap forward towards a single Euro-state could worsen the very problems that have wreaked such calamity since 2008.

Conversely, there is little reason to think that full national autonomy and an unwinding of European cooperation would remedy the factors driving the EU's poly-crisis. Despite the emerging official rhetoric about transcending the binary divide between Europhiles and Eurosceptics, both camps still tend rather haughtily to dismiss the possibility of a qualitatively different kind of European integration.

MORE OF THE SAME

In response to the crisis, there has been no shortage of calls for stronger unity and cooperation between European nations. Indeed, for most EU leaders, governments and politicians the instinctive, default response to the crisis has been to call for deeper EU integration – and these calls have become more numerous and vociferous in the improved conditions of 2017. The crisis has reinforced rather than dented the conviction of many in the EU that an extension of existing patterns of cooperation is required. The EU's problem is certainly not a lack of blueprints for centralising more policy-making powers at the European level.

Perhaps most high profile was the already-mentioned Five Presidents' Report that was presented in June 2015 and pushed for a process of change leading from economic union to financial union, then to fiscal union and finally to political union.[2] The Italian government has for several years called particularly forcefully for fiscal centralisation and the creation of an EU finance minister to run economic policy across the continent.

The several dramatic moments of the eurozone crisis have triggered a wave of proposals for further integration. These proposals have nearly all contained the same elements: a centralised budget and fiscal competences, along with a political union based around a primary role for the European Parliament. Many politicians have argued that the fragile economic context requires tighter, more bureaucratised rules to prevent problems from resurfacing in the future. Politicians' speeches, officials' memos and analysts' articles follow a standard playbook: greater Europe-wide infrastructure spending combined with EU job-creation initiatives, supplemented with ideas for deeper integration to manage refugee flows.

In many studies, ministers and experts advocate an extension of the existing structures of European integration.[3] While governments may often talk of the need for novel approaches, the EU continues to introduce plans and laws that follow the existing top-down and regulation-oriented means of centralising more powers – in areas from information technology to services, energy and banking. Many in the EU have pinned considerable hopes on the 'Energy Union Strategy' agreed in 2015. They believe this could be the core element of a relaunch and deepening of European cooperation, based on the model of how integration in coal and steel kick-started integration in the 1950s.

In May 2016, a group of notable European politicians, writers and public figures issued a manifesto for a 'new Europe', again consisting of calls for a common EU budget, more centralised spending and redistribution, more defence integration and a directly elected Commission president.[4] The morning of the UK referendum, the Spanish foreign minister, José Manuel García-Margallo, wrote that whichever way the result went the EU now needed to move forward to full political and economic union and a 'United States of Europe'.[5]

A manifesto put out by the French and German foreign ministers after the Brexit vote advocated pushing ahead with political union. The plan acknowledged that

> We have to be more focused on essentials and on meeting the concrete expectations of our citizens [...] we have to strictly focus our joints efforts on those challenges that can only be addressed by common European answers, while leaving others to national or regional decision making and variation.

But, somewhat at odds with this apparent willingness to rethink, the document then boldly announced that, anyway, France and Germany 'will therefore move further towards political union'.[6]

At their August 2016 meeting, the French, German and Italian leaders raised the need for deeper commitments to cooperation in defence, migration and economic growth. In particular, they presented a 'Europe of Defence' as a core proposal for regenerating the EU project. Building on this meeting, at yet another supposedly make-or-break summit in Bratislava in September 2016, EU leaders insisted on the need for a post-Brexit relaunch based on similar ideas for security integration. In June 2017, the EU set up a 'Military Planning and Conduct Capability' to facilitate the management of conflict resolution and counter-terrorism missions. In the same month, the Commission launched a new Defence Fund to draw money for the first time from the EU budget for military projects. The plan is for up to 1.5 billion euros to be spent each year from 2020, with smaller amounts to kick-start military-technology collaboration before then.[7]

Meanwhile, in the European Parliament two high-profile reports on the future of the EU were agreed at the beginning of 2017. They followed a standard pattern of running through every area of policy in turn and advocating deeper, supranational integration as the solution to problems in each area. The reports urged more, not less binding EU rules; measures to undercut the role of national governments; more resources for various parts of the EU budget; more European Parliament power over the Council; and less scope for flexible forms of cooperation outside existing, formal EU procedures. Neither report acknowledged any need to consider new approaches – indeed, they gave no clue at all that recent events might have raised questions over these stock policy recipes.[8]

Debate then centred on the sixtieth-anniversary Rome summit in March 2017. To provide ideas for this summit, the Commission presented a long-awaited white paper offering scenarios for the EU's future. This document refers to the need to look beyond existing templates and combine different integration logics. Yet its scenarios – basically: more cooperation, less cooperation or variable-speed integration – in fact still define the question of the EU's future mainly in terms of *degrees* of integration.[9] More widely, in debates leading up to the crucial series of European elections in 2017, parties offered few detailed or radically innovative ideas on EU reform.[10]

At the Rome summit, leaders put off any major decisions until the end of the year, stressing the need to wait until elections in France and

Germany had been held. Their logic was that with these elections out of the way, leaders would then be less restrained from moving forward. And indeed, there is now a widespread feeling that the results of the Dutch and, especially, the French elections dramatically improve the prospects for reviving the EU. The Commission is set to present a programme for deeper integration at the end of 2017 that many believe can now be taken forward in 2018.

The British election in June 2017 has fed into this conviction. The UK's post-election uncertainty seems to have reinforced unity among other member states. EU politicians now assert that Brexit has worked as an antidote to Euroscepticism and populism across the continent. In many settings, maximalist, federal options are back on the table – a buoyant self-confidence in the EU is now displacing talk of the need for alternative models of integration.

Since his election in May 2017, there has been much talk of President Macron being a catalyst for deeper integration. Macron has talked astutely about how fundamental change is needed to the way the EU works and has even recognised that the UK vote to leave reflects the Union's current shortcomings. The new president has suggested an innovative series of 'democratic conventions' on the EU's future (a proposal we will return to in Chapter 5). At the same time, he calls unequivocally for deeper integration and full economic union. Eyes have been trained on Germany's reaction. Even if most observers doubt that significant convergence on economic policies will occur, the French and German governments have suggested they may now be willing to contemplate treaty change to usher in some areas of deeper integration. At the end of summer 2017, Chancellor Merkel made positive comments about economic union, but clarified that she favoured a very limited version of this.

With their national rehabilitation so tied to the postwar model of integration, the French and German elites still seem to show little appetite fundamentally to question the status quo and explore less formal, less hierarchical, more open forms of cooperation. They have both supported a tilt towards intergovernmental power in recent years. German politicians often stress that they dislike disruptive politics within Germany itself, preferring smoothly managed trade-offs – and they tend to believe the same style of politics is best for Europe and the EU too. With Angela Merkel now obliged to begin difficult talks to form a new government, this caution is even less likely to change.

Moreover, the external context in 2017 has not been propitious for ambitious, new thinking. Donald Trump's mercurial and erratic actions have encouraged a 'banding together' mentality among EU member states – with much talk of the need to deepen current integration plans as a response to a US president now openly critical of the EU project. While this is welcome, insiders acknowledge that this has once again diverted attention from any 'risky' rethink of the integration model.

Just as much as policy-makers, writers, academics and think-tankers have also advocated a centralisation of similar sets of policies to existing EU institutions and processes. For instance, the much-cited if controversial Bernard-Henri Lévy argues that only deeper political integration and common policies can now save Europe, as he sees the choice as an existential and binary one: 'Europe or barbarism, Europe or chaos.'[11] In one illustrative example of the standard set of reforms generally espoused, an influential project carried out by the European Policy Centre has called for a 'New Pact for Europe', comprising a package of large-scale stimulus investment at the EU level, more union spending on social policy, centralised fiscal capacity, a centralised unemployment insurance scheme, and EU-wide voting for single lists of European Parliamentary candidates.[12]

Author Ulrike Guérot agrees that integration needs a new start, and calls for a 'Republican Europe'. This would involve power being taken away from governments in the European Council; voting on a pan-European rather than national basis; voters defining themselves as citizens of Europe as much as national subjects; and Europeanised taxes and social rights.[13] More subtly, Sergio Fabbrini argues that powers should be centralised, albeit without a single EU government: a federal union rather than a federal state.[14] I could cite many more articles and reports in the same vein. In general, analysts may suggest slightly different terminologies and different policy mixes, but they insist that more formal, institutionalised cooperation is needed.

Many writers and reports start by acknowledging that old-style federalist visions are no longer feasible, but then advocate measures that in most senses look very similar to traditional models of supranational integration – even when dressed in the different language of confederalism (the notion of cooperation flowing from states that retain ultimate sovereignty) or republicanism (whereby political authority flows from citizen consent). They invariably map out a form of political union that is still based around much greater centralisation of powers. The impression is that at least some seek to drop the term 'federal' mainly for presentational reasons.

PARALLEL WORLDS

Despite their many judicious ideas, these calls suffer from several shortcomings in how they relate to the context of the current crisis. First, they do not work with the grain of member states' and citizens' actually existing concerns and positions. Proposals invariably take the form of injunctions that can appear to be plucked from thin air. Europe must be more united. Governments must have more common policies. Powers must be transferred to the EU centre. Ideas are replete with a litany of 'shoulds' untethered from political and social reality. They build castles in the air. If unity and solidarity were so easy to conjure up, one imagines that governments would already have implemented these 'shoulds' and the EU would not have found itself in the current morass.

There is a nagging air of unreality about some such proposals: member states that have fought tooth and nail over the last decade are expected suddenly to give up huge chunks of power in the name of a shared vision of economic development. These blueprints never seem to explain *how* governments are likely to make this step. And even if it does now, from late 2017, prove possible for governments to follow through on steps towards deeper integration, they would risk misidentifying the structural drivers of the poly-crisis, deepening divisions and exacerbating citizens' feelings of disempowerment.

Generations of political elites have been acculturated into thinking of European cooperation in terms of one set framework, and of holding a specific model of EU institutions and rules to be synonymous with European solidarity. Understandably, this makes it difficult for them to think outside these parameters, even when many of them now insist they are favourably disposed to doing so. Elites' rhetoric is counterproductive in ratcheting up the level of aspiration and making more ambitious promises in response to the crisis. If the EU were more modest in its level of ambition, citizens might be less frustrated and angered when results fall short. The Energy Union provides one concrete example: governments committed to this in a blaze of high-level promises, before they realised that member states have increasingly divergent notions of what energy security means and that the sharper competition for ever-more finite resources could be a source of major disunity rather than a new platform for EU success.

Of course, it is entirely logical and desirable to call for stronger European unity. After all, who would aspire to disunity? But the ubiquitous and habitual calls for deeper integration implicitly understand 'unity' in a very particular form. All governments preach 'unity', but each state wants unity in the sense of its own interests being supported by others in Europe. Few mean they are willing to relinquish vital interests of their own in the name of European unity. Appeals to unity and solidarity may strike a desirable note, but they have become vacuous – that is, they add little in terms of understanding how we map a practical path out of the quagmire in which the European dream finds itself.

The standard proposals fail to explain why we should expect support for the concept of European citizenship to materialise now, after such a divisive period of crisis. Analysis uniformly posits the resurfacing of local or national identities as a problem. Ideas for moving forward rarely get to grips with the practical need for a new Europe to work with the grain of local identities rather than against it. Any desire to reclaim local ownership from the EU is now widely dismissed as nativist nationalism. Often it may indeed be so, but this is not always and certainly not necessarily the case. I will return to this point later, in drawing out what legitimate and productive roles such local identities might play in an alternative Europe.

A second concern is that the standard proposals may risk aggravating the causal drivers of the poly-crisis. They suffer from a kind of circular hollowness. They call for an extension of the same integration model that has been the cause of the EU's current crisis. Simply calling for more unity and convergence is unlikely to be productive when the crisis has revealed the very opposite – divergence and a creeping distrust between European peoples. Council president Donald Tusk has realised that 'A vision of a federation does not seem the best answer to euro-scepticism, euro-pessimism and the spectre of a break-up that is haunting Europe.'[15] This is not to argue against deeper cooperation per se but rather to suggest that more focus is first needed on improving the basic structure of integration that is to be advanced. 'More Europe' may be desirable, but 'more Europe' of the wrong type will be counterproductive.

Many recent reform blueprints are repackaged from previous, very different periods. Proposals now seek to replicate the institutional model of the European Coal and Steel Community in areas – such as the digital market – that could not be more different in their basic economic dynamics from the heavy industries of the 1950s.[16] The new European defence plans also return to proposals tried decades ago and put forward many times since then. While citizens are undoubtedly concerned about security, they have hardly been demonstrating in the streets for shared defence procurement as the means of restoring their faith in the European project. The new Defence Fund is at the least somewhat insensitive in committing 1.5 billion euros of new money per year to help arms manufacturers develop prototype military equipment at a time when the EU is forcing member states to cut pensions, education and health spending. When Federica Mogherini now regularly talks about the possible development of a common Euro-drone, one wonders if this is really what citizens want as a means of feeling reconnected with their EU. Indeed, a focus on the notoriously opaque policy sectors of defence and intelligence-sharing risks taking the EU even further away from people's desire for more transparency and accountability.

The standard proposals misdiagnose what is needed to get to the root causes of today's Eurosceptic populist surge. An unfortunate dynamic is at work: as rightist populists appropriate the discourse of redemocratising the EU – they gathered together in Germany in January 2017 under the banner of 'Freedom for Europe' – this makes mainstream politicians more reluctant to deviate from the current model of integration. They fear that to do so might be seen as a defeat, playing into the hands of right-wing populists.

However, for all the simplistic, intolerant and parochial positions held by populist parties, their rise cannot be dismissed as an errant anomaly. The standard pro-integrationist prescriptions struggle to understand the depth of citizens' concerns and underlying social change. European governments and officials work to an overly simplistic trope that unhappiness with the EU is coming from those 'left behind' – implying that all the EU needs to do is to extend the benefits of existing integration to more people. Centrist, liberal, internationalist politicians have increasingly talked of the need to rethink how to defeat the nationalist right; but few of them have suggested that devising different ways of doing European cooperation could help towards this end. Prime minister Mark Rutte defeated Geert Wilders in the Dutch election by promising to rebuild patriotism and national identity – but he did not spell out what kind of reformed EU he would seek in order to fulfil these promises.

The EU poly-crisis is the manifestation of a broader clash between, on the one hand, changes in the international economy and global political order, and, on the other, citizen empowerment. It is well known that people turn away from cosmopolitanism to nativist identity as protection against uncertainty and turmoil. Current EU policies and integration models seem to have accentuated the economic, political, social and cultural disorder that drives such fretful insularity. These are deep-rooted trends, not mere popular caprice – and as such, it is unlikely that they can be excised simply by pushing ahead with more of the same from the EU. The point is that there are profound, structural reasons why the traditional templates for deeper EU integration need to be rethought.[17]

Flowing from this, a third weakness is that many calls for 'more Europe' flow from a questionable assumption that the key change required is for stronger political leadership to push forward with deeper integration against misinformed and irrational doubters among the population. If only national governments would stand aside, the narrative runs, citizens would cooperate across borders free of petty national rivalries. The premise is that cooperatively minded European citizens are being held back from EU harmony by devious and feckless national governments.

This is, surely, a dangerous caricature upon which to base a vision of the EU's future. It is dependent on an understanding of power, agency and political change that is discordant with ongoing social change – a pervasive problem with much EU analysis to which we will return many times during the book. A common argument has been that Europe needs strong leaders to push on with integration against populist opinion. But if done too heavy-handedly this may risk widening the increasingly striking disconnect between leaders and citizens even further.

With polls showing that the more citizens engage with EU debates the more doubts they express about the EU, solutions cannot simply be about explaining or communicating the EU better – as elites often claim.[18] In the wake of President Macron's election, there is again much talk of a repaired Franco-German motor being the key to reviving the EU. While this is clearly a welcome prospect, it once again risks detracting from the underlying changes in political process that are required. It should be remembered that for many other member states, the hauteur of the Paris–Berlin duopoly has been one of the causes of the EU's crisis, not its potential remedy.

In a similar vein, to conclude that Brexit shows the need for EU leaders to push forward to political union, if necessary against public ambivalence, must be a mistaken reading of what caused the poly-crisis. There is significant risk in the emerging argument that the UK's apparent self-immolation will unlock the doors of full political union. Forging unity by using Brexit Britain as the EU's antonymic 'other' will not address the structural roots of the poly-crisis. Indeed, EU leaders may be using a perfectly understandable antipathy towards Britain's truculent Conservative government as a convenient distraction from their own inability to rethink integration. It might be entirely reasonable for the EU to feel little sympathy for the UK's self-inflicted pain, but it is hardly an inspiring message to reignite deeper integration on the basis of fear – that is, by stressing that citizens should be afraid of the consequences of questioning the status quo.

A fourth point: there is a certain intellectual and analytical atrophy that prevents ideas about the EU's future keeping pace with the way that European societies, economies and political processes are changing. The calls for more of the same do not flow from a theory of social and political change that captures the complexities of how politics and societies are evolving. The process of change upon which European integration has long been based looks simplistic today: it assumes that interdependence deepens, that it works, and that therefore states and citizens automatically fit into a pattern of wanting more of the same kind of integration.

These existing models of integration were fashioned over half a century ago. Since then European societies have changed out of all recognition. The relationship between citizen and state has undergone a far-reaching transformation. It is hardly surprising that the EU's institutional processes also need updating in tune with these underlying shifts. We will pick up this crucial analytical issue in Chapter 4, when I attempt to set the parameters for a more rooted, bottom-up concept of change and power – and to tease out how this might lead us towards an alternative form of deeper European cooperation.

Among commentators and researchers, there is surprisingly little plurality of views. Most analysts stick closely to a very traditional way of interpreting the European project. There are journalists who are profoundly Eurosceptic, but few experts who question the basic premises of the integration model from a more positive standpoint. Writing commonly takes the form of journalists, intellectuals, think-tankers and former politicians calling for today's leaders to adopt bold new ideas – without the writers themselves going beyond the familiar range of very old ideas about the EU project.

Academic work on European integration has focused on established concerns like the debates between intergovernmentalism and supranationalism (cooperation between governments versus policy powers being vested in EU institutions), between rationalism and constructivism (governments carefully weighing up their interests versus cooperation flowing from values and identities), or about multi-level governance (the coexistence of different levels of policy-making authority). These debates have deflected scholars away from the big questions about Europe's future. The inadequacy of current concepts gives birth to a paradox: the crisis has deepened both supranationalism and intergovernmentalism, and both of these have intensified the turmoil and dissatisfaction now at hand. Ian Manners and Richard Whitman have drawn a link between these conceptual shortcomings and the ongoing EU crisis: they suggest that 'more pluralism, productive dissent, inclusivity, robust scholarship and engagement with the EU political field would help address the yawning chasm between scholarly theories and the political realities of the EU.'[19]

More radically, critical thinkers lament that the standard solutions are failing because they simply mimic the forms and practices of the nation state. The EU has failed in its mission to map out a different kind of political system and in its post-modern promise of a deterritorialised politics. Post-structuralists – who search for power interests behind political concepts – say the EU project has come to replicate the same kind of exclusionary actions of the nation state, especially in terms of how it runs pro-market economic policies, how it seeks to develop European identities and now through its search for 'harder' borders around the Union.[20] Ben Rosamond sums up the state of debates: the search for alternative approaches to European integration now requires analysts to set themselves against the rather limiting conceptual boundaries of accepted scholarship in EU studies.[21]

BEYOND ANTI-AUSTERITY

There is a specific strand of calls for deeper integration that has assumed particular resonance and force within post-crisis debates. Among analysts, the most common call is for future EU integration to be based on centralised measures that counteract austerity. Many understand deeper EU cooperation and solidarity to be synonymous with a Union less wedded to financial austerity. Many equate an alternative Europe with an anti-austerity Europe – and an EU capable of taming the unaccountable power of global markets and finance.

Hundreds of articles have been written arguing the same line: that saving and changing the EU is a matter of Germany allowing more inflationary and expansionary policies, and allowing wages of German workers to rise as a means of strengthening the competitiveness of periphery countries. Centre-left parties in France, Spain and Italy have pressed for a single EU-wide minimum wage, retirement age, unemployment fund and treasury. In some member states, conservative and other right-wing parties have also pushed back against stringent austerity.

The anti-austerity argument is well-grounded and essential, but in some ways has clouded debate about future models of integration. The questioning of austerity might be a necessary part of reinventing European integration, but it is not sufficient for this purpose. While the criticisms of austerity are well made, they do not reimagine the core political processes of European cooperation. There may be powerful reasons to sympathise with the economic and social aims of the anti-austerity line, yet this line does not proffer a model of integration. It advocates different policies, not a different form of EU integration. My concern here is not to enter in detail into the long-running debate about whether fiscal prudence has been too harsh; rather, it is to distinguish this debate from the broader reflection required to reset the EU integration model.

For some leftist critics, the crisis was and remains a crisis of market capitalism more than of the EU as such. They berate governments for failing to curtail financial organisations, the real perpetrators of the crisis. Many writers strongly urge more centralised integration as a means to embed a more social-democratic or socialist set of economic policies. Their concern is not with the qualitative, political features of the integration process in itself. Rather, their goal is to change the nature of the EU's policies – in order to bring about the creation of a more effective, supranational welfare state.[22] A common assumption is that a commitment to fostering growth would suffice to resolve the EU's crisis of legitimacy.

There is then a tendency to suggest that creating an anti-austerity, social Europe is the same thing as achieving a more workable way of organising the process of integration – rather than being a preference for one type of policy. The crisis has engendered endless debate about whether austerity is necessary or counterproductive; whichever position turns out to be right from the retrospective viewpoint of the *longue durée*, for now both will retain adherents. This means that in practice the EU needs to find a form of political process capable of dealing with diametrically opposed positions on this question.

This issue is now very much centre-stage in policy debates, as the newly elected President Macron calls for a fully centralised economic and fiscal union. It may be that Macron's political momentum wins some concessions from Germany on economic policy and that the EU is now able to take modest steps towards deeper economic union. Many predict that Germany will feel pressure to show greater flexibility if Macron advances on domestic reforms within France. Even if there is a limited degree of rapprochement around some of Macron's proposals, however, it will not negate the need for deeper political changes. A mild, welcome dose of Franco-German convergence on economic, fiscal and banking union would be beneficial, but not a panacea. Slightly more flexible spending rules and steps towards some redistributive union would not suffice to 'refound' the EU, as Macron himself has suggested is necessary. For the moment, the president's early efforts to meet EU fiscal targets have dragged down his approval ratings.

Social Europe is invariably presented as a solution, a means of making the EU more popular and meaningful to its citizens. Again, however, it is by no means certain that there is common agreement on social Europe any more than there is on monetary policy. One might reason that if social entitlements are so dear to citizens, they are unlikely to cede control over these to EU decision-makers.[23] One poll of eight member states shows that the areas of policy where citizens most strongly support competences remaining at the national level are budgetary policy and unemployment benefit – in these policy areas 73 and 66 per cent of people, respectively, want national sovereignty retained.[24] Another late-2016 survey shows that those people fearful of economic interdependence are the most sceptical that more centralised integration is the best antidote to globalism.[25]

Leftists have not yet advocated or designed a new political model of integration. In Spain, Podemos speaks against 'the bankers' EU', but does not have a vision of integration that is any less centralist than what currently exists; indeed, it came out against the notion of flexible integration. So-called 'new' parties like Podemos and Syriza in Greece, which promised to transform Europe, for the moment look to be as mired in the arts of trade-offs and power-seeking as the *casta* they so fiercely excoriate.

If it is to serve as the basis for a common EU identity, the European social model needs updating. A strong and convincing argument has been made in recent years that the state needs to switch its role from compensating losses to pre-emptively investing in what is necessary to make the EU globally competitive.[26] Yet this has rarely been the focus of governments' proposals for deeper integration. The main debates in recent years appear to have got struck on the single question of whether to increase or decrease state spending, replaying discussions from several decades ago, as if nothing had changed in the structure of global economic relations.

Both sides of the austerity debate seem stuck – constantly bewailing either the narrowness of German policy visions or, conversely, the free-rider rule-breaking of debtor states. If a magical, breakthrough summit should suddenly conjure up a new consensus, so much the better. But for now this seems unlikely. What is needed is a different *process* – one that can deal with the current divergences, work around them and explore new avenues for and understandings of solidarity.

SIREN CALL: DE-INTERDEPENDENCE

If generic entreaties for 'more Europe' fail to address the particular characteristics of the poly-crisis, neither do positions at the other end of the spectrum: the increasingly shrill calls for 'less Europe'. My purpose here is not to offer a general or exhaustive evaluation of the anti-EU case, but rather to explain why it fails to speak to the specific drivers of the multiple crises witnessed since 2008.

Those rejecting the 'deeper integration' mantra overwhelmingly urge 'a Europe of nations': a winding back of European cooperation, not a new form for advancing collaboration. The option of national autonomy may have won support in response to the crisis, but it is out of sync with the factors that have caused it. Those pressing for a simple, blanket recipe of 'less Europe' misdiagnose the underlying causal drivers of the poly-crisis just as much as those calling for the opposite.

For sceptical analysts, the EU has simply become too ossified to reform in any significant way and therefore detachment from the European project is the only viable way forward. The ship is sinking and the best course of action is to jump overboard early enough to grab a lifeboat. The crisis shows that the only viable alternative now is to disband the integration project altogether. The underlying 'deceit' of the incremental method of cumulative integration has been laid bare and all its unresolvable contradictions rendered more acute by the crisis. There are no feasible different models of integration to consider. Disintegration is inevitable and governments can only cause harm by swimming against this unstoppable tide.[27]

Doubters predict that the EU may survive in vestigial form, but will no longer be central to the European conduct of affairs, as it will simply be bypassed. This is especially so because new technology has resulted in cooperation occurring on a completely different plane from that on which EU institutions are based.[28] Some analysts insist that the EU's dissolution would enable fully sovereign states to deal with security threats – from Russia to refugees and IS – more effectively than they are doing at present.[29]

Yet unspooling European cooperation would not address the underlying reasons why the poly-crisis has been so serious. The dynamics of the EU's recent difficulties do not in themselves demonstrate that nation states are now more able to meet policy aims by freeing themselves from regional cooperation schemes. Europeanness may have lost some of its sheen in citizens' eyes, but states have hardly gained the capacities needed to provide solutions without European cooperation.

Isolationists' solutions fail on their own terms. Sceptics insist that either diluting or exiting the EU is the way to recover effective control and accountability. They equate 'representing the people' with defending a supposed national interest against the intrusions of European-level decisions. They wrongly see reviving democracy as synonymous with limiting European cooperation. In practice, national isolation or radically diminished degrees of EU cooperation would leave nation states vulnerable to the influence of deepening interdependence with even less say over the external constraints to which national economies are subject. It is a perspective on control and autonomy that contradicts its own premises and is unjustifiably pre-emptive in equating more democracy with less integration.

National isolation is not a guaranteed way of recovering democratic control. As we will see in the next chapter, the legitimacy of national political systems is waning just as much as that of EU institutions. Polls now regularly show that in several member states citizens have lost faith in national institutions just as much as – if not more than – in EU institutions. There are only a handful of exceptions to this trend, including the UK, Germany, Austria and the Netherlands.[30]

If the EU had not existed, it is by no means clear that citizens would have found better national political avenues to ensure effective remedies to the economic and political as well as security- and identity-related aspects of the poly-crisis in recent years. While concern has rightly grown over European integration producing marginalised 'outsiders', the strategies of national autarchy that predominated before the 1980s were hardly a resounding success in preventing this phenomenon. Perhaps reflecting this, central and Eastern European states have angrily huffed and puffed against the EU, but then in practice press for more benefits from the existing model of integration rather than mapping out any alternative.[31]

The argument put forward by Yanis Varoufakis is instructive, as a politician whose direct and punishing experience of the EU's democratic distortions gave him more reason than most to campaign to leave the Union. He cautions:

> I wish that we could [...] have a degree of autonomy, autarky [...] You can't [...] if you exit, then you will always be subject to a market that is run by technocrats and you will have even less degrees of freedom than you have now [...] I believe in staying in [the EU] to subvert the rules.[32]

Leading French political philosopher Pierre Manent has elegantly traced the lineage of democracy's historical development to conclude that the EU project has detached self-governance from its necessary moorings in the nation state. He argues for the reassertion of the nation state, not as a cultural construct that generates antagonistic nationalism, but as the entity that is necessary for organising self-government – a self-government that has to be about mediating political differences and not simply a set of formal rights enshrined in EU treaties.[33] While such analytical frameworks represent a vital contribution to the debate over the EU's future, it is striking that they invariably eschew any discussion of how nationally based self-government is to be combined with the democratic management of interdependence – and tend not to acknowledge that this latter imperative has unavoidably to be tackled.

The poly-crisis is not a reflection of unravelling interdependence. Anthony Giddens points out that while the crisis has brought sharp divisions to the surface, it shows how interdependent member states and societies are and how deeply they share a single 'community of fate'. The only viable way forward is for citizen-led models of integration to emerge based on the principle of 'mutuality' – the recognition that shared responsibilities are unavoidable in today's closely interwoven patterns of social, economic and political relations that stretch across national borders.[34] This reflects the fact that national isolation rubs against deeply entrenched patterns of cultural diversity and social linkages that have been built up across European borders.[35]

For example, many studies demonstrate the enormous cost of reinstalling national border controls. One calculates that over a decade the EU would lose the equivalent of Italy's whole GDP.[36] Some writers believe today's most successful states are those that embrace the geopolitical advantages of migration.[37] The startling growth in cross-border digital networks makes it especially clear that purely national governance is unlikely to be able to regulate modern social and economic activity.

Neither is it clear that national isolation would bring politics into line with the popular will, despite the gains registered by Eurosceptic parties. Overall, opinion polls show that while few citizens support deeper integration across the board, few support a dramatic unwinding of integration. The apparent paradox is that citizens seem to want to keep the basic level of integration more or less the same, yet they also express growing dissatisfaction with the way the EU works.[38] An extensive polling project carried out by the Bertelsmann Stiftung found that 'Europe's citizens may be dissatisfied about the current state of affairs in Brussels, but they are equally unhappy with the situation in their national capitals' – that is, citizens do not see the nation state as a vastly better alternative to European cooperation.[39]

The idea has taken root that support is holding up for the EU only among a privileged, urban and cosmopolitan elite; but the figures do not show that it is only an 'elite' who acknowledge the need for interdependence to underpin national interests. The debate is being reframed in a misleading way – as if a less liberal Europe would be less elitist. A common notion suggests that liberalism is some kind of disease specific to this same self-serving elite. But if liberalism is understood as tolerant protection for the voiceless, then surely it is clear that a less liberal Europe would be even more elitist, not less so.

Anti-EU populists' division of society into 'the good people' versus 'the bad elite' does not correspond with views on Union policies. Among 'the people' there are huge variations, between those doing well out of European cooperation and keen for more integration and those less at ease with its cosmopolitan ethos. The populist dichotomy does not in itself help map any particular form of EU reform capable of commanding consensual support. Both leftist and rightist populism contain elements of genuine grievance, but both tend to an extreme. An alternative Europe cannot realistically be one that undoes economic interdependence, as some on the left advocate, or one set up to defend a supposed European civilisation, as some conservatives want.

Despite their support for prime minister Viktor Orbán, Hungarians still profess a favourable attitude towards the EU. Orbán's Fidesz party only turned critical after the EU rejected its pleas for more flexible austerity; it also felt that the EU was biased against the conservative values of the voters it represented. Similarly, in Italy voters have switched to Eurosceptic parties while polls show they apparently still support the general aspiration of deeper union. All this suggests that disintegration would hardly address the problems of social frustration among may parts of the population. It would be no magic wand.

History does not suggest that weaker regional cooperation results in stronger nation states, as if there were a zero-sum trade-off between the two levels. Realists often celebrate the 1648 Treaty of Westphalia as a European security system based on national sovereignty. However, under the Westphalia system, France, Prussia, Spain, Austria, Britain, Russia and others tried just about every combination of alliances and enmities without stemming bloody conflict. Maintaining a balance of power came at a huge cost in terms of lost lives and societies' constant mobilisation for war. Could Europe really expect to be free of such fraught geopolitical dynamics today if integration evaporated?

CONCLUSION

After such a chastening poly-crisis, many policy-makers acknowledge the need for fundamentally different approaches to integration. Yet beneath the rhetorical calls for experimentation, most formal reform proposals in fact tread well-worn paths. Even as they now talk of a new era of deepened cooperation, governments have failed to address the structural failings of the EU integration model as successive crises have hit the continent. Leaders work with the mindset that a leaking boat cannot be fixed in the middle of a storm. Yet the EU boat is constantly battered by gales and the moment of repair never arrives. There never will be a perfect, becalmed opportunity for designing and implementing a grand template for the future EU as an all-defining, all-clarifying solution. At the risk of over-extending this metaphor, it might be suggested that leaders should stop trying to add more and more layers to their heavily leaking boat and instead transfer to a more seaworthy vessel. Different ways must be found of recovering ground on the journey towards European solidarity – along with a more convincing conceptualisation of how positive, constructive change is likely to come about.

CHAPTER THREE

The Democracy Problem

One element of the poly-crisis cuts across and through all the different policy areas in which the EU has struggled to find unity and effective solutions. This is the EU's democracy problem. This warrants special attention as it sits at the heart of all others aspects of the crisis. Finding a way to overcome this problem will need to be the central pillar of an alternative Europe.

It has become increasingly clear that the EU suffers from major deficiencies in democratic accountability. Analysts have been writing about the EU's so-called democratic deficit for many years, alluding to the fact that as policies are centralised to the EU level, national democratic controls are lost without being replaced by effective European-level democracy. While the problem is not new, however, the EU's democratic shortcomings have now come to have a more tangible impact, contributing in a major way to citizen revolts and political upheavals within member states. In 2004, the number of Europeans who believed that their voice counted in the EU was 39 per cent; by 2014 it had dropped to a worryingly low 29 per cent. Over the same period those who felt 'disempowered' by the Union increased from 52 to 66 per cent.[1]

This chapter unpacks the EU's democracy problem – and in doing so shows that this is not quite as straightforward a phenomenon as often assumed. While much attention has focused on the opaqueness of EU institutions and the standard notion of the Union's democratic deficit, Europe's democracy problem also arises from trends at the national level. The chapter also points to governments' increasing tendency to prioritise 'practical results' over democratic improvements in European integration. After dissecting the different levels of the democracy prob-lem, I question the widespread assumption that solving this issue is primarily about boosting the role of the European Parliament and national parliaments.

EUROPEAN DEFICIT

The first component of the democracy problem flows from the way in which the crisis has been managed at the EU level. Several important areas of decision-making have been centralised at the European level without strong accompanying democratic oversight. The EU is a micro-cosm of particularly acute tensions between cross-border markets and democratic politics. The harsh effects and disciplines of economic crisis have done much to limit effective democracy across Europe. This is the part of the democracy problem that is best known and to which writers most routinely allude.

Even before the crisis erupted, experts were warning that EU policies would inevitably become more controversial and politicised, as the Union began to engage in issues that affect the distribution of economic and other benefits.[2] In the aftershocks of the euro crisis, the dearth of democratic legitimacy behind EU policies has become more evident and more extensive. The crisis has aggravated the political economy of Europe's democratic deficit. It has sharpened the tensions between liberal economics and a liberal politics that seeks to operate on a trans-national, pan-European basis. Colin Crouch influentially defined this situation as 'post-democracy': policy responses to the financial crisis have reinforced the embedded power of economic elites and further eviscerated popular accountability.[3] The EU's long-present distortion of running 'policies without politics' has become increasingly serious and problematic.[4]

Increased supranational powers of oversight and intervention have transferred more powers to the EU's centre with little effective demo-cratic control – indeed, in some cases after national governments have expressly restricted debate and scrutiny. The Fiscal Compact treaty obliges member states to introduce constitutional provisions to limit deficits and to submit budgets for scrutiny to the EU institutions ahead of any debate in national assemblies. The ceding of more powers to the EU level has been done without treaty change that would have required the consent of all member states.

France won more time to reduce its deficit on condition it pushed through labour reforms, which the government did using special powers that circumvented opposition in parliament. When Greek voters chose an anti-austerity Syriza government, Jean-Claude Juncker bizarrely warned them that 'there can be no democratic choice against the European Union treaties'. German finance minister Wolfgang Schäuble helpfully quipped, 'Elections change nothing.'[5] When Angela Merkel talked about 'market-conforming democracy', this sounded to many across Europe like a notion that would restrict free democratic choices, not enable them.

The European Central Bank has become the most powerful actor in deciding the fate of the euro without any efforts to introduce democratic accountability over its decisions. Moves towards a limited form of banking union merely increase the degree of opaque decision-making by unaccountable bodies, increasing the powers of the bank. The banking union is often presented as the key to reassembling an effective post-crisis EU. But its rationale – single supervisory processes for European banks – is hardly a rallying cry to enthuse citizens in the stirring nobility of the European project.

National politicians have borrowed from the fragile legitimacy of the Union in order to implement difficult austerity measures. This has tainted the EU. In the eyes of many citizens, the EU has become akin to the adjustment-imposing IMF, rather than a project of solidarity. In the middle of Spain's tense elections in 2015 and 2016, Commission statements about the risk of the country reversing labour reforms and falling behind on deficit reductions met with an angry response from Spanish party leaders – who saw the EU as upsetting delicate talks to form a government.

The poly-crisis has changed the structure of the integration model. It has not just changed a few EU-level competences, but has redrawn the very type of polity that the EU operates. During the crisis, the EU moved beyond being a primarily 'regulatory state', limited to correcting market externalities through regulations. And as this has happened, profound uncertainties and imbalances have come to dominate policy-making challenges. EU-level decisions have created a range of surveillance mechanisms that have consequences for fiscal and macroeconomic policies. Such integration by stealth raises uncomfortable questions for the sustainability of future European cooperation.[6]

Moreover, such consciously surreptitious centralisation has extended beyond economic measures. The Commission proposed centralising federal powers over asylum to circumvent national opposition. Poland, Slovakia, the Czech Republic and Hungary all complained at the lack of accountability over the EU plan to relocate refugees. New measures to channel humanitarian aid within the EU for the first time were structured to avoid democratic control by the European Parliament. A new mechanism for funding Turkey likewise sought to neuter concerns over Turkey's deteriorating human-rights situation. Civil society groups protest that EU decision-making is now more opaque and subject to closed-doors dealing than ever before: in 2016 not a single piece of legislation received a second reading in the European Parliament, effectively short-circuiting established democratic procedures in every policy sector.[7]

In short, across a number of policy areas, new European-level crisis-management bodies have become autonomous from governments in de facto terms, undercutting national accountability.[8] Some theorists worry that these moves have upset the delicate balance between national-level accountability and European-level processes.[9] Christopher Bickerton conceptualises the current EU as a 'union of member states': states' most basic authority is inseparable from their EU membership in a way that has dragged authority away from local forms of popular legitimacy. The poly-crisis is not due just to one or two policy challenges but to a change in the whole essence of European nation states.[10]

Growing criticism of the EU pulls Europhiles into a siege mentality that militates against prioritising democracy. A vicious circle has formed: to circumvent the dangers of national democratic processes impeding EU business, EU elites have resorted to low-visibility ways of adding to the *acquis communautaire*, which merely fuels further popular mistrust, and in turns pushes elites into even more opaque avenues of decision-making.[11] Europhiles are increasingly tempted to band together to combat newly empowered Euroscepticism in ways that cut across democratic legitimacy. Governments are increasingly enticed by measures of 'covert integration' that are clearly incompatible with their own rhetoric about the need for stronger democratic accountability.[12]

BACK TO OUTPUT LEGITIMACY – AGAIN

As the democratic deficit at the EU level has worsened, the problem has been effectively left to fester as governments increasingly invest their hopes in reviving 'output legitimacy' – the idea that a few good policy successes are far more important than new ideas to boost democratic accountability. Behind their talk of wholesale political union, leaders are in practice now focused on select policy changes – that is, on centralising cooperation in familiar terms in a few choice areas that can deliver quick, tangible results.

Many argue that the poly-crisis requires governments and EU elites to push ahead with deeper integration to get the management of financial interdependence right – and expressly not to be held back by a constant series of national democratic elections that now give space to Eurosceptic parties.[13] Some prominent experts reject suggestions that the crisis reveals any deep democracy problem at all and insist that the EU should stick to delivering better output.[14]

After Brexit and Donald Trump's election, many European politicians, advisors, journalists and thinkers muttered even more forebodingly about the risks of letting the people have their say – and the need instead to 'get practical'. In recent policy proposals and meetings, the tendency has been towards a so-called 'practical union'. This reflects the reality that many member states now look at the EU in terms of careful cost–benefit analysis, not as an all-encompassing political project whose value transcends immediate, tangible gain.[15]

Since the shock outcome of the UK referendum, pro-Europeans have routinely asserted that direct democracy is a bad idea and that EU policy-makers need to focus on sensible suggestions for modest policy changes. Matteo Renzi's referendum defeat and resignation heightened these concerns over the effects of consulting society. According to one insider, the December 2016 Council summit principally took the form of leaders 'venting their frustration at referenda'.[16] Such democratic doubts have increasingly been expressed on both the left and the right, with a new wave of calls for strong leadership to push the EU forward against errant popular concerns if necessary – a trend evoking Robespierre's now-voguish, sinister rumination: 'The people: are they good enough?'[17]

European leaders increasingly seek tangible progress on deliverable changes in a small number of policies rather than a genuine rethink of EU integration's fundamental tenets. Their assessment is that Brexit and other elements of the crisis call for focused action on borders, shared defence procurement and infrastructure investments rather than for any restructuring of the basic EU model. The desired end state of political integration is left unmodified, while in the short term leaders focus pragmatically on a few areas of deeper integration they believe capable of delivering concrete benefits.

Many new proposals now swing decisively back to a hunt for output legitimacy. This is true of a battery of recent ideas and proposals, including for a digital union, a clampdown on corporate taxes, an enhanced EU social-rights pillar and further increases to infrastructure spending. A 'social summit' is planned for the autumn of 2017. By May 2017, the European Strategic Investment Plan had spent 180 billion euros on economic projects and EU officials proclaim its expansion as central to reviving the Union's fortunes. The Commission and several member states have pushed to boost EU trade defence instruments, while in September 2017 Juncker proposed measures that would undercut national and regional parliaments' say in new trade deals. Italy and others are calling for a huge boost in the Erasmus budget. Some recent suggestions have a populist tinge to them, like the European Parliament's proposal that young people be given a free Interrail ticket to explore Europe and also the idea of creating 'ambassador schools' in which to cultivate the notion of European citizenship – ironic when elites are busy excoriating populists for peddling 'simplistic solutions'.

One set of interviews revealed that policy-makers have come to see a 'flexible union' overwhelmingly in terms of using existing treaty clauses for 'quick-win' results and very expressly not as part of any far-reaching set of reforms.[18] Seeking to rejoin the 'inner core' of large member states in the run-up to the Rome summit, the Spanish government highlighted that it saw a number of big projects in areas like transport, energy and defence cooperation as the way to revive the EU's fortunes.[19] The Commission's March 2017 *White Paper on the Future of Europe* contained no mention of democratising the EU, focusing instead on policy delivery.[20]

The tilt towards output legitimacy is also evident in governments' accelerated move towards a 'Security Union'. As part of these plans the Commission has moved to set up a new research programme for defence issues. This plan triggered a 60,000-strong petition by people concerned about millions of euros being diverted from other parts of the budget and about the broader lack of public oversight over new defence-related funding. In some senses, these proposals are the very antithesis of citizens' pleas for an EU more responsive to everyday concerns over jobs and economic conditions.[21]

As conditions improve, elites bring forward these kinds of new proposals for more cooperation, while their erstwhile promises to reboot citizen-oriented democratic participation are once again disappearing from view. The conclusions of the European Council summit in June 2017, for example, ran through a long list of policy areas where new activity is afoot, but made no mention at all of the democracy challenge.[22] Governments, elites and policy-makers recoil from what democratising integration might entail and clutch for the certainties of 'an EU that delivers results'. This is an entirely familiar historical pattern. When times are good, EU leaders see little need to address the democracy shortfall; when times are bad, they want immediate results and insist they have no scope to focus on the democracy problem. Despite many years of experts and policy-makers agreeing that the EU cannot rely on output legitimacy, policy responses do exactly this.

NATIONAL GOVERNMENTS

The EU's growing democracy problem is not just the result of EU institutions' disconnection from democratic oversight. It also flows from
the way that national governments function within EU debates and the
way they have responded to the poly-crisis. An important component of
this is that national governments – separately and collectively through
the European Council – have assumed more prominent roles in a way
that makes decision-making more opaque. This trend makes it more
difficult for citizens to exert accountability over both EU institutions
and national governments' decisions related to European coordination.

The democracy problem is not just a matter of the economic crisis
or of markets restricting citizens' choices. It reflects a broader approach
to EU policy-making that is increasingly top-down in nature, within as
well as beyond the national sphere. Indeed, in some ways it reflects the
growing role of national governments in such decision-making dynamics, not their eclipse or the creeping power of supranational Brussels
institutions. National administrations have lost legitimacy just as much
as EU institutions for being associated with decisions responsible for
the poly-crisis.

For over two decades now, since the 1992 Maastricht Treaty, many
advances in European cooperation have occurred on an intergovernmental basis. The EU has resorted increasingly to informal procedures
of cooperation – whereby governments agree to coordinate through
setting targets and exerting peer pressure, rather than giving powers to
supranational EU bodies. To help implement cooperation, governments
have created new bodies – like the External Action Service, the European
Stability Mechanism and Frontex – over which they retain leverage.[23]

As a result, popular frustration is not simply a reaction against distant
and opaque EU bodies like the Commission, the European Parliament
and the European Court of Justice. It also reflects disconnects between
national governments and their own citizens. The point is that in some
areas governments have already responded to the lack of enthusiasm for
centralised EU bodies. And clearly, the way they have done this has not
succeeded in mitigating citizens' feelings of disenfranchisement. The

implication is important: solutions to the democracy problem will not be found by simply restoring sovereignty or returning powers back to national governments.

The crisis has in some areas pushed national governments into the driving seat of EU affairs. Many theorists say the period since 2009 has been one dominated by hard bargaining between national governments, in which the influence of both shared ideals and standards of democratic legitimacy has diminished.[24] Commission president Jean-Claude Juncker has interpreted his 'political' mandate in terms of a need to centralise power to push forward certain government-backed policy dossiers. If anything, this approach amplifies concerns over accountability and means that the Commission's new powers have gone hand in hand with – rather than being eclipsed by – ascendant intergovernmentalism.[25] It is generally agreed that this trend has deepened even further in the wake of the Brexit vote, as nervous governments seek a tighter grip on the EU's political direction at this potentially watershed moment.

All this is in turn linked to the much-commented-on turn towards nationalism in many European states. The relationship between democracy and nationalism is complicated and varied. The deepening of democracy has often depended on the emergence of national identity. However, when nationalism extends too far, it can undermine democracy. This debate is complicated further in the EU by the need to understand what democracy means in a context of shared sovereignty. This context means that what analysts and journalists now habitually describe as a turn towards nationalism in Europe does not involve the same kind of bellicose and expansionary 'nationalism' that has blighted previous periods of European history. Rather, it seems more defensively tied to a perceived loss of democratic inclusiveness.

This has less to do with formal national powers or national identity per se than with the real practices of day-to-day politics. The Lisbon Treaty formally made the EU confederal, legally enshrining a state's rights of sovereignty and of withdrawal. But this was about legally fixing nation states' role, not about freeing up national-level democratic participation in the day-to-day functioning of EU policy-making. In practice, legitimacy shortfalls have deepened at the national level as many decisions have been given over either to technical bodies or to markets outside the sphere of political debate. Polling shows that citizens' trust in national institutions has declined almost in parallel with declining trust in EU institutions.[26]

Few parliaments have *ex ante* scrutiny powers over national decisions that relate to EU matters – Denmark's legislature is the main exception, as it must approve the government's negotiating mandate prior to each summit. Citizens do not feel that national parliaments are that much more responsive to their interests and concerns than is the European Parliament. Decision-making on many issues like trade is just as opaque and technical within national governments and parliaments as it is at the EU level. Indeed, it is instructive that those member states where parliaments are most active on EU affairs – the UK, Denmark and the Netherlands – are those with high levels of Euroscepticism. This suggests that national legislative scrutiny over EU matters is hardly a catch-all antidote to discontent with the EU.[27] The so-called yellow- and orange-card procedures introduced by the Lisbon Treaty – which parliaments can raise against Commission legislative proposals – remain virtually unused as a means of influencing EU decisions.

The core message is that both European- and national-level democracy is suffering a worrying depletion – a harsh duality that contrasts with the tendency to see these two levels of democracy as zero-sum trade-offs against each other. One of the most important analytical developments of recent years is the concept of *demoicracy* (government by 'peoples' – *demoi* – as opposed to government by 'the people' – *demos*): some analysts believe that prior to the poly-crisis the EU had begun to develop a *sui generis* mix of national- and European-level democracy.[28] Experts talk about the EU becoming a unique 'compound union', combining democratic channels at the EU level with those at the national level. The concept of demoicracy has gained currency to express the idea that citizens participate both in the national democracies of their countries and in the common democracy of the EU. The optimistic reading is that the EU was moving towards being 'a Union of citizens and member states' with a unique model of transnational governance consisting of a 'common democracy'.[29]

However, the poly-crisis appears to have left these notions on the defensive. Richard Bellamy worries that the EU's 'republican inter-governmentalism' – its identity as an 'international association of democratic states' – has been undermined. This is most clearly due to creditor domination over debtors, but also to other developments such as cases in the European Court of Justice that begin to confer rights of European citizenship, and the instrumental engineering of pan-European political networks.[30] EU demoicracy is premised on the idea that citizens can retain national identities and enjoy democratic accountability at the national level while also expressing empathy with other member states. The crisis has undercut the role of parliaments at the national level, while weakening empathy and effective engagement of citizens at the European level. Both parts – the national and the European – of the EU's incipient demoicracy have been put under strain simultaneously.[31]

ILLIBERAL TURN

The European democracy problem has a potentially even more serious dimension. Since the poly-crisis began, some governments have taken a further step towards illiberal politics – of a kind that represents a more direct and profound threat to the quality of European democracy. In several member states, governments have diluted checks and balances and democratic quality has suffered. The EU now struggles to deal with its own budding autocrats. National-level democracy is experiencing serious problems in many parts of Europe.

The most dramatic and well-known case is that of Hungary, where Viktor Orbán's Fidesz government has repealed many democratic checks and balances, seized control of the judicial process through constitutional change and tightened control over the media and civil society. In summer 2017, Orbán passed legislation severely restricting non-governmental organisations. The government even moved to close down one of Hungary's most prestigious, independent univer-sities, the Central European University. This case unleashed a storm of international media attention, but is only one part of a far broader assault on civic freedoms in Hungary.

In Poland, the government led by the Law and Justice party (PiS) is now following suit with several similar measures – even though the illiberal turn in Poland is for now tamer and narrower than that in Hungary. The PiS has progressively tightened its control over a number of senior judicial and media appointments. In 2016, it introduced a new security and anti-terror law that further short-circuits democratic checks and boosts state surveillance powers. Notwithstanding their differences, Fidesz and PiS openly challenge political, social and economic liberalism.

Even mainstream pro-EU parties in central and Eastern Europe often show ambivalent commitment to core liberal norms of tolerance and the rule of law. Governments in most of these countries have pushed towards more majoritarian forms of democracy, weakening checks and balances and the rule of law. They may still be formally democratic, but increasingly combine ethnic nationalism, social illiberalism and clientelistic, personalised and somewhat predatory politics – a style taken up by both centre-left and centre-right mainstream parties. In the Economist Intelligence Unit's *Democracy Index 2016*, central and Eastern Europe recorded the most dramatic democratic regression of any region at any time since the index began in 2006. For 2016, the region suffered more country regressions than any other region. The index does not now rank a single central or Eastern European state as a full democracy.[32]

If Poland and Hungary talk of leading a wider 'cultural counter-revolution' to challenge the liberal tenets of EU integration, Czech president Miloš Zeman has pursued several illiberal policies from a social-democratic angle. He has been vehemently hostile to Muslim migrants and advocates a major thinning out of EU laws. The Croatian Democratic Union's victory in Croatia has brought several liberal rights commitments into question. All this suggests that central and Eastern European and Baltic states' democratic transitions were always rather shallow, as they sought formally to align themselves with EU conditionalities but did so without deeply internalising liberal norms.[33] Mass protests in Romania in early 2017 forced the social-democratic government to withdraw a law that would have freed politicians accused of corruption from legal sanction – an inspiring testament to civic power but also a reminder of just how far dysfunctional governance has spread within the EU. In May 2017, similar corruption-related protests erupted in Slovakia.

In 2014, the Commission felt obliged to a draw up a new *Framework to Strengthen the Rule of Law* because of these worrying trends.[34] To date, this is essentially a mechanism for dialogue on concerns about the rule of law and has brought forward no new concrete means of dealing with illiberal populism. Since the Commission activated the framework against Poland in January 2016, PiS attacks on judicial independence have merely worsened. The Commission issued its first opinion under this framework in June 2016, criticising the PiS for undermining the judiciary's independence. In the autumn, the Commission moved to a second stage of the process by listing the specific reforms it expected the PiS government to introduce. On both occasions, the Polish government angrily rebuffed the Commission's intervention. Member states have not given strong backing to the Commission's moves against the Polish government; indeed, France, Spain and the UK have on occasion questioned whether the framework really lies within the Commission's competences. At a council meeting in May 2017, a majority of member states for the first time called for firmer action against the PiS government. Yet far from being cowed by the EU, in July 2017 the PiS government passed laws constricting judicial independence even further; the state of these laws was left uncertain when Polish president Andrzej Duda vetoed some of them. The Commission drew up a third opinion under the rule-of-law framework and also at this stage threatened legal action against the Polish government.

The EU has had to fend off PiS accusations of double standards. Previous, more overtly pro-EU governments in Poland also sought to control judicial and media appointments, albeit in more subtle ways. As the EU did not react at all on these occasions, many in Poland feel the Commission is not impartial, and this has stirred further resentment against the Union. The PiS argued that the changes to personnel on the constitutional court were needed to reverse the moves made by the previous Civic Platform government to load the tribunal in its favour shortly before the 2015 elections. The Polish government also complains that the EU is leaning far harder on PiS measures when it did virtually nothing in response to the far wider range of democracy-limiting measures adopted in Hungary.

The mood is brittle: any intrusive EU pressure may stoke the fires of incipient nationalism and Euroscepticism in Poland. A movement called the Committee for the Defence of Democracy has organised large-scale protests against the PiS government – protests that regularly gather more than 100,000 participants and have rumbled on into 2017. When the PiS government introduced rules restricting certain public demonstrations and bypassed parliament to push through its budget plans, the protests managed to get some measures diluted. But Poland's illiberal turn is still getting worse.

The EU has not yet designed effective policy tools to get to grips with the illiberal turn seen within national politics. In May 2017, pressure from the European Parliament seemed to chasten Viktor Orbán and the Commission drew up legal proceedings to challenge the Hungarian government's new civil society laws. While the Hungarian government did react by slightly softening its proposed NGO law, it did so through relatively cosmetic changes. With both Poland and Hungary now subject to Commission legal action, Germany has raised the prospect of reducing EU funds to governments in breach of fundamental democratic norms, but this possibility would only kick in under the new EU budget after 2020 and the idea would still need to gain the support of other member states.

In general, there have been few instances of meaningful leverage. The Agency for Fundamental Rights simply monitors member states' application of EU laws and cannot intervene to limit a general deterioration of democratic quality. The Commission framework is limited to rule-of-law questions and so far seen as relevant only to the current cases of Poland and Hungary. In late 2016, the European Parliament proposed a new mechanism to defend democracy and rights in the Union because of the ineffectiveness of the Commission framework and the Council's rule-of-law dialogues.[35] In March 2017, the Commission and Council rejected this proposal. At the same time, several member states got the Commission to drop a report looking critically into rising corruption across Europe.[36] Some experts argue that the EU's most serious democratic deficit today is the way that political parties in the European Parliament have accepted authoritarian dynamics for partisan reasons – especially in the case of Hungary, given Fidesz's contribution to the European People's Party majority in the Brussels chamber.[37]

Illiberal trends are not limited to central and Eastern Europe. Spain and other states have forced through restrictions on protests and freedom of assembly. The Council of Europe has criticised the creeping political control exerted over the judiciary in Spain.[38] The UK and other governments have given themselves extensive new surveillance powers. France and others have brought in restrictions on minority rights, especially with respect to Roma people. The space for civic activism is narrowing across Europe, in the face of both government restrictions and the rise of intolerant social values. While politicians and EU leaders deliver endless speeches about the need to bring society into a more inclusive process of integration, governments' own actions have in practice begun to make life more difficult for civil society organisations.[39]

The trend now extends well beyond one or two parties with particularly high-profile leaders. A YouGov poll in October 2016 found that around half the people surveyed across 12 member states espoused somewhat illiberal opinions – a combination of anti-immigration sentiments, nationalism, hawkish views on international policy and opposition to human-rights laws, EU institutions and European integration policies.[40] Shocking data from the 2016 World Values Survey suggests that over a third of young voters in Europe believe military rule could be legitimate. These data show declining support among younger voters for a whole series of core liberal-democratic values – among the well educated and rich just as much as those 'left out' of the benefits of EU integration. (It should be pointed out that some experts question these data.)[41] Over the last decade, EU member states are the group of countries whose democratic quality scores have fallen furthest within the Economist Intelligence Unit's Democracy Index, and the regression is not due only to central and Eastern Europe: between 2006 and 2016 democracy scores in 13 out of 21 Western European countries worsened.[42]

Illiberal populists recoil angrily against the EU and liberal values, but their response is to undercut political liberalism at home, not to forward a constructive or innovative vision for European integration. These parties may accurately capture some of the popular frustration with the EU, but they do not embody any kind of reform programme that is compatible with their own narrative of 'letting the ordinary people speak'. To the extent that they menace the quality of liberal democracy in their own national contexts, they cannot be convincing as putative architects of a European-level democratic transformation.

EMPOWERING PARLIAMENTS?

Much current debate centres on ways of enhancing the influence of both the European and national parliaments. Many politicians and analysts see such options as the principal means of boosting democratic legitimacy at the European and national levels. Yet these formal, institutional routes have shown limited potential to deepen the democratic component of European integration – in some ways they even amplify aspects of the EU democracy shortfall.

In most official templates, the main focus for enhancing democratic control has been on boosting the powers of the European Parliament. The 2015 Five Presidents' Report proposes more powers for this institution as the means of legitimising the onward march to fully centralised economic and political union.[43] Ideas that are frequently debated include authorising the parliament to select a combined post of Council and Commission president and selecting commissioners from among its own members.[44] Another standard call is for European Parliament elections to be based on Europe-wide constituencies.[45] In September 2017 a campaign has gathered steam to use transnational party lists to fill the seats vacated by British MEPs.

Enhanced powers for the European Parliament might be desirable on some specific issues, but cannot be the main pillar of a solution to the EU's democracy problem. Debates in the parliament still take place around a division between pro-EU and anti-EU camps, not around different models and ideologies of integration. Most members act as lobbyists for deeper integration, showing little appetite for critically exploring alternative ways of organising integration. In consequence, the argument that the European Parliament is not the solution to the democratic deficit has been prominent for many years. Yet the institution has gained incrementally in power, while other forms of democratic accountability and participation in the EU have not been supported.

As the parliament has gained power in each successive new EU treaty, its legitimacy with citizens has decreased. Thus its weakness today is hardly its lack of formal powers. It has long stood as the purveyor of a particular type of formal, centralised integration rather than as a chamber promoting new and exciting ideas on how to reinvent the EU. The parliament's stake in the existing institutional system is greater than its commitment to finding more effective ways to legitimise the European project. Europhiles point to a tightening Commission–parliament nexus as evidence of stronger democratic accountability. To member states and citizens this nexus looks like Brussels insiders colluding constantly to push more integration – a new form of opaqueness, not democratic openness. Alternatively put: while the European Parliament's democratic role has strengthened upwards, in relation to the Commission, it has weakened downwards, in relation to citizens.

The parliamentary elections in 2014 offered voters an effective choice and leverage as parties agreed that the winning party would select the Commission president; far from enticing voters, the turnout dipped to a record low. Many politicians and experts still argue that the European Parliament's greater powers are helping to generate a common demos.[46] However, polls have found that European public opinion is not favourable towards the idea of a directly elected EU president or to the idea of the European Parliament being the main forum for democratic accountability.[47]

The second standard proposal is for national parliaments to be granted a stronger role in providing the EU with democratic legitimacy. Such calls have grown notably in the wake of the crisis. There is a growing recognition that national democratic processes should be part of the solution for EU democracy, not something to be usurped by purely European-level institutions. It will certainly be essential to design ways for all national parliaments to be better plugged in to EU decisions that affect their countries directly or indirectly. One extensive survey of debates in national legislatures concludes that the crisis has made governments realise that 'the era of de-parliamentarisation' has to end.[48] In the 2017 French election campaign, Socialist candidate Benoît Hamon proposed – unsuccessfully, of course – a treaty for democratising the EU though transferring significant powers from the European Parliament down to national parliaments.

Better national-level democracy is not a zero-sum alternative to European cooperation, but is likely to give firmer grounding and legitimacy for measures agreed at the European level. EU-level legitimacy cannot be achieved by leapfrogging national democracy, but must be built on bettering it. Empowering national parliaments in EU affairs will be vital to reinstalling a kind of republican democracy between member states – where governments treat each other as equals and are also fully accountable to citizens.[49] Yet more is needed than simply having national backstops to vet EU powers. And simply calling for more powers to be given to national parliaments does not help determine what is to be done when no agreement can be found between these parliaments.

While there is widespread agreement on the principle of national parliaments playing a greater role in monitoring EU affairs, in practice doubts and hesitancy persist. A sizeable number of member states rejected David Cameron's bid to increase national parliaments' powers of scrutiny over EU affairs as part of the 2016 UK renegotiation package. The so-called COSAC (Conference of Parliamentary Committees for Union Affairs) is still very opaque. It was created in 1989 but has made little impact. It provides a forum for national MPs and MEPs to share views twice a year but does not allow national parliaments a proactive lead. The public knows nothing about COSAC so it does not serve as a way to bring EU affairs closer to the people – rather it is simply another invisible Brussels committee.[50] The yellow and orange cards will never be a significant means of democratic control because national parliamentarians are unlikely to move explicitly against their own governments to stop new laws.

Intensified consultations between and within national parliaments on EU issues may be useful, but will not suffice to bring about the Union's democratic regeneration, given how disconnected citizens are from mainstream political parties – not only on the European level, but also on the national level. A simple reallocation of European powers down to the national level alone will not restore democratic accountability. A few additional scrutiny committees would hardly be enough to rescue the European dream. A forum of national parliaments is unlikely to solve the challenge of fragmentation and diversity.[51]

As already indicated, it is certainly the case that the nation-state political arena will be one important component of a reformulated EU. But this national-level input cannot be reduced either to an antiquated notion of formal sovereignty or to beefed-up parliamentary scrutiny powers. Rather, it will need to be expressed through many aspects of more active civic participation, organised and articulated at the national level – as explained in the following chapters.

These difficulties reflect a general and crucial point: resolving the EU's credibility shortfall is not just about slightly reshuffling formal competences between different institutions. There is no institutional magic bullet to address the current political malaise in the EU. Focusing on formal processes of democratic control and representation will not be enough to recast the EU as a democratic project. The EU needs to shift from an ethos of legal constitutionalism to one of political participation. The need for democracy is not so much about committees simply blocking laws but about citizens being able to engage more positively and suggest new lines of cooperation.

The EU's complex web of institutions already has multiple points of accountability built into it – indeed, so many as to gridlock decision-making very often. It is not these formal checks and balances that are lacking so much as participative forums that connect citizens to the EU project. The different EU institutions now communicate with each other much more to reach compromise solutions in order to unblock new policies; while this is broadly welcome, it makes decisions even more dependent on bargaining between institutions that have almost taken on a life and identity of their own, beyond any regular citizen guidance.[52]

CONCLUSION

All politicians and political elites say they support ideas to democratise the EU. Such an aim has long been part of the official rhetoric. Yet in practice, the concern with democracy never seems to be deemed important enough to catalyse concrete change. More urgent policy imperatives always appear, crowding the democracy question from the EU agenda. Innovative analytical frameworks have presented the EU as a dual-level democracy, with representation and identities being safeguarded at the national and EU levels. The sobering point is that the crisis has weakened *both* these dimensions of democracy at the same time.

The aim of injecting the EU with greater democracy is often assumed to be a kind of secondary add-on to effective substantive policy coordination. That is, governments and EU institutions endeavour to find agreement on the 'right' policies, and then search for means of legitimising the pro-integration measures they have adopted. Conversely, Eurosceptics disingenuously claim that more democracy necessarily entails less integration. On both sides of the debate, current proposals foreclose discussion over fundamentally different policy choices and fail to provide for the kind of proactive citizen involvement in fundamental political choices that the Union so evidently lacks.

Democracy has not yet become part of the DNA of how the EU seeks to manage contemporary interdependence. The EU must become a democratic project as its very core rationale. It has reached the limit of what it can do without far more meaningful and proactive democratic engagement. European Central Bank governor Mario Draghi was credited with effectively saving the euro when he declared that the bank would do 'whatever it takes' to prop up the currency. The EU needs an equivalent 'whatever-it-takes' in the realm of democracy: a commitment to do whatever is necessary to give citizens a participative stake in the project in order to stem its haemorrhaging support and legitimacy. Donald Tusk issued a forceful reminder at the Rome anniversary summit: 'The unity of Europe is not a bureaucratic model. It is a set of common values and democratic standards.' Policy proposals that do full justice to his emotive call are long overdue.

CHAPTER FOUR

Europe as a Citizens' Project

We have unpacked the different elements of Europe's democracy dilemmas and explained why existing, formal routes to a democratic EU are part of the problem as much as a solution. What then is the remedy? In this chapter I lay the groundwork for approaching the democracy problem from a less familiar angle. This entails exploring new ideas for accountability and participation that have already begun to take root in many emerging democratic processes. The framework I offer here lays the foundation for a series of more concrete policy recommendations that follow in later chapters.

While many articles and books make standard pleas for democratising the EU, they draw from concepts that are very specific to the rarefied world of EU integration and its very distinctive theories and terminology. As we saw in the previous chapters, this reinforces the tendency for specialists to think about future options in terms of existing integration concepts and for EU debates to become unhealthily self-contained. I believe it is necessary to tackle the democracy debate in a less self-referential way and not purely in terms of the standard EU conceptual lexicon.

Standard proposals still see a more democratic and participative EU coming about *through* formal governmental and supranational institutions. In contrast, I contend that the most pertinent avenue of research is to explore whether newly energised civic impulses can also take place *around* these formal, top-down institutions. This is not to deny the importance of top-down decision-making dynamics or the need for robust institutional powers, but rather to examine how civic processes can better feed new ideas into formal institutional reform debates from a vantage point of more proactive autonomy. The many idealistic visions for EU reform fail to explain exactly *how* we are supposed to get from the current stalemate to a better version of European cooperation. My conceptual approach is different from the many others written on the EU's crisis in focusing on the real-life political processes from which an alternative Europe must emerge.

In essence, I am concerned to search for avenues and processes of political change that are more grounded in actually occurring social processes – and therefore more likely to deliver new forms of European integration in practice. In this sense, I explain why there is potential for an alternative Europe to work with the grain of bottom-up processes of civic empowerment. But the chapter also points out how much more needs to be done to maximise such citizen-based potential – and indeed to overcome its limitations and contain its downsides.

DEMOCRACY FROM THE GROUND

The shortcomings inherent in existing approaches to the democracy problem strengthen the case for a more bottom-up and open-ended model of European integration. The EU needs an understanding of political change that highlights the role of citizen agency as opposed to enlightened elite paternalism. It needs to bring its approach to democracy into line with the fluidity of civic activism, new social movements and the changing nature of electorates. The EU's democratic legitimacy will hinge less on controlling or limiting what comes out of Brussels, and more positively on empowering citizens. The insufficient empowerment of citizens is the crux of Europe's current legitimacy malaise, and this goes well beyond the specific configuration of EU institutional procedures. European integration must be run in a way that is more citizen-centred. The new EU must be a project that fosters and allows active citizenship – not one that curtails the exercise of citizenship in the name of a predetermined notion of the greater pro-European good.

With hopes pinned once again on output legitimacy, a common line now widely heard is that the EU must reflect the concerns of 'integration's losers' or 'globalisation's malcontents'. This is too easy a refrain. It gives the impression that a few policy adjustments can solve an issue that is actually far more deeply rooted and behoves us to rethink the structural relationship between citizen and state. It ignores the fact that polls and research show populism to be driven by a complex mix of economic concerns and deep-seated shifts in identity. The populist surge is not the result of temporarily bad economic conditions but a more structural change in identities – of a kind that poses a profound challenge to European integration.

Demand is certainly high for such an approach. In one survey citizens ranked direct public participation as the element of European democracy that is currently most absent from the Union.[1] Asked which actors should gain most influence in EU decision-making, 70 per cent of respondents to one poll said citizens, far above support for any other actor gaining power.[2]

The case for a novel and citizen-oriented concept of EU democratic legitimacy has strong analytical grounding. Theorists concur that injecting more meaningful democracy into the Union will require deviation from the institutional forms of the nation state and must harness looser, cosmopolitan networks of participation.[3] For a project that prides itself on having rethought the whole nature of interstate relations, the EU is disappointingly slow and reluctant to accept novel thinking on democracy and elite–citizen relations. In some ways, the Union is fiercely post-modern; in other ways, it is almost a throwback to nineteenth-century elitism.[4]

Simply replicating national-level politics a notch higher at the European level is not the right metric for an EU democracy. A prominent strand of new theoretical work suggests that democracy gains meaning not so much through its formal rules and rights as by being 'performed' in practice. Democracy is shaped by many continuous acts undertaken by a variety of different actors. This is relevant to the EU since such thinking questions the need for a single 'people' to be defined before democratic politics can function satisfactorily. A political community comes into being by 'performing' democracy in a regular and meaning-ful way.[5] Calls for a Republican Europe are not fully on target because Europe needs more focus on a liberal as well as republican concept of citizenship – that is, rather than the republican emphasis on formal entitlements and identities, what is also required is a liberal concern with active, played-out citizenship.

With citizens recoiling from representative politics at the national level, fixing the EU democratic deficit cannot be simply a matter of granting national parliaments extra powers of scrutiny. Rather than a few additional parliamentary committees, the EU needs a whole new social contract that remoulds the relationship between citizens and the public sphere. Today's populist surge is in essence about citizens' desire to push back the boundaries of the prevailing status quo and encourage elites to explore hitherto uncontemplated and undefined changes.[6] Contrary to much commentary, Brexit was not driven simply by the poor working class or a major rebellion against globalism as such, but was about non-metropolitan areas clamouring for a voice – with a similar trend seen in other member states.

Governments need to reconstitute the Union's grand bargain, this time from the bottom up. The EU requires better ongoing and continu-ally invoked mechanisms of accountability – to hold decision-makers to account on a regular basis, away from party and electoral politics. Accountability needs to be extended to a broader range of stakeholders and civic organisations beyond the formal vote, while being linked more specifically to the management of interdependence across bor-ders. Trans-governmentalism must be accompanied and bolstered by trans-citizenism.

An often-quoted refrain says that 'the EU must be big on the big things, small on the small things'. Many political leaders and policy documents – including the Rome declaration agreed at the March 2017 anniversary summit – have used this phrase in recent years, and the maxim is now widely accepted as a guideline for future integration. Yet it does not answer the crucial question of what precisely the 'big things' and 'small things' actually are in European integration. Politicians and officials sometimes use this expression in a way that suggests that power should be centralised to the EU level for important matters, and exercised at the local level for less important, almost residual, questions. However, there are many vital questions that need to be close to locally participative and vibrant decision-making. Surely, some of the things that 'really matter' are those that need to be kept open to local, popular accountability.

When many analysts call for more democratic debate and participation they betray their real intent by then suggesting that this debate should inexorably lead to support for deeper integration or conversely for less integration – democracy becomes a mere means to a predetermined end.[7] For example, some say it is necessary to deepen economic union, and that securing this through a referendum in all states would give it the requisite legitimacy.[8] Rather than any set of less standard forms of cooperation emerging organically, the end is preordained and then opened for verification.

More open-ended democratic regeneration must allow for the fact that deeper citizen engagement might not always bolster elites' particular policy preferences. This is liberalism's standard test: to restore credibility to the EU it will be necessary to offer more space to its doubters, malcontents and ambivalent hesitaters. Decentralisation, reimagined forms of representation and civic empowerment should not be seen as an anti-EU agenda. Quite the opposite: they offer a more oblique way of saving the integration project from itself – by ensuring that different populations still buy into a form of risk-sharing and solidarity, even after a crisis that has revealed a new multiplicity of varied perspectives.

ALTERNATIVE THEORIES OF CHANGE

The bottom-up route is vital because the EU is stalled by divergence on so many issues, but also because of underlying social and organisational shifts. The lingering elitism in federalist visions rubs uneasily against the sociological dispersal of power.[9] The rise of individualism in social and political action makes activism more disruptive and citizens' trust in big collectivities weaker. More fragmented social activism and political identities reinforce the case for a less monolithic institutional form of EU integration. The EU model has failed to keep pace with these underlying social and political changes. This helps explain why standard visions for deeper integration today seem to be plucked out of thin air, rather than being rooted in a theory of political change that is attuned to social realities.

Some theorists talk of a whole paradigm shift as loosely organised, grass-roots citizen movements have come to be the primary drivers of political, economic and societal change.[10] These new forms of change and agency require us to revisit models of democracy beyond heavily institutional templates.[11] Thicker participation and consensual deliberation lie at the heart of the much-cited notion of 'liquid democracy' – a concept that many believe captures the wave of active, participative initiatives seen across Europe in recent years.[12] A whole body of literature has come to focus on and celebrate these kinds of incipient moves towards 'post-representative politics'.[13]

Analytically, the focus has switched from the strict understanding of liberal democracy protecting individual rights to citizens gaining the capacity and effective independence to exert influence and hold decision-makers accountable.[14] Some theorists argue that moves to relegitimise democracy must be built around these very loose forms of deliberation and localism, cutting across the traditional container of the nation state but also in resistance to centralised institutionalisation.[15] Change, it is suggested, is most likely to be sustained through civic monitoring processes rather than through formal representational avenues on their own.[16]

In line with this, it must be acknowledged that the EU's democracy problem is not just the sign of a temporary surge in Euroscepticism; it is also the result of a profound mismatch between new social mobilisation and citizens' disengagement from standard representative channels. Without a balanced reconciliation of participative and representative dynamics, piecemeal moves towards deeper union risk simply solidifying the elitism that lies at the root of the EU crisis and that has gradually sapped democracy's emancipatory spirit in the member states themselves. Thus, a reimagining of forms of representation within the process of integration is not only essential for legitimising transnational interdependence; it is a prerequisite for regenerating democracy per se. The need is actively to engage citizens and national governments through a combination of local participation and national democracy to influence the way that interdependence between nations is managed.

The local perspective is so necessary because it is rooted in actual economic and social trends. A powerful ethos of localism is emerging, and this is radically different from previous conceptions of local politics – it is not based on the old federalist-inspired 'Europe of the regions', but a grass-roots contestation of hierarchical forms of governance. This kind of localism today outstrips any sign of uniform Europeanisation. The EU has not grown into a single, homogeneously integrated market so much as into a cluster of interconnected islands surrounded by largely unlinked economic spaces. The picture is one of variegated interdependence, dominated by integration between metropolitan nuclei resembling city states. These clusters often have more links with similar communities on the other side of the continent than with small towns nearby in their own country. Moreover, recent evidence suggests that Europeans have increasingly sought a rootedness among local family and community connections.[17]

Crucially, these dynamics shed light on the appropriate concept of *citizenship* that is needed to underpin a reformed model of integration. Democratic citizenship across Europe needs to flow from what citizens actually do and how they act in trying to advance their interests, rather than – as at present – from formal citizenship rights included in EU treaties or new institutional arrangements that seem to have little tangible effect on people's daily lives. What matters is whether citizens are beginning to organise and mobilise in a way that enacts a common democracy in practice, not whether the EU is more intergovernmental or federal at a macro-institutional level.

Initiatives and processes are needed to give concrete expression to a more dynamic form of multilevel citizenship. Debates about citizenship have tended to focus on the formal division of rights between the national and European levels, and the question of which level should have primacy. But the more urgent challenge is to make all levels of citizenship practically more *active* in the way that options for future integration are debated. The aim must be to ensure that the local, national and European levels of citizenship are better linked to each other, without any one prevailing over the others. EU reform should be based on getting democratic participation at the local level to inform debates at the European level, rather than beginning with an idealised notion of European citizenship that then sits uneasily with local concerns. To the extent that an alternative Europe will also need to rest on more active national-level participative forums, this would help ensure that patterns of European cooperation emerge out of active national citizenship, rather than subjugating it. The practical arrangements suggested in the next chapter attempt to embody these citizenship principles.

More broadly, electorates today are far more fluid than they were a generation ago. Individuals' identities are not so rigidly determined by class, professional or corporatist groupings. Democracy is no longer based on or rooted in mass-membership bodies or firmly categorised labour sectors. The original European project was predicated on a core assumption about the way organised interests operate: very specific economic and social sectors would band together across borders and cooperate in pushing for integration because they saw common benefit in doing so. This was the social basis of the so-called neo-functionalist pattern of self-sustaining integration.

But national democracy works very differently today. Opinions are more disparate and the very specifically organised forms of interest-representation less dominant. The notion of a cohesive collective will has given way to a more disaggregated form of civic politics. Beyond all the different policy dimensions of the poly-crisis, the underlying structural predicament is this: the EU rests on a corporatist understanding of political development, in an era marked by the individualisation and atomisation of social organisation. The current model of EU integration is heavily predicated on a functional logic that no longer corresponds to the structure of social interests – and because of this, it no longer offers a realistic theory of political change. The search for 'non-mediated' politics should be an EU strength – as the Union lacks the standard channels of representative democracy – and yet has become its Achilles heel.

Notions of citizen-led change are also in tune with the times to the extent that they flow out of the growing influence of *digital activism*. Of course, it is well known that digital technology has begun to change the basic nature of political activity, as it offers multiple tools for online campaigning, petitioning and voting. While the changes injected by these forms of digital activism have been exhaustively analysed, however, they remain somewhat separate from mainstream debates about the EU. Today, digital tools or 'civic tech' give citizens vastly better organisational capacities and broaden the scope of participation. They allow more people to get involved in decision-making and to hold elites to account, while raising citizens' expectations of how their politicians should be responding to popular demands. Such tools herald such far-reaching change to political activity that their influence clearly needs to be better incorporated into theories and models of European integration.

None of this is naively to posit that citizens can generate political change on their own. As in any process of political restructuring, EU reform will happen only if bottom-up and top-down efforts eventually interlock effectively. The need to combine direct and representative democracy is now well established; the key is to harness both these avenues to foster better-quality deliberation that goes beyond narrow self-regard. The disconnect between direct and representative democracy is a general problem, but is especially acute in the case of EU debates – within both national- and European-level political processes.

My point here is not that formal, national and EU institutional dynamics are unimportant, but that an autonomous impulse towards defining the reform agenda must also come from the civic sphere – instead of the civic sphere having to mould itself to parameters of change that are predefined at a higher, political level. The aim should categorically *not* be to supplant elite-level routes to reform, but rather to add a civic component better to *complement* the standard focus on summits, intergovernmental deals, legal changes, conventions, and the like. Participation is in no way a substitute for solid institutional powers, but rather a way of setting these on a firmer footing. The challenge is to get the conditions right for a benign use of participative and direct democracy, aligned with more open and responsive formal pathways to EU reform. Whatever flaws the use of direct democracy may have had to date – seen especially in ill-conceived referendums – this concept needs to be perfected, not surrendered and suffocated.

The grass-roots level cannot work miracles – and there is a risk today that some analysts and activists may be overly romanticising hyper-localism, seduced by the notion that harsh policy trade-offs can somehow be avoided. Yet it can and should play a primary and generative, not secondary and merely validating role in debates over the EU's reinvention. The next chapter takes up the question of how the vital interlocking between the civic and political spheres might be facilitated.

One other point in parenthesis: while this book is concerned with the future of the EU, the basic spirit of such reflections could also be applied to post-exit Britain. It would hardly fulfil Leavers' supposed mandate of having UK citizens 'take back control' if powers were simply transferred from one opaque, unresponsive power centre in Brussels to another in London – from one underperforming system of democracy to another. If the UK is serious about harnessing Brexit to revive democratic accountability and participation, then innovation will be needed in the way national democracy works in Britain. In the absence of such change, Brexit will hardly usher in a stronger UK democratic identity – indeed, it will simply empower national elites to the detriment of British citizens. This is for now a separate question from democratising the EU, of course, but it might be that in the future ways can be found to interlock democratic innovation in the 'EU 27' with similar reform in the UK.

LOCALISM: PROMISE AND PERIL

An alternative Europe can and should harness today's spirit of intense localism – not to replace, but to accompany and nourish other levels of political dynamics. Most of the interesting innovations and dynamism in democratic forms are currently occurring within local communities. Debates among democracy, human-rights and civil society experts and practitioners today invariably dwell on the paralysis of multilateral institutions and the consequent need to 'go local' in mapping out practical solutions.

The range of novel initiatives fostering citizen participation at a local level across Europe is impressive, embracing the wider use of referendums on community and neighbourhood matters; informal tools of consultation to help decide such issues; new forms of local voting; the spread of neighbourhood councils; and civic complaint mechanisms. The number of cooperatives and other initiatives based on the principle of mutualism has increased many times over during the last five years. Community shops, time-banking organisations, skill-swapping forums and other kinds of initiative involve increasingly dense collective networks mobilised around a spirit of solidarity-based civic participation and have expanded particularly in the Netherlands, Spain and the UK, as well as in other European states.[18]

A large number of participative initiatives have gained momentum at the level of city governance. Initiatives in places like Barcelona, Bologna, Helsinki, Paris and Madrid have made a discernible difference in germinating public involvement in very concrete day-to-day matters outside the channels of mainstream politics. Municipal participatory budgeting is also spreading dramatically. In Paris in 2016, the allocation of 100 million euros was decided by citizens, with 158,000 residents voting on the budget. Portugal is now offering such a mechanism on a national scale with the novel provision for citizens to vote through cashpoint machines.[19] The Barcelona city council crowdsourced a whole collaborative economy plan in 2016. In March 2017, the G1000 initiative in Madrid gave 1,000 randomly selected citizens the chance to debate and advise on spending priorities for the city administration. Another initiative in Spain, 'Municipalismo, Autogobierno y Kontrapoder' (MAK2), aims to get local communities to hold town authorities to account and bolster 'cross-border municipalism' through Europe.

An especially thick network of civic associations has taken root in Denmark and other Nordic states, and this has deepened at a local level in recent years. The Dutch and Belgian parliaments are building several city-level participatory processes. In early 2017, the Civic Innovation Network and CitizenLab ran an online platform called 'Openwall' for people living in Brussels to vote on ways to improve the quality of life in the city. A Eurocities initiative and a Network of European Municipalities have both gained traction and momentum. Solidarity Cities is a network focused specifically on the issue of refugees.

Fundamental social and ideational changes drive these initiatives: the idea of a big, central state has lost legitimacy, but so has the belief in the free market. And many citizens say they are looking for solutions in localism, in citizen-led initiatives based around the notion of the 'civic commons' – initiatives that involve people sharing resources and mutual assistance outside formal policy-making structures, often even using informal means of bartering to move outside the currency turmoil of the euro crisis.[20] The rise of at least some populist parties is part of this trend and should be interpreted as a call for more 'contact democracy', reflecting citizens' desire to build on the already-incipient use of citizens' juries, citizens' assemblies and the like in countries such as Belgium, the Netherlands, Norway and Ireland.[21]

All this incipient localism comes with a striking silence, however. It offers great potential for political renewal; and yet it is for now largely disconnected from EU-level debates. The local initiatives and debates that have taken shape in the cauldron of the poly-crisis do not speak strongly to Europe-wide democratic regeneration – at least not yet. While not directly about the EU crisis, they are implicitly concerned with European developments to the extent that they have emerged to deal with the consequences of that crisis. But concerted efforts will be needed if local networks are to play a full role in a reset Europe.

Attend events like the Global Forum on Modern Direct Democracy to hear about all this exciting new action and one is struck by the contrast with the downbeat gatherings of EU experts these days – and also by the fact that those experts are completely absent from these forums, which are designed to inform attendees about local-level participation. This is the great paradox of the crisis: there is both a hollowing out of democracy at the EU and national levels and more intense civic empowerment at a local level – and yet the latter gets no look-in when leaders gather to discuss 'the future of the EU'.

The activists and what some term 'party-movements' engaged at the local level have not yet signalled any strong interest in contributing new ideas on European integration. There are clear tensions between their municipal-level aims and existing EU structures and norms. Most municipal activism is an implied way of circumventing the failings of the EU model. Local activists and officials are generally pro-EU, and yet their whole narrative is about reclaiming powers for the local level from higher levels of authority. As yet, there are few effective connections between such localism and the democratic management of transnational interdependence. Some critics worry that a growing phenomenon of populist localism is inward-looking and unlikely to contribute to a healthy regeneration of European democracy.[22]

Social movements' concerns have been very different from each other and invariably quite parochially focused on local economic problems and corruption scandals; the protests and broader movements that took shape in the wake of the economic crisis have reinforced the centrality of national-level political processes, rather than transcending these in the name of pan-European notions of democracy.[23] Most citizen-based initiatives that have sprung up during the crisis are firmly rooted in specifically local debates. Crisis-induced social movements have often berated the EU as a problem rather than as a creative space for reimagining common European democracy.[24] In Naples, a mayor closely linked to social-movement activists took power and resisted EU economic rules very directly.

While the trends in local participation and collective action are important, they can sometimes be overhyped. They are generally limited in scale and still far from having the dramatic, structural impact on macro-level economic and political systems that their supporters claim. While a rich set of participatory processes has spread in recent years – something that is often dubbed 'the participative turn' – it has had fairly small-scale impacts. Many citizen initiatives have gradually become diluted from the originally emancipatory concept of participative democracy. In their very recent forms they can involve much co-option, as people have input without much guarantee of having an effect on decision outputs.[25] Radicals lament that local empowerment has so far been about individuals defending their own entitlements and not a genuinely progressive internationalism.[26] Some initiatives overseen by committed activists have suffered from infighting and run up against opposition from the broader citizenry.

Much work remains to be done in fine-tuning democratic localism. Citizens' assemblies have so far been used for single issues, for specified periods of time – one example being their role on abortion laws in Ireland. They need to be broadened so as to expose citizens to the need to contemplate trade-offs between different policy aims – the complex nub and essence of democratic politics. As one local democracy innovator in Barcelona admits, many participative mechanisms have been introduced across Europe, but citizens still need the capacity and awareness to take advantage fully of these within EU-related debates. The talk is now of an emerging phase of localism in which citizens are involved more proactively in setting political agendas rather than simply and somewhat passively being asked to vote or engage online on set questions relating to predetermined issues. The focus is also on ensuring that local votes are framed and used in such a way as to foster debate on common community goals rather than narrow individual interests.

There are pan-European networks and initiatives that link together formal city- and local-authority representatives. These tend to gather together people from big cities that are already internationalised and cosmopolitan, rather than involving the smaller towns and villages across Europe where the harder questions are being asked of the current EU model. One Eurocities representative admits that a link has not yet been made between city-level concerns and the future direction of European integration. And a Commission representative admits that EU officials have not yet sought to borrow from local-level participation techniques to enliven the Union's decision-making processes.[27]

In sum, while trends in localism and the participative management of the 'civic commons' offer great potential for citizen empowerment, they still need to be plugged into debates about the future model of EU integration – through both nation-state and European-level processes. Nascent local-level initiatives must be harnessed to cascade upwards into a revitalised debate about the EU's future. Civil society leaders now talk of the need to create a new 'translocalism' that would scale up links between highly localised forums. This translocalism must not be seen simply as a source of pro-EU support for existing integration policies, but will also need to reflect the more critical edge that has emerged in many localities across the continent.

The trend towards local citizen engagement and empowerment is a powerful one. For all the limitations of the community forums that have taken shape so far across Europe, something is changing at the local level and in the way society is organised. It is a serious omission that articles and think pieces on EU reform invariably fail to engage with or even show any awareness of these trends. Such democratic localism often appears to be unfolding in a parallel universe to debates about the future of European integration. The result is that there is much potential for democratic renewal being wasted.

DEMOCRACY, DISINTEGRATION AND MARKETS

Two counterarguments are now routinely made against this focus on citizen participation. While these raise valid warnings, neither makes a fully convincing case against a more democratic integration model.

Nativism. The first is that opening Europe to greater popular participation would amplify the influence of illiberal, Eurosceptic populists and risk killing off the whole EU ideal. There are rising concerns that the call to 'bring the people back in' is simply the disingenuous talk of destructive populism. Many in the EU today fear that more meaningful democratic responsiveness will simply open the doors to anti-European voices – and they suspect that many of those calling for a more democratic EU have this very aim in mind.

It is true that some recent trends shake one's faith in democracy. European citizens either turn inwards with chauvinistic meanness of spirit or they watch passively while political and economic elites grasp even more greedily at the sinews of power. Recent years have seen a re-emergence of an old line of reasoning that defending liberalism – in its economic, political, social and international forms – requires that democracy be held at bay.

However, this does not mean that the liberal principles of the European project can be rescued by denying more meaningful democratic participation. While fears over what popular participation might produce are well grounded, they are based on an overly static understanding of democracy. Anti-EU populism has its very roots in the lack of citizen voice. It is in large measure because policy debates happen 'elsewhere' and beyond citizens' influence that nativist identity politics fills the gap. Populism at least opens up the opportunity to politicise the EU.

We should not be so idealistic to suppose that an effective citizens' democracy would magically turn every voter into an ardent liberal cosmopolitan. But neither should we forget that participative democracy is a process that moulds and remoulds citizens' preferences and world views. Local democratic dynamics would certainly not dissolve all the tensions of the poly-crisis, and in some ways might raise additional challenges, but it is difficult to envisage a successful way forward today that does not cultivate a better sense of popular ownership over European integration – in the sense of both what it can achieve and where its limits lie.

There are well-grounded concerns that populists are antagonistic to pluralism and democratic compromise.[28] More broadly, populists have in general eschewed any radically new thinking on European integration. Many populists in fact follow fairly mainstream positions on EU integration, beyond their two or three red-flag issues. They do not seem to make a connection between their domestic radicalism and the need for a concrete redesign of the integration model. European populist parties nominally hold a range of views on participative and direct democracy.[29] Leftists now preach localism and conservatives support the Catholic-inspired doctrine of subsidiarity. They both still need to work through these community-centred principles to embellish more original ideas for Europe's future.

While feckless populist leaders may enflame and stir opinion, citizens' concerns are genuine – and not merely the result of misinformation or beguiling, charismatic leadership. Parties should not be dismissed as radical or extreme simply because they are critical of the EU. Some populist parties are exclusionary and feel empowered enough to resist cooperation with mainstream parties, while others impact politics mainly through entering into coalitions and through their organic links in civic networks; some are influential mainly through municipal politics rather than through any wholesale subversion of 'the system'.[30] Populists' policy prescriptions might be simplistic and unachievable, but then surely so are many of those proposed by mainstream parties.

Referendums have certainly been misused and have delivered bruising shocks to the European project. Yet there is an important distinction between direct-democracy mechanisms that are generated by citizens and those deployed for self-serving purposes by elites. Encouragingly, today's active citizenship is leading to more of the former. In this sense, there is incipient potential to deploy bottom-up direct democracy more productively. It can be used to enrich representative democracy and it can help set the direction for future political options in a way that makes it harder for special-interest groups to hijack decision-making.[31]

Some degree of balance is required. Reform must chart a course between populism and the self-assured rightness of the existing EU narrative. The challenge is to ensure that the democracy-enhancing potential that drives citizens' turn against elites wins out over populists' illiberalism. It will be to cultivate non-mediated participation without this leading to unbridled majoritarianism. Deeper citizen participation would not be populism's victory but its antithesis: while populists lay claim to one single vision that supposedly represents the will of the true people, an alternative Europe needs to be based on a multiplicity of visions – precisely because it is fanciful to think that one notion of the European general will exists or can be concocted.

Market constraints. The second critique relates to political economy. Ceding more systematic democratic input would not remove the constraints on policy options that come with market and financial interdependence. Doubters insist that all the talk of citizen participation is largely window dressing insofar as the very structure of market-led globalism militates against any meaningful democratic choice and accountability. They assert that effective democratic control and market-financial integration cannot go hand in hand – and that an alternative Europe must clearly prioritise one of these to the detriment of the other.

It is certainly the case that a more democratic process of integration would not remove the constraints of interdependence or magic away the very difficult choices that governments and citizens face in wanting the benefits of both cooperation and control. Yet scope surely exists for citizens to have a greater say in setting the aims towards which markets are channelled. In some areas, they may wish to see markets tamed, while in others they may deem deeper economic interdependence beneficial. They may put the onus on other, non-economic areas of policy as the leading edge of pan-European cooperation. An alternative EU may need a different balance between open markets and local democracy.

The dilemma is not simply one of absolute trade-offs between democracy and the market. It is also a question of democratic owner-ship building a firmer support base for whatever forms and degrees of economic and financial integration come to be adopted. Citizens will still have to grapple with balancing the malign and the benign of trans-national interdependencies. But if they are to take difficult choices to accept globalism and market disciplines they should at least feel some kind of ownership over these decisions; and conversely, if and when they prefer to curtail markets radically, theirs should be the responsibility of managing the consequences of this option. Democratic participation should not be about conjuring up unfeasible, false panaceas that ignore the harsh realities of Europe's challenges, but about giving citizens more meaningful say in the way the EU deals with constraints, trade-offs and power imbalances.

It is often pointed out that the root of the EU's malaise lies in Europe's increasingly oligarchic set of social and economic structures. An alternative EU needs to address this imbalance above all else if it is to demonstrate that citizens' voices matter; and that is why structural change to its proto-polity is needed and not merely a bit more fiscal leeway, more cross-border infrastructure spending or EU-branded job-creation schemes. Some may indeed think that the basic spirit of the European project can only be honoured by a pushback against market-led globalism. But, alongside this, the democratically crucial ingredient is that citizens are able more proactively to shape the mix of pro- and anti-market policies and that this mix is no longer presented to them as a predetermined given.

EURO-CIVISMO

Defining the dilemma in these terms helps us to frame a particularly important aspect of the EU's democracy problem – and to identify the criteria for a successful, democratic integration process. Today's rising popular frustration does not result simply from a few institutional imperfections or policy inadequacies, but is a product of citizens' rootless particularism and modernity's thinning of recognisable collectivities. The challenge is to reconstruct community without illiberal excesses, through a kind of interdependent self-government or localist cosmopolitanism.

Democracy in today's deeply interdependent economic and political spaces requires citizens to take into account the impact of their choices on citizens in other localities and states. Those affected by one state's decisions should have some voice in that state's democratic processes. Self-determination requires us to make ourselves heard in the decision-making processes of other states that affect our interests. This is what would constitute transnational self-determination. There needs to be strong national-level democratic legitimation; but national political processes themselves need to reflect the interests of EU citizens from other states that are affected by 'our' national decisions. This is what is required to reduce the sensation that European integration now consists of others controlling us, not of us having influence over our own choices or indeed those of others.[32]

Part of this must be about further developing the concept of demoi-cracy – the most influential and helpful adjustment to democratic ideas over the last decade. Demoicracy rightly focuses on the need to combine the formal democratic channels of national and European democracy in tandem with each other. Some of the concept's foremost proponents have begun to focus on the need for a more concerted development of demoicracy's bottom-up dynamics in the wake of the poly-crisis.[33] If European solidarity is to be rebuilt it must be regenerated on the basis of citizens' own voluntary will; pan-European solidarity must feel more genuinely desired and less imposed through opaque formalised rules and requirements. Mutual solidarity must be by choice. It needs to be the basis of a more flexible social contract among European citizens of many different nationalities and social identities.

But is such cross-border empathy really possible? Of course, sceptics would insist that, given the distrust and divergence that is now so pervasive, the idea of citizen-driven solidarity is simply an over-idealised contradiction in terms. The poly-crisis has undoubtedly sapped the 'Europeanness' of democratic debates and procedures. It has undercut the idea that citizens from different member states should have a reciprocal voice in each other's affairs. A 2012 survey found that, in a long list of features describing the desired qualities of democracy, EU citizens put 'responsiveness to other EU governments' in last place.[34] And a more recent project shows that in nearly all member states citizens express far less willingness to extend solidarity across borders than they did a decade ago. Citizens want 'more Europe' in the sense of expecting the EU to recognise and address their particular problems, but they are now less inclined to make concessions to reach common positions or make sacrifices in the name of citizens elsewhere in Europe.[35]

Given this, many proposals do indeed have an air of fantasy. Clearly, it is unrealistic to think that citizens will suddenly cease to think in terms of their own interests and express their democratic preferences in the name of some imagined collective European will. The poly-crisis casts doubt on the many writings claiming that voters already have a strongly embedded and unshakeable European conscience and outlook. Indeed, constructing an alternative EU should very much *not* be about simply stepping up highly instrumental attempts to engineer a model European citizen or a single European public space – ideas that have been on the policy agenda for many years, to little avail in terms of their practical resonance in the depths of the poly-crisis. The existing juridical principle of the European 'citizen' was supposed to be the foundation of a new transnational and distinctive form of democracy. It clearly has not worked.

However, the relevant aim and measure of democratic success is not that of an idealised European citizenship. Rather, it is for citizens to gain a better appreciation of how their own interests are affected by European-level externalities. The need is for a spirit of mutual recognition of communities' different preferences and interests – not for diverse interests to be shoehorned into a common set of prescriptions. This might be expressed as a spirit of *euro-civismo*, a more flexible and open notion than that of engineering a supposedly common European identity. This could be defined as a general inclination to take the broader set of European contexts and challenges into account beyond one's own narrow interests.

Integral to *euro-civismo* is the idea that citizens need the ability directly to debate what duties they are willing to bear as quid pro quos for EU citizenship rights – the lack of any such popular deliberation on this crucial balance between duties and rights is a startling lacuna after 60 years of integration, when it is such a fundamental premise for any well-worked notion of citizenship. None of this would imply the need to engineer any single 'general will', but rather denote a much thinner and democratically rooted version of Rousseau's famous concept. Concrete reform options should be targeted towards this aim – a more realistic and achievable objective than breezy talk of pan-European identity and identikit citizenship.

A key concept here is that of externalities: the need to recognise that citizens' choices have an impact on the interests of citizens from other member states, and that the interests of these citizens in turn are important to one's own interests. Democratic input needs to be informed by such externalities. The key is to devise ways to encourage this kind of pragmatically rooted other-regarding behaviour. If they were given greater participation and the opportunity to put forward their opinions, citizens might be likely to take more rounded views than those that now underpin Europe's ascendant populists. While the EU's democratic legitimacy must be rooted in national and local political processes, the poly-crisis makes clear that these can themselves only be effective when they acknowledge the myriad connections that condition today's European space.[36]

To an extent, some citizens may have begun to do this. Many Germans have realised that helping Greece is a way of protecting Germany's own interests. Many Spaniards voted for a government that accepted austerity requirements as they realised that a stable Europe was vital for their own interests. It is not clear that citizens are really frustrated because they want an old sense of the nation state to regain control; rather, they more concretely despair at their lack of say and sway over EU affairs as individual citizens – citizens with very specific and local concerns not related to the abstract questions of a supposed ideal-type national identity.

This suggests that some – albeit shallow – foundations are in place upon which European societies can develop this fragile but crucial ingredient of mutual empathy. Member states could agree to any number of democratic reforms, but if these fail to foster greater empathy between citizens from very different parts of the continent, they will not get to the core of the EU's current malaise. This is the key standard by which more democratic forums must be judged. Do they increase the likelihood that citizens will better understand and appreciate the positions of those elsewhere in Europe? This is not a question of citizens coming to agree on every aspect of EU policies, but of them at least beginning to empathise beyond their own national context. This is an exacting standard of measurement – but not beyond the realms of what is achievable within real-life acts of citizen engagement.

CONCLUSION

Vibrant social and political change is taking shape at the level of cities and local communities across Europe. These trends point towards a theory of EU change that flows with the current of contemporary social concerns, agency, organisational forms and power shifts – quite unlike the heavily idealised calls for elite-led deeper European integration. Yet it is important not to romanticise such civic initiatives. Successful processes of change will depend on the local, national and European levels linking together more tightly than they have to date. Bottom-up change should not be seen as a substitute for national-level democratic influence, good European leadership and formal institution-driven reform; rather, it must serve as a complement to elite-level rethinking and needs an effective interface with the latter.

Moreover, reformers will need to fashion forms of engagement that temper the risk of citizen influence generating disintegration, as opposed to a new integration. A healthy, alternative EU will need to build links between cosmopolitan and nativist factions, as neither of these will win out exclusively. It will need democratic ways to bridge the divide that currently dominates European politics: cosmopolitans deride localists as parochial and chauvinistic; localists deride cosmopolitans as elitist and out of touch. An alternative Europe needs to mediate this divide.

This must certainly not be about idealising citizens, especially at a moment when they seem to be making some surprising and disturbing choices. Indeed, quite the contrary: a deep-rooted democratisation of the EU is necessary precisely because differences and uncertainties are so profound today. At present, the formal EU vision of 'increasing democratic consultation' is shallow: it assumes that the EU gifts civic consultation to the people, and that citizens will then readily agree on new cooperation in line with the standard notion of centralised integration. In contrast, today participative processes are needed to manage ongoing difference and divergence, and in a way that gives fair hearing to fundamentally revised understandings of integration.

In this sense, the EU's broadest challenge is to cultivate democratic accountability and legitimacy at several different levels: within national political processes; through local, citizen-centred democratic vibrancy; but also in the transnational management of interdependence between member states. No single level of democratic improvement will be enough on its own. The challenging question is whether these levels can be combined through an ethos of mutual empathy or *euro-civismo*. The next chapter suggests how these broad principles and conceptual yardsticks for a process of EU reform might be put into action.

CHAPTER FIVE

A Compact of European Citizens

While many politicians, policy-makers and thinkers say they favour the idea of democratising the EU, they rarely lay out exactly how they would cultivate more popular participation. It is now often asserted that EU leaders need to engage citizens and especially to take on board the concerns that lie behind populists' rise. The question that is most pertinent but invariably left unanswered is exactly how this can be done in practice. The challenge, in particular, is to open the way for a popular participation capable of germinating mutual empathy and *euro-civismo*, rather than simply giving vent to angry anti-elite spleen that may bring about the Union's disintegration.

This chapter delves deeper and lays out a practical set of recommendations for what I call a 'Compact of European Citizens'. This offers a concrete policy framework for rebuilding European democracy and solidarity from the ground – not as a substitute for, but as an accompanying counterweight to formal institutional capacities and top-down reform pathways. It is a modest contribution towards making sure that the EU is able to transcend the solipsistic gloom of the last decade and firmly leave the poly-crisis behind. My aim is to explore how the principles for reform laid out in the previous chapter can be implemented. Before detailing the compact, I first show why current initiatives aimed at bolstering citizen participation are either misconceived or fail to innovate sufficiently. Any new compact must build on the civic engagement already under way across Europe, while understanding precisely how this needs to be modified and extended.

CURRENT POLICIES: REACHING CITIZENS?

Many policy-makers would reject my critical analysis by insisting that the EU has already taken on board the need for democratic renewal and opened the door to citizen participation. For a number of years, the Union has been ramping up efforts to engage with citizens and to expose decision-making to more meaningful democratic accountability. Many diplomats concur that enhancing European Parliament and national parliaments' powers is not sufficient and claim that the EU institutions have already been exploring a wider set of options for mitigating the democracy problem – options that revolve around more extensive consultations with civil society organisations (CSOs).

The concern with bolstering the EU's democratic credentials is certainly not new. But it has gradually taken on a different hue. For a long time, the EU generally believed that a so-called neo-corporatist approach was most appropriate, with the Commission consulting well-established, pro-European CSOs as favoured, quasi-insider partners in efforts to push integration forward. Civil society consultations were more about communicating pro-integration aims than any critical or countervailing agenda-setting participation. In many sectors, civil society became a vehicle for specialised lobbying of EU institutions, but not for any mass organisation of a broader political community concerned with the overarching direction of the European project. Indeed, the insider CSOs discouraged any wider inclusion, so as to prevent competing civic influences undercutting their own privileged role.

This approach dominated through the convention that drew up the ill-fated EU constitution in the middle of the last decade. French and Dutch voters' rejection of the constitution revealed the inadequacy of this bounded and controlled notion of democratic participation. The structured consultations with specified civil society actors and social partners that developed as a response to the Maastricht Treaty's troubled ratification process have quite clearly failed to halt a worsening of Europe's democracy problem over the last two decades.

EU institutions oversee an increasingly dense web of engagement with CSOs, and officials claim that there has been a host of efforts to reach out to local organisations about the future of Europe. The Commission has held structured sector dialogues regularly over the last decade. It held 704 open public consultations from 2015 to 2017, applying stricter transparency requirements and conflict-of-interest prohibitions to those participating in such processes.[1] The Commission is now funding a large research project on legitimacy questions related to the financial crisis.[2] For its part, and on a broader scale, the Council of Europe has set up an 'Incubator for Participatory Democracy', grouping together democracy innovators from cities across Europe.

However, the EU still has a highly functional notion of civil society's role, based on the search for partnerships towards a certain set of shared goals. This is not an especially liberal understanding of the role that civil society plays in political development. A relatively fixed set of civic actors and NGOs remains the system's fulcrum. These actors tend to think very firmly inside the box of existing integration options rather than agitating assertively for fundamental reform.

EU institutions today roll out many initiatives that ostensibly consult civil society about reforming integration, but they still engage overwhelmingly with insider groups that are part of what outsiders believe is a self-serving network. These civic groups provide services or functions to advance a model of integration that benefits the very institutions that support these civic organisations. The battery of exchange programmes, mobility schemes and grants that the EU has developed in recent years benefits only a small percentage of the population, leaving behind those less prepared or less financially equipped to take the opportunities that European schemes offer.[3]

While the Commission has moved beyond its de facto accreditation system for CSOs, research finds that in practice the transition from the 'registered insiders' model to a more open model of consultation has been relatively circumscribed. Open initiatives have not generated large-scale, highly plural civil society input and the Commission most often still deals with select CSOs within very focused consultations.[4] The Commission has used its funding expressly to push CSOs to Europeanise; this means that civil society engagement at the EU level has been shaped through a top-down process rather than being allowed to develop from grass-roots policy priorities.[5] One eminent democracy expert fears that in the name of democratic participation these consultations have actually created something akin to a circle of captured special interests.[6] In 2016, the Commission made 30 million euros available for political communication; while it insisted this was part of its democracy-enhancing efforts, in practice it looked more like a marketing exercise.

Ask anyone in Brussels about policies to democratise the EU and you are likely to be referred to the European Citizens' Initiative (ECI). This allows citizens to petition the EU for reforms, and is widely seen as the Union's vanguard initiative in the realm of democratic accountability. But the ECI has had an extremely limited impact. In the five and a half years since it began in April 2012, only three petitions have won sufficient support to be accepted by the EU institutions, on water access, vivisection and stem-cell research. None of these managed to push the Commission into any concrete action or response. When the ECI came up for review in late 2016, the EU refused to expand the scope of this supposed flagship of participatory democracy; after severe civil society criticism, in April 2017 the Commission agreed to reconsider this refusal.

The ECI has gained little traction and is not widely known among European citizens. It allows citizens only to suggest an expansion of legal powers already enjoyed by the Commission in a given policy sector. And in practice it is professional NGOs rather than locally rooted civic movements that have engaged in the initiative. The Commission declined to allow an ECI petition that gathered the required million votes to strip the Commission of its mandate to negotiate a free-trade deal with the United States (the so-called Transatlantic Trade and Investment Partnership, or TTIP). One survey finds that few citizens are aware of the ECI, and that those citizens who do know of it do not believe the initiative makes the EU more open, democratic or responsive – indeed, many believe it reinforces the limits to EU accountability.[7] The number of attempted petitions has been falling since 2015.

In a similar vein, the EU Charter of Fundamental Rights was supposed to reanimate citizens' enthusiasm for the EU, and convince ordinary people that the Union is a vehicle for protecting important freedoms that make a difference to everyday life. Yet this charter remains low profile and quite unable to deflect the tide of scepticism and disillusion that has swept over the European project. Of limited reach, the Fundamental Rights Agency is only advisory and consultative, and has no mandate to propose major new approaches to integration or building democratic legitimacy.

In 2009, the European Commission ran a series of 'European Citizens' Consultations' that promised broader involvement to ordinary citizens. This initiative only covered economic issues like vocational training for young people, however; it was not about the EU per se. Moreover, there was no follow-up. The EU then named 2013 'Year of the Citizen', and launched a number of civic consultations. But this was precisely when management of the eurozone crisis seemed to be undermining citizens' voices more than at any previous moment in the history of European integration.

The kind of approach the EU generally favours can be shown with one example. A large project funded under the ECI supported the Institut Français des Relations Internationales' idea of bringing together representatives from six European cities (Amsterdam, Athens, Birmingham, Budapest, Lisbon and Paris) to discuss how local politicians could help to develop European citizenship, integrate migrants and 'defeat populism'. The project has been mainly concerned with the excellent work being undertaken by these municipalities in fostering tolerance and inclusiveness; it is not essentially directed at rethinking the EU as such.

Jean-Claude Juncker promised his Commission would be the most 'political' ever and acknowledged the need to assuage citizens' concerns. It soon transpired that this would take the form of commissioners visiting national capitals more frequently to 'communicate better' in justifying the EU project. Since 2014, the Commission has held 125 Citizens' Dialogues, in which commissioners meet ordinary people in town-hall meetings. Yet it is difficult to pinpoint any tangible impact from all this consultation. Democracy was not mentioned in Juncker's top ten priorities for his commission term. There is still much denial from officials that the EU even has a democratic shortfall. Despite all the official promises to listen more to citizens, bring the EU closer to 'the people' and democratise the EU, each time leaders have the opportunity to do something concrete to fulfil these promises they fail to do so.

Commission vice president Frans Timmermans launched a new initiative to weed out unnecessary legislation. Among institutions in Brussels, this initiative is seen as key to making the EU more responsive and legitimate with citizens. Yet it does not entail any systematic engagement with those citizens. The Commission has introduced a strict set of controls to judge whether any new piece of legislation is really needed, and this has resulted in many proposals being dropped. The number of legislative proposals decreased from 165 in 2011 to 50 in 2015, while 48 EU laws were repealed between 2015 and 2017.[8]

However, decisions on which measures to drop and which to advance are made by officials and on criteria related to the potential added value of EU measures in a given policy sector. This may be entirely sensible, but it is difficult to see how it is really about a more proactively participative EU. Some businesses and unions have mobilised to complain that the Commission now decides which regulations to remove without any transparency and completely outside the sphere of political debate. The fact that officials insist the 'Better Regulation' initiative is already adequately reforming the EU reveals much about how they understand the concept of 'reform'.[9] Plans mooted in 2017 to streamline 'comitology' – the web of committees in which member states meet to make decisions – reflect the same kind of sensible but unambitious, partial approach.

The EU's 2017 Citizenship Report on what it is doing to promote a union of democratic engagement covers several areas: activities that raise awareness of EU rights and common values; exchanges and volunteering schemes; EU communication strategies; access to documents; and cutting red tape. These are all valuable and important, but they are clearly not about a fundamental democratisation of the Union – indeed, that they are presented as such again says much about how the current EU elite misunderstands what democratic renewal should entail.[10]

In sum, new initiatives and proposals invariably emanate outwards from the EU centre; they seek to engage networks of civic activists within existing European-level channels and initiatives. They are valuable, but are not about building up a store of genuinely new ideas from outside these structures and networks. Even when leaders, politicians and officials acknowledge the need to engage the wider public they do so in a way that betrays a lingering elitism: such citizen input is seen as something gracefully gifted by elites and largely on their terms.

Many of the initiatives the EU labels as 'grass-roots', including those supported by non-governmental foundations concerned with shoring up the European project, are in fact not rooted in local communities at all. As one expert summarises: EU institutions seek forms of 'limited democratic politics' – options safely within the purview of formal reform templates and speaking little to the need for radically participative and different forms of cooperation.[11] Existing participative consultations are about communicating formal EU narratives downwards to citizens more than conveying popular demands upwards to decision-makers – and for this very reason they are spurring the creation of more confrontational 'outsider' civic initiatives.[12] Some MEPs have even tried to curtail EU funding for civic organisations that 'engage in activities running counter to EU interests such as advocacy against EU policy'.[13] Euro-paternalism abounds – if anything aggravated by the poly-crisis.

Perhaps the most interesting new official proposal is the promise made by Emmanuel Macron to hold a series of 'democratic conventions' on the EU. This commitment arguably goes further than any other to date in recognising the need for a broad set of public consultations. (The German foreign ministry sponsored post-Brexit citizen dialogues in cities across Germany, but these did not produce substantive input to reform plans.) However, Macron's proposal is for these conventions to run for a few months only rather than for them to be a permanent means of democratic input. And the new president has not waited to see what the conventions might produce before indicating his desire to press ahead with deeper fiscal and security integration. The one area of democratic control his manifesto specifically mentioned was that of citizens being able to limit free-trade accords. Notwithstanding the 'democratic conventions' idea, the underlying theme of his electoral programme was an output-oriented one of 'strengthening European identity through concrete achievements'.[14]

CITIZEN INITIATIVES: NEW IDEAS?

Complementing these official initiatives, pressure and ideas for EU reform have increasingly come from civil society actors themselves. It is worth examining these civic initiatives and the proposals they bring to the table about EU integration and citizen-oriented democratic legitimacy. An illustrative sample helps shed light on what kind of reform momentum is already flourishing within the European civic sphere and how the poly-crisis has unleashed a wave of new initiatives.

The *European Civic Forum* includes more than 100 NGOs from across all member states and encourages civil society dialogue to increase 'popular ownership of European matters'. In the wake of the crisis, the forum has developed a 'Plan C for Europe', the C standing for citizenship. Its activities focus on education about citizenship rights, information sharing between NGOs from different member states and 'Democratic Citizenship Awards'. The forum has broadened its activities away from advocacy within EU institutions to direct-democracy initiatives that embrace the new social movements spurred into action by the crisis. Its primary focus within Plan C is on getting associations to be given a formal say in EU institutional procedures and for pan-European NGO networks to be granted stronger formal recognition. The organisation is pressing for an EU commissioner for civil dialogue and an EU Observatory to monitor dialogue with civil society.[15] Another concern is to get civic voices in Eastern Europe into EU debates to contain growing illiberalism on the periphery.[16]

European Alternatives supports local-level activities and participation to 'build another Europe'. Its projects include the Transeuropa cultural festival; training for CSOs especially on citizens' rights; dialogues involving 'cultural activists'; and a 'Citizens' Pact' to develop proposals for post-crisis EU reforms. This last project ran a series of 'Caravans' across Europe to engage citizens in the preparation of a manifesto ahead of the 2014 European Parliament elections. The manifesto proposed stopping privatisation, a right to clean drinking water, votes for migrants; more power to the European Parliament; Europe-wide political parties; more green policies and an end to shale-gas fracking; no bank bail-outs; debt write-offs and a financial transactions tax; controls over media empires; more generous asylum rules; more gay and abortion rights; and a basic income across all member states. European Alternatives expresses a concern with local democracy and breaking the current model of decision-making, with a primary agenda of anti-austerity advocacy.[17]

The *European Association for Local Democracy* (ALDA) promotes citizen participation at the local level, and focuses on activities that facilitate cooperation between local authorities and civil society. It groups together a range of local authorities with NGOs and works on the interface between these actors, with a mandate to get citizens involved in local-level decision-making. It runs projects for youth exchanges, local environment policies, education and anti-discrimination policies. A large part of its focus lies outside the EU, in neighbourhood states and especially the Balkans, where the organisation offers expertise and training to local democracy agencies on models of participation.[18] Its DECIDE project – whose name stands for 'DEmocratic Compact: Improving Democracy in Europe' – set up a network of towns to coordinate on EU affairs, with NGO and youth councils to bring civil society into local municipal policy-making.[19]

The *European Students' Forum* began a 'Bridging Europe' project in the wake of the crisis to enhance the democratic participation in EU affairs of young people, and their empowerment through exchanges, courses, debates and advocacy. One of its current projects runs a range of activities aimed at teaching young people about their democratic rights as a step towards getting them more involved in politics.[20] The *European Citizens' Initiative Campaign* pushes for the ECI to be expanded in scope, to allow more bids and oblige the Commission to respond more tangibly to petitions. *A Soul for Europe* runs forums in local communities to get more cultural issues taken on board within EU integration policies and also oversees a Euro-regional Centre for Democracy.

FutureLab Europe began in 2011 and has funded more than 100 young people to design a 'paradigm shift' in the EU integration model. It focuses especially on how to use new technology and social media to get citizens involved in EU politics. Proposals call for a 'citizen-centred governance model' and a 'truly European political culture' through direct elections for the Commission and Council presidents, and transnational party lists in the European Parliament. The organisation calls for a scaling up of direct democracy, through extending the ECI. Finally, it pushes for better access to information from EU institutions, along with more programmes to educate young people in EU affairs and explain the Union to them. FutureLab Europe is now trying to broaden its activities to include new types of social movement and the kinds of sectors so far disengaged from EU debates.[21]

Citizens for Europe coordinates a team of around 300 organisations, such as the European Movement and the European Citizens' Initiative Campaign. It also funds new social networks, especially to foster collaboration between civic initiatives across European borders, all on the theme of increasing citizen participation in EU affairs through grass-roots activities. The initiative's spine is an online platform sharing information about new types of citizens' projects and democratic ideas. On the back of this project, *European Movement International* (EMI) has launched a new initiative called 'Reframing Democracy', to explore the use of new methods like randomly selected assemblies. This initiative expressly seeks to push the boundary beyond the EMI's traditional type of project. The aims of the project are ambitious: to 'get rid of our traditional mindset […] challenge the status quo […] reclaim the political space […] reinvent the system […] experiment with alternatives.'[22] EMI also calls for a Europe-wide constituency in European Parliament elections and individual membership of European political parties as a direct link between citizens and EU-level politics.[23] In 2017, EMI began a new citizens' platform, 'On Our Watch', to monitor the European Parliament and push for more open democratic access to its proceedings.

The *Dialogue on Europe* project, funded by the German foreign ministry and overseen by Das Progressive Zentrum, ran town hall meetings in Greece, Spain, Portugal, Italy, France and Germany. From these, it called for more European cooperation to meet the EU's core challenges. *Our New Europe* runs online referendums on key European matters. The group's questionnaire invites respondents to choose one of three options: more centralised integration on a business-as-usual basis; less integration and withdrawal from the EU; or flexible, democratic and multi-speed Europe. Other questions are about specific policies, including enlargement, Ukraine, refugees and fiscal coordination. Results in mid-2016 showed that 39 per cent want a reformed EU, 30 per cent a more centralised, federal EU and 31 per cent a reduced EU. A commanding majority want citizens to have more of a voice and 80 per cent want each state to elect a constitutional council to draw up a fundamentally new set of EU treaties.[24]

Civil Society Europe was formed at the end of 2014 to group together CSOs from all member states. Its stated aim is to 'work towards regenerating the European project around the shared values of equality, solidarity, inclusiveness and democracy'. It does this by coordinating a range of dialogues between European CSOs and policy-makers. It also assists CSOs in improving the effectiveness of their advocacy work with EU institutions. In October 2016, the initiative ran a European Civic Academy, together with other civic organisations, to promote and debate the issue of democratic effectiveness in Europe. High profile but not so rooted in grass-roots civil society, *Civico Europa is* a group of MEPs, politicians and celebrities that has called for deeper integration and a round of participative debates among citizens.[25]

The *European Democracy Lab* tries to connect national parliamentarians to EU debates, with the aim of promoting more European ways of thinking among national parliamentarians. It advocates a European Republic as a means of shifting power towards the European Parliament and bringing in regional governments more systematically. It calls for common transnational elections and a pan-European social system.

The *European Institute for Public Participation* provides advice and services to civil society and other organisations on how to design participatory processes. Its main focus is on citizen participation in local service consultations, around issues like environmental controls. *Project for a Democratic Union* is a small think tank overseen by students and young academics in several member states, running occasional events and posting blog comments. The initiative is generally supportive of a federal Europe. *Puissance Europe* is beginning to call assemblies within twinned cities in different member states. *Democracy International* got nearly 60,000 signatures on a petition for an EU 'relaunch' to be presented at the Bratislava summit in September 2016. The Cologne-based organisation has aimed to mobilise an informal ECI for a new convention to reform the EU and also a campaign more broadly to inform citizens of the ECI and to increase their use of this instrument.

WeMove.eu defines itself as a new 'online citizens' movement' campaigning for a 'citizen-led democracy' to overcome powerful vested interests. It sets itself against the current trend of governments' infringing citizens' rights and building more intrusive surveillance. By 2017, nearly half a million European citizens were signed up to the site. WeMove.eu runs online campaigns, with the stated aim to use digital campaigning to generate grass-roots, offline networks mobilised around European policy issues. The movement generally speaks in favour of more cooperation, more EU commitments on social questions, economic policies, climate change and foreign policy. It has run recent campaigns against the free-trade deal with Canada, against the Polish government's proposals on abortion, on human-rights abuses in Turkey, against arms exports, on different cases of corporate corruption and on several environmental issues.

The 2016 *European Youth Event*, run in partnership with the European Parliament, gathered 75,000 young people from across Europe and resulted in a sizeable compendium of their ideas for relaunching integration. Young people called for more migrants to be accepted; more schemes for helping refugees to integrate; more religious tolerance; more diversity; more teaching about the EU in schools; more student exchanges; more young people in political office; more help to reduce youth unemployment; EU-wide labour laws to prevent wages and workers' rights being undercut; more funding for youth organisations to build links across borders; a programme for young leaders; stronger rights for the disabled; a universal citizens' income; more mobility;

alternative economic models; a stronger commitment to mitigate climate change; and better communication from the European Parliament and Commission about the benefits of EU programmes. To generate better democracy, they called for e-voting, more contact with MEPs through Twitter or specific apps, deliberative workplaces and more transparency of EU documents.[26]

The *Funders' Initiative for Civil Society* (FICS) is a new initiative that symbolises the spirit of the times: it groups together funders who have for a long time worked to protect CSOs in developing states, but who have now focused their attention on reversing incipient democratic restrictions within Europe itself. The initiative's leaders berate EU officials and member-state governments for still failing to see how far civil society needs protecting inside, and not only beyond Europe. The FICS team argues that, far from more intense citizen input into high-level policy-making, Europe is witnessing a constriction of civic space, with current EU civil society dialogues too tepid to get anywhere near addressing this. In a similar vein, the *European Citizens' Rights, Involvement and Trust Foundation* (ECIT), which was started by a small group of academics, offers a portal and events to raise awareness of EU citizenship rights.[27]

The *European Citizen Action Service* (ECAS) offers legal advice, training and consultancy, especially to CSOs. It focuses on advice over EU legal rights and gaining better access to EU decision-making, and runs services and events on these questions for EU institutions. The organisation began a new project in 2017 called 'EUCrowd', looking at how crowdsourcing can be used to generate ideas for the future of Europe.[28] Also in early 2017, a new citizens' initiative called *Pulse of Europe* was formed to galvanise pro-European opinion ahead of the Dutch, French and German elections. The initiative organised weekly demonstrations in more than 40 European cities in the run up to the March 2017 Rome summit. Its remit says: 'The European idea must be better appreciated and understandable for the man in the street. It must start at the bottom and be carried upwards.'[29] The *Our Europe* initiative also mobilised successfully around the Rome summit, with calls for solidarity, protection of social rights and help for refugees, although it did not specify any aims on how to organise a new EU.[30] At the same time a group of new, self-styled grass-roots and participative think tanks – Argo in France, Polis 180 in Germany and Foraus in Switzerland – have begun advocating a more citizen-oriented EU.[31]

A cluster of initiatives has been more radical in nature. *Decentralised Citizens Engagement Technologies* (D-CENT) was a three-year EU-funded project for technological infrastructure to develop smart cities for citizens' involvement in service delivery. It was billed as the EU's biggest project on direct democracy. It was pan-European in the sense of building links between new initiatives in different countries, albeit very much outside formal EU processes. A post-capitalist rhetoric was integral to these new platforms. The project's events and works were based around debate about changing the economic system and criticism of EU-imposed austerity. The focus was on new politics at city level, rather than on EU integration as such. The project was about fostering movement-based parties, and working with these on the use of new technologies. Crowdsourcing legislation was a main focus, implicitly as a means of recovering power from opaque formal channels of democratic representation.

¡Democracia real YA! is an anti-austerity group that organises strikes and marches against austerity, and seeks to revive popular democracy and the use of referendums. It began in Spain and spread to other countries.[32] *Another Europe is Possible* is a UK organisation set up for the referendum, led by left-wing parties and unions, and with a generic advocacy of a 'social Europe' based on justice, equality and democracy. It calls for better workers' rights, environmental standards, free movement and minority rights. It is strongly critical of EU austerity. The focus was initially on getting the UK to stay in the Union, rather than mapping out an alternative model of integration in general. The line was that the UK should vote to stay and then use its position to lead a fight against multinationals.

Perhaps the highest-profile new initiative is *Democracy in Europe Movement 2025* (DiEM25). This is headed by Yanis Varoufakis and billed as a 'pan-European citizens' movement' aimed at building a 'democratic Europe' beyond the current institutions of the European

Union. DiEM25 pushes for a constitutional assembly by 2025 to decide how to design a full European democracy. 'Constructive disobedience' is a key tactic, Varoufakis citing the lesson of Sophocles's Antigone, 'who taught us that good women and men have a duty to contradict rules lacking political and moral legitimacy'.[33] Varoufakis issues a clarion call: 'Instead of starting at the level of the nation-state and forging an alliance, which is flimsy and brittle, how about starting a movement throughout Europe on the basis of a very clear manifesto that binds us together?'[34] Formally, the movement spans all political ideologies, although in practice its participants are almost exclusively left-wing.

Most of DiEM25's concrete policy ideas are relatively centralist and familiar: a supranational parliament; Europe-wide parties; an EU public investment bank; a common EU social insurance fund. As DiEM25 celebrated its first anniversary in February 2017, it kicked off a consultation exercise among its now 40,000 members to draw up 'white papers' on the economy, labour, migration, green investment and what an EU constitution should include. Its New European Deal proposes a route towards economic stabilisation using pan-European poverty, housing, jobs and debt-conversion programmes, and maps longer-term 'plans for a post-capitalist Europe' based on forms of commons-based economic activity.[35] In May 2017, the movement announced it was transforming itself into a Europe-wide political party.

This is an illustrative sample of the civic initiatives that have sprung up or intensified their activities since the EU's crisis began. I could have listed more such organisations. My aim in presenting this selective list is to show that the density of civic activity now provides a promising platform for an alternative EU. How far these initiatives have focused on really innovative models of integration is more open to question. This is not to suggest that all such initiatives should have this as their main concern, of course. But there is a risk of self-confirmation bias, as many simply pursue predetermined policy preferences under a label of 'reforming the EU'. A new wave of pro-EU initiatives and protests surged in the weeks leading up to the Dutch and French elections; these helped rebalance the civic momentum away from anti-EU populists, but did not add detail to debates over precisely what kind of EU should be engineered for the future.

It is striking that there are few citizen initiatives that have grown out of a desire for or interest in looser forms of integration and diversity. Europe is replete with highly idealistic citizen initiatives, which are in practice largely about bringing young people together for cultural and social events and tend to support some degree of deeper, centralised integration. Most of the initiatives have a certain Erasmus-like flavour about them. Many discussions and seminars about young citizens' participation end up being a discussion of the need for more EU exchanges and youth programmes. Most efforts focus on youth and students, even though this is the part of the population that is already engaged and least needs convincing of the European ideal – certainly, no 'workers' Erasmus' is in sight.

There is still a lot of window dressing evident, with connections between civic initiatives and EU institutions that do more to shore up the existing model of integration than to foster critical and open debate. There is a lot of new dialogue between specialists and activists already sharing very idealistic visions for deeper European integration, but few avenues for getting divergent voices and opinions together. Most initiatives still centre on proposals for things like pan-European parties and constituencies, which hardly excite the average citizen. Citizens' initiatives still need to expand beyond their own set of 'usual suspects'.

One standard type of initiative pushes for more Europe through centralisation of redistributive policies and more powers for the European Parliament. These organisations propose idealistic policy changes and talk about solidarity and equality. They generally see the problem in EU integration as being the power of the rich, of companies and banks; they see governments as the guilty culprits, and citizens as united and sharing aims across borders. If only governments and multinational companies could be swept aside, their message normally runs, Europe would be democratic and united. Some observers involved in new movements note that these seek to build a common European cultural identity based on disputation and grass-roots resistance to top-down notions of cooperation.[36]

In short, new and dynamic civic activities are blossoming because of the poly-crisis. While some of these explore novel approaches, most espouse fairly standard policy recommendations. And many initiatives have an instrumental view of 'democratising the EU'; that is, they press for this as a means of winning greater influence for their work on particular topics – justice, equality, environment, refugees. Relatively few are engaged in assessing the nature of the integration model per se. One exception that proves the rule: a group of practitioners under the rubric of the 'Network of European Foundations' has tried to kick-start a whole new approach to projects about EU reform that is about 'seeding the future' and 'collaborative value creation' rather than 'engineering a particular solution'.[37] This form of radically open-ended reform initiative is still relatively rare.

Undoubtedly the civic sphere is changing and casting around for a wider net of ideas. Activities aimed at local participation and linking non-party groups are beginning to take shape; they originate mainly in the anti-capitalist left around anti-austerity agendas – a vitally important and legitimate angle, of course, but not one that represents the entire political spectrum. A common narrative has formed from social movements: hacking the political system; 'we' the citizens reclaiming power from the political class; 'institutions for the twenty-first century'. But it is for the moment difficult to identify what these broad slogans and principles mean in terms of movements' detailed prescriptions for a different model of European integration.

A COMPACT OF EUROPEAN CITIZENS

What then is the way forward? We have seen that many civic initiatives, within the familiar EU framework, are highly promising but arguably not innovative enough. We have also seen that recent trends in civic empowerment provide a propitious context for different kinds of citizen involvement – with this potential still relatively untapped within EU debates. A radical and mould-breaking set of initiatives is required, and civic trends make this increasingly possible. The EU's remodelled future should be mapped out through a Compact of European Citizens.

This initiative would draw from a number of core principles and approaches. Unlike the standard range of reform pleas, this Compact would dovetail with incipient social trends. It would not simply be launched with groundless hope, in a societal vacuum. Rather, it would be consistent with ongoing social and organisational changes within many communities across Europe. It would also resonate with and be able to draw from a raft of new thinking about democratic quality and effectiveness.

The Compact would not be about magically conjuring consensus out of divergence. The EU does much, admirably, to seek consensus – between nations, between different sectors of society, between faiths. But this is often the consensus of expedient and superficial convenience. European cooperation needs to be rooted in a deeper notion of dialogue that finds mutually acceptable ways of managing diversity and means to express solidarity that are compatible with citizens adopting different policy choices. The Compact would not be about simply substituting easily assumed citizen consensus for government bickering.

The aim must be to combine a reclaiming of powers from the abiding ethos of EU institutional centralism with a thicker form of democratic citizenship carried out in practical ways across borders. Political thinkers have talked for a long time about 'Europe' needing to be defined not in terms of a fixed set of institutions but as an idea – a set of values that are flexible and open, and capable of rooting a notion of integration that is no longer about replicating a uniform set of nation state-like practices. The Compact would echo and borrow from the emergent model of 'monitory democracy' – scrutiny outside the channels of formal representative bodies, which underperform in the context of EU decision-making.[38]

The Compact would also be able to encompass emerging ideas about 'deliberative democracy'. Sceptics have tended to dismiss the whole notion of deliberative democracy as overly idealistic, pointing out that political reality is a long way short of the conditions needed to make deliberation work perfectly – since, as doubters claim, citizens are not interested in more engagement, rarely think beyond their own narrow interests and do not come together on equal terms. In response, theorists have suggested a more modest concept of deliberative democracy: not a perfect absolute, but mini-public forums serving as loose brainstorming opportunities that then filter into representative bodies.[39] This should be the kind of feasible model that inspires the Compact of European Citizens.

The Compact would also take on board the practice of 'sortition', which has been gaining support in recent years. This notion dates from ancient Greece, when lots were drawn to fill places in citizens' assemblies. For its supporters, sortition offers the prospect of broadening the range and type of citizens involved in politics. Elections return professional politicians – people who are socially privileged, highly educated and self-confident; sortition ensures that more 'ordinary' citizens get their chance to influence decision-making. Proponents insist that long-form deliberations such as citizens' juries and reference panels make decisions in more genuinely democratic ways. Randomly selected citizens – chosen from electoral rolls – are brought together numerous times to become better informed, to deliberate with one another and to propose serious recommendations.

Crucially, while sceptics will predictably doubt that such provisions are practicable, there is now a rich collection of real-life experiences that suggest otherwise. The best examples are from Australia, Canada, Iceland and Ireland, where these methods have been used dozens of times in recent years.[40] Experts have done much work on the practical details of how to make citizen forums filled by lot both effective and logistically feasible. Such bodies have been used to some effect already – scuppering the objection that sortition would not be at all workable in today's complex and large-scale polities. In these real-life experiments, citizen bodies have not always been allowed to exert a really decisive influence over policy, as elected politicians have been reluctant to let go of their own power, but the evidence suggests that deliberations can help soften tensions between citizens' different positions and begin to work towards shared understandings of common challenges.

Sophisticated models now exist for splitting such forums into sub-groups at appropriate stages of their deliberations, involving some qualified experts, amplifying wider citizen input through social media, and feeding forums' results into the decision-making of elected bodies. Proponents like David Van Reybrouck rightly stress that sortition should supplement rather than replace elections and formal representative channels.[41] A sortition forum would be especially suited to mapping out the future of European integration – a body looking at the broad direction of the EU rather than immersing itself in highly technical day-to-day matters.

The Compact might also harness the similar method of 'sociocracy' that is being increasingly used by private and public organisations searching for internal decision-making that is inclusive without holding up all decisions. This is a system based on circles of debate that continue deliberation until all give their consent to a certain measure, not in the sense of full agreement but of their having no serious objection. Sociocracy is increasingly used as a managerial tool, but might also be explored as a means of fostering shared proposals for Europe's political futures.[42]

Taking all these trends and principles on board leads us towards ideas for the precise form of the Compact. There could be a cascade of lot-filled assemblies from the local to the national to the European level. That is, a fully elaborate and densely knit structure would consist of calling assemblies at a very local level by lot; then drawing lots to select representatives from these local bodies to fill an assembly at the national level in each member state; and finally drawing some citizens from each of these national assemblies to a European-level citizens' forum.

A process of deliberation could initially run for two years and prepare a civic blueprint with ideas to ensure democratic input into a new process of integration. The crucial requirement is that these deliberations should involve citizens imagining what kind of Europe they want from scratch – rather than being prompted towards modifications of existing institutions, policies and processes. 'Participation' should move away from being code for simply registering 'objections' to policies that touch upon very specific interests, to a more positive dynamic of deliberative circles constructively empowering new ideas.

The Compact must function in a more political key than existing deliberations that occur within functional sectors of integration
and struggle to extend beyond a kind of technical lobbying role.
Governments should commit to receive the civic blueprint and react
to it with tangible change. A deep, meaningful and ongoing interaction
between the Compact and formal institutional processes will be crucial
if the EU is to draw positively from a comprehensive and balanced
combination of bottom-up and top-down reform dynamics. At the
two-year point, governments could agree to hold a summit specifically
around the Compact's output. At this juncture, national and EU officials
could consider the formal 'how' of putting its ideas into practice – for
example, addressing the question of whether or not they would require
formal treaty changes.

The Compact will then need to involve continued engagement –
unlike current exercises in citizen consultation, it should be multilayered,
strongly structured and ongoing. A forum of representatives from the
different levels of citizens' assemblies should shadow whatever formal
institutions exist in the new Europe. They should have an equal right to
initiate proposals as well as the right to comment on policy decisions.
A lot-drawn citizens' assembly could displace today's unloved MEPs
as the European Parliament's primary chamber for matters concern-
ing the long-term planning of European integration. A less ambitious
possibility would be to append the European-level citizens' forum as
a second chamber of the European Parliament or use it to fill the 73
seats to be vacated by UK deputies – a matter on which there is much
current debate. Or the Compact could be linked to the incipient efforts
of a small number of MEPs to use crowdsourcing for ideas for legislative
amendments.

The Compact would be multilevel in order to resonate with the
different tiers of the current democracy malaise. Starting at the local
level, it would tap into emerging community mobilisation and help
project this outwards to larger-picture issues. One step up from this,
the Compact would marshal debate at the level of regions, harnessing
regional identities as a vital component of integration – but in a far
more participative manner that currently happens within the EU. By

then agglomerating deliberations at the national level, the Compact would give a new lease of life to nation states' role in the EU; it would enable the nation state to play an influential role in European affairs that extends well beyond the current primacy of government-to-government relations. In its pan-European dimension, the Compact would provide for the long-overdue citizen lead in EU-level reflections on how integration needs to be rethought.

The cascade from local to European levels would help very specifically address one of the major problems in current EU debates: the unfulfilled potential of democratic localism, which is mobilising local communities but is still dislocated from European-level deliberations. Hence the importance of joining together local citizens' assemblies and a process that feeds into national and European discussions, and that also links local issues with big-picture questions of the EU's future design. In particular, small, local forums would act as a link between the isolated individual citizen and the Brussels machinery – making a significant contribution to relegitimising the European project in a way that, again, is very much in line with recent work on deliberative democracy.[43] In short, the Compact would be structured as a multilayered initiative in order to help redress the current disconnect between participative localism on the one hand, and debates about the future of European integration on the other.

This cross-cutting schema for citizen participation could be crucial for articulating a new way of tackling the EU's 'different levels' dilemma. The question normally asked of different EU integration models is what balance they strike between the nation state and the European level of decision-making. The Compact would enable an alternative Europe to transcend this standard yardstick. Participation would become the most meaningful measure. It would flourish at local, regional, national and European levels simultaneously, rather than there having to be a zero-sum trade-off between these different arenas. In light of mounting pressure for nation states to regain influence, it is important to note how the Compact would lock in more vibrant engagement at the national level. It would create space for national-level identities and influence, but without the role of the nation state being reduced to formal institutions supposedly safeguarding absolutist notions of sovereignty.

Perhaps the most immediately practical question relates to who would run the Compact. As indicated, one option would be for governments to launch it, buy into its civic spirit and commit to taking on board the outcomes. However, if governments decline to accept the need for a far-reaching citizen-led initiative, then civil society could and should consider setting up a fully structured process of its own. One admirably broad and exploratory initiative concluded that any new EU-level citizens' assembly could be constituted outside the formal network of institutional initiatives in order to avoid the co-option that dilutes so many promising new forums.[44] As there are lots of officially sponsored civil society initiatives, it might even be most productive for the Compact to stake a different route – albeit seeking eventually to link up with formal institutional debates over EU reform.

The Compact could incorporate and bring together the kind of civil society initiatives described above that are seeking ways to rejuvenate the EU. These organisations could even take charge of the Compact jointly and organise its logistical elements. If CSOs launched and ran the Compact they would not have to wait for official blessing or funds, or need to fit these new deliberations into existing consultations. The Compact could then stand as a new flagship civil society initiative that goes much further than existing programmes in generating a radically open-ended process of participation and producing fresh ideas on Europe's future. If governments or EU institutions refused to engage at all, the Compact could serve as the platform for citizens' summits, organised at the same time as formal EU summits.

None of this should be taken to idealise sortition, which is a concept that still has significant limitations. Rather, it is to suggest that it could play a supplementary role in reviving the European project among other levels of reform. So far, sortition has been tried out mainly for very local issues. The real challenge is whether it can be used in a modest way to link together the micro and macro levels, and thus help inject more concrete meaning into EU reform plans. There would need to be carefully defined procedures for locking together the different levels of the Compact to channel widely supported ideas towards concrete operationalisation. The Compact would not aim to rival but would rather nourish efforts to improve the EU's formal institutional powers and capacities.

The onus should be on pre-emptive and ongoing participatory democracy, not referendum-style direct democracy. Analysts have long called for a tighter merging of the best qualities of direct and deliberative democracy; this should also be the aim of the Compact as it fosters careful and open deliberation but also catalyses direct forms of campaigning and social movements. The Compact would feed into better national- and European-level representative democracy; it might well supplant some of the European Parliament's current powers, but the aim would be to enrich, not hollow out, existing channels of accountability and debate. The EU would move towards a mutually enhancing combination of participative, direct and representative democracy, and mix informal and formal reform impulses.

CONCLUSION

Current EU initiatives to give citizens some voice in decision-making are narrowly drawn and carefully scripted. They assume the basic parameters of the EU are already set in stone and then offer citizens the ability to influence policies at the margins. The Commission expressly keeps its range of citizen-engagement initiatives away from the EU's big, existential questions.[45] A range of new, post-crisis civil society initiatives offers greater promise, but these could also be more ambitious, more innovative and more open to prompting a fundamental redesign of European integration.

The Compact of European Citizens suggested here would adopt a radically different approach and encourage ordinary people to bring forward new ideas and propose innovative solutions. A more democratic Europe is not about co-opting civic actors into a preset Europeanisation rhetoric, but about channelling their engagement into more open-ended conversations about the European project. The Compact should, in this sense, be seen as an incubator – a space for genuinely new and challenging ideas for an alternative Europe.

The Compact could lend a new sense of possibility to European integration – and a sense of excitement to dissolve today's fatalism. Recent experiences in citizen-led policy input suggest it would be too easy simply to dismiss these ideas as unworkable – a familiar and predictable line that has constantly narrowed the menu of reform options being seriously debated in recent years. Indeed, what is surely unworkable today is the very opposite, namely the standard approach to reform that excludes such citizen input. Aiming for an ambitious and liberating Compact of European Citizens would both energise the EU and bring the whole process of integration into line with developments within local communities. This European–local alignment is the central pillar upon which future reforms must be based if they are to have any chance of succeeding over the long term.

CHAPTER SIX

Divergent Europe
Towards Radical Flexibility

A cross-cutting theme of today's EU crisis is divergence. For many decades, convergence has been the cornerstone of European integration: the EU project is designed to channel states and societies towards similar policies, similar rules, similar ideals and similar identities. Undoubtedly, the EU has smoothed the roughest edges of difference and confrontation between European countries. Yet in recent years Europe has become a more diverse political, economic and social space. Preferences, aims and values have pulled apart, among both governments and citizens. While it may be possible to identify very generic common European values, the poly-crisis has widened variation in what different governments and peoples want from EU cooperation. It does not appear that states or citizens will agree any time soon on a standard, uniform set of policies or single EU institutional template. Today's challenge is to manage a looser bandwidth of European diversity.

Fairly broad agreement has taken shape that cooperation between states and societies in Europe needs to occur on a more flexible basis. Flexible integration is the watchword of many reform proposals. But what would a more flexible EU really look like? Do those who agree on this question also agree on what it would entail? These issues have been debated for many years, and yet the EU has become less rather than better able to deal with divergence.

My aim is to argue that flexibility must be understood in a more innovative way in the future. It should not be equated with a two-speed or multi-speed Europe: this widely touted way forward is another false solution. Rather, an alternative Europe must be flexible in the sense of offering states and citizens the ability to opt in to a cluster of integration choices, where feasible on a reversible basis. The EU should set broad goals and leave states and societies to find their preferred paths to meet these. It should explore the possibility of modest forms of differentiation within and not just between states. And as a broad guiding principle, the flexibility debate must be connected more integrally to the democracy debate; in other words, in the future, the EU's flexibility must be a fully democratic flexibility. These measures could help European states find a different and common core of solidarity better and more harmoniously able to bind the EU together over the longer term.

MULTI-DIVERGENCE

The poly-crisis has presented member states with contrasting concerns. The eurozone crisis has hit some states but not others. The refugee crisis hits a different selection of states, while again leaving others relatively untouched. For some, Russian actions in Ukraine and other Eastern countries represent an existential threat, while for others they are no more than a minor annoyance. Conversely, while some states worry more about Middle Eastern challenges, for other governments these southern security problems are a lower priority. One project concludes that in today's splintered Europe, everyone believes they are shouldering an unfair share of other states' burdens.[1]

Some of the foremost commentators on the eurozone crisis speak of an unprecedented divide on economic policy and argue that this is now unbridgeable by standard efforts to reach single, coordinated policies.[2] The last big leap forward in European integration, enshrined in the Maastricht Treaty, happened at a moment when national policy preferences had converged. The euro came into existence because member states had clustered around broadly similar ideas about economic and monetary policy. The poly-crisis has corroded this consensus.

A common claim is that the way to save the EU is to move away from orthodox economic policies and develop strongly redistributive measures at the European level. This clearly makes sense, especially from a Greek, Spanish or Portuguese perspective. But in Germany and other parts of Europe, the feelings of grievance and distrust that have arisen undermine support for the idea that large-scale cross-border financial flows can be the European project's central pillar. Yanis Varoufakis lays out an admirable plan for new rules to combat poverty and debt that would decentralise decisions within a still-common Europeanised policy framework.[3] One might concur with the ideas, but it is doubtful that they are capable of gaining universal appeal and legitimacy. Trade unions have mobilised in the crisis to protect their own national workers' rights but not for pan-European solidarity – indeed, in response to some efforts to get them to do so, they have generally refused. The eurozone crisis has not led to a uniform wave of anti-neo-liberal social democracy across Europe but to a retrenchment into national and local identities and to the appearance of divergent specificities.

On the question of further fiscal integration, polls show a mix of divisions: opinions are divided along national lines, in accordance with individual circumstances and, within countries, between generations as well.[4] The European Social Survey reveals that northern Protestant states are more likely to support European integration the less redistribution it entails, while for citizens in southern member states exactly the opposite is true.[5] Bertelsmann polls show that citizens in the south and east want an EU that is mainly about economic growth, while citizens in the north favour one dealing primarily with peace and security.[6] And differences between self-defined cosmopolitan classes and a working class within each member state are as significant as those between countries.

Another yawning divide is between euro members and those outside the single currency. The former have been caught up in an endogenous dynamic of deeper cooperation just to keep the euro from collapsing. Conversely, those member states that are not members of the euro have not adopted these commitments, making it harder for them to converge in the future.[7] Statistical testing confirms that recent steps in political integration are associated with deepening inequalities across Europe.[8]

Influential theorist Peter Hall observes that the crisis has accentuated the degree to which member states have fundamentally different structures of political economy – a development that renders a uniform set of centralised economic policies less viable than it was before the crisis.[9] Member states do not simply follow different policy preferences, but subscribe to quite different models of capitalism.[10]

Moreover, there are many axes of divergence. Divergence is prevalent in political as well as economic debates. Multiple fault lines now cross the continent: the economic crisis splits northern and southern Europe; the refugee crisis splits a potential inner Schengen core from everyone else; an increasingly non-liberal Eastern Europe seems to diverge from Western European political values. There is no single direction to the bubbling discontent: the eurozone crisis has pulled many angry citizens to the left, while the refugee surge and security fears have enticed them to the right.

The Dutch are dissatisfied because the EU does too much, the Spanish because it does too little. Yet the Dutch want the EU to do more on the environment, while Poles believe the Union already imposes too many green rules. Bail-outs brought down a government in Slovakia for being deemed excessive, and another in Greece for being too miserly. While many in Greece, Spain and Portugal want full fiscal union in order to increase their own European revenues, Ireland sees the prospect of common EU taxes as a risk to the competitive advantage the country gains from its low corporate tax rates. For some, centralised tax resources are the means of restoring the EU's legitimacy; to others they are even more unthinkable now than before the crisis.[11]

The crisis has highlighted profound schisms between the historical trajectories that have brought member states to support the European project. One can understand why German politicians might instinctively want to overcome today's tensions by fleeing even further from the nation state and nationalism. But central European states insist their political journey is quite the opposite: joining the EU was equated with the recovery of national sovereignty. Politicians from these states argue that they never had the chance to complete a process of nation-forming and now need a stronger national identity to weather current challenges.

Even those member states that share an aspiration for political union have divergent views on what this should look like. For instance, in economic terms some assume a political union would be able to exert stricter control over the periphery, while others see its whole rationale as being about drawing resources away from the centre. The French understanding of political union is a confederal and *dirigiste* political system led by governments, and capable of mobilising state resources. For Germany, it means the strict application of law and rules, and control over price stability. The crisis has pushed Germany towards an even more legalistic view of European integration and a conviction that there is already too much wiggle room for national governments to evade foundational principles. In direct contrast, many in France are now even more convinced that EU integration has to be led by elites with significant political space to manoeuvre. All proponents of political union see it as an instrumental route to their own particular policy preferences. The result is stasis: while German politicians still subscribe to political union, in practice they are holding back because they distrust French intentions and fear full union would leave Germany exposed to be being outvoted on core monetary issues.[12]

On the other side of the ledger, Euroscepticism is equally varied. Some of today's growing scepticism is rooted in a kind of soft modern nationalism: a view that the EU contravenes national sovereignty. Some of it is anti-state, against the EU as an unnecessary layer of regulation and intervention. Some is anti-market, uneasy that the EU is too rooted in free-market ideology. Some is democratic, concerned that the EU hollows out democratic legitimacy. Some is localist, unhappy that the EU undermines local self-sufficiency and community identity. To some extent, it was ever thus. But the poly-crisis is so broad that it has intensified fears in all these different ideological strains of doubt simultaneously. This produces a complex web of party preferences across Europe, making it difficult to identify any one set of positions on the EU held by a particular nation or party family.[13]

The point is not that governments simply have different policy preferences – this much is well known. The crux is that the crisis has widened discrepancies over relegitimising European integration and has sharpened existential dilemmas over what that is fundamentally about. One comprehensive survey explicitly hunted for substantive policy initiatives that would relegitimise the EU project across all countries: it concluded that no such initiatives exist.[14] Jan-Werner Müller notes that the crisis may have fostered the long-awaited European public sphere – as EU developments become the staple fare of national media and political debates – but one that seems to be driving a divergence and not convergence in understandings.[15] Of course, there have long been divisions at the EU's core; the difference now is that these appear to have widened beyond what can be mediated through existing political institutions. Europhiles have become more ardent in their convictions, EU-doubters even more hesitant; this pulling apart has shrunk the middle-ground 'permissive consensus' that for so long sustained European integration.

There is also a cross-cutting divergence over how to react to Germany's growing power. Hans Kundnani notes that differences have widened among other member states over what to do about Germany's rise. He argues that this divergence is amplified by Germany being dominant but not quite preponderant enough to exert absolute control or a shared sense of European order.[16] Some analysts believe that Germany has built a non-hegemonic leadership based on networks of consent and 'willing followership' from other member states.[17] However, many EU governments self-evidently do not willingly follow, but rather resist, Germany's conceptualisation of European integration. Any acceptance there might have been in the crisis's early moments of a benign German leadership is now wearing thin. In short, Germany's changing position at the heart of European affairs adds further diversity among governmental and popular opinions across the continent.

HARNESSING DIVERSITY?

Leaders frequently pay lip service to diversity, suggesting it is now a core aspect of the EU's future. Yet their policy ideas fail fully to advance this principle. The question is whether a form of EU integration can be fashioned that allows member states greater scope to pursue different policy preferences without completely breaking the ethos, rationale and necessary institutional solidity of the integration project. A form of diversity is required that helps rebuild solidarity, rather than undercutting it. Europe needs to make divergence work to its advantage, and shape a model of integration less dependent on forcing multifarious preferences into homogeneous sameness. Most diversity is benign; some of it is harmful. A flexible Europe would get away from the attempt to quash divergence and be able to guard more tightly against those specific elements of diversity that are malign.

Integration can no longer be based on an assumption that governments and societies will move smoothly along a unilinear path towards similar preferences or similar understandings of what the EU's core rationale should be. Multiple levels of divergence now appear to be firmly rooted across national borders, as well as between EU elites and citizens. If European integration is to survive, it must find a way of dealing with this. This is more realistic than breezily assuming that the incremental processes of EU cooperation put diversity on a long-term path to disappearing.

For five decades, the working analytical assumption has been that integration moves in one direction, incrementally increasing – more or less quickly, but always onwards. There is no analytical framework for describing, explaining or predicting the path of integration as a more varied and fluid back-and-forth process.[18] Member states are constantly exhorted to look beyond their own interests to reduce divergences. Yet if they were willing to look so readily beyond short-term interests, Europe's current problems would not have arisen in the first place. We need a model of integration that is somehow able to work with rather than against the grain of divergent national and societal preferences.

This must be a more fruitful way of proceeding than assuming that common European constitutionalised norms are imminent, like dormant buds on the cusp of blossoming in the crisis's wake. The notion of a fully common European political culture is divorced from citizens' sharply contrasting experiences since the crisis began. It is frequently said that the EU needs to create a new narrative. But given the diversity of views across the EU today, it is unlikely that any one single alternative can replace the 'EU as a peace project' narrative. Instead, in the future, European integration will need to be underpinned by a plurality of narratives.[19]

A profoundly analytical challenge sits at the heart of these debates about flexible integration. The dilemma is that the concept of liberalism – upon which the whole European project rests – is fracturing, and this opens up tensions. Some want to drop economic liberalism but retain social liberalism; others push back mainly against social liberalism, but not economic liberalism; for some less social liberalism means challenging political liberalism too, while for others it does not. The question that arises from all this diversity is whether the EU can be flexible enough to let parts of European society choose their preferred combination of economic, social and cultural liberalism. If not, one wonders how the EU can stifle the ominous creep of all-embracing post-liberalism. In essence, to prevent this from happening a reset Europe will need to shift towards understanding liberalism as self-ownership and mutually tolerated variation.[20]

The realist view is that diversity and dispersed autonomy underpinned the Westphalian system of rules and statecraft – and that now the EU has got its strategic thinking backwards in seeking to maximise unity through limits to diversity.[21] Even if such old-style realism can hardly be the way forward for an alternative Europe, history certainly reinforces the conclusion that diversity is unlikely to evaporate any time soon. Each time there has been a European crisis in the last 500 years, some states have sought to overcome it through deeper centralisation, others through more pluralism.[22]

Naturally, the fact that the EU crisis has unleashed such dissonant and deviating perspectives presents an enormous challenge. And there will be no easy answer to combining diversity with effectiveness in European cooperation. However, Europe's diversity can no longer simply be wished away. Doubters point out that too much flexibility encourages states to free-ride, and takes away the incentive to engage in trade-offs or to make sure that decisions taken in one area of policy do not cut across those in others. Yet while it is certainly vital to be aware of the limits to viable and healthy flexibility, a more elastic concept of integration is surely necessary.

OPT-OUTS, SPEEDS AND CORES

To some extent, the EU is already a system of differentiated integration. Policies are centralised at the EU level to different degrees and include different sets of member states. There is both policy and territorial differentiation.[23] More than 30 forms of differentiation within areas of EU policies already exist, having developed incrementally over many years.[24] Some writers suggest that this very messiness is what makes the EU's development very different from the more uniform dynamics of history's other examples of regional integration and policy formation.[25]

Yet this differentiation has clearly not been enough to avert the poly-crisis. Today's variation exists where one or two member states have objected to a new area of policy or some states need time to meet entry requirements for a new sphere of integration. This is flexibility by ad hoc tactical necessity, not as a proactive organising principle for EU integration as a whole. It is not a type of flexibility capable of dealing with far-reaching divergence, where states differ in their basic aims and some want to unwind their existing EU commitments.[26]

The idea of slowly accumulating, pragmatic sector cooperation has been the spirit behind the so-called open model of coordination for over a decade. The results of this have been negligible. The principle of subsidiarity – taking decisions at the closest practicable level to citizens – has been present in EU politics for more than 20 years and has clearly not succeeded in shoring up the Union's legitimacy. Asymmetrical integration is generally touted as a means of adding to an 'untouchable core' of the EU's existing political system, and is hence a way of preserving rather than rethinking the fundamentals of integration.[27] Governments now debate flexibility very much within the parameters of existing treaty provisions, and nothing more radical.[28] Far more innovative and original forms of flexibility are needed.

When politicians, policy-makers and analysts talk about flexibility as a response to the current EU crisis, they most commonly advocate different speeds of integration. Calls for a two-speed or multi-speed EU have become common in the wake of the crisis. Foreign ministers of the founding six member states met in 2016 to discuss options for a 'core Europe'.[29] The illiberal and confrontational tone of the Polish and Hungarian governments has intensified interest in a smaller 'core Europe' – the mood among many politicians in Spain and France is now very strongly one of impatience with central and Eastern Europe. In the run up to the sixtieth anniversary Rome summit in March 2017, the idea of a multi-speed Europe gained prominence and lay at the heart of several governments' proposals, as well as the Commission's *White Paper on the Future of Europe*.[30]

The former director of the European Council's legal service argues that a two-speed Europe can be formally structured not to create long-lasting divisions but rather to create the flexibility necessary to keep the whole European project together.[31] *The Economist* proposes a 'multi-tier' model; it sees this as more fluid and innovative than the current batch of two-speed proposals, but still envisages a more fully integrated core around the eurozone, a second tier of non-euro member states, and additional tiers of current non-members.[32]

Some academics insist that managing divergence is essentially a matter of engineering a formal split between eurozone and other member states, with the former proceeding to political union.[33] Joseph Stiglitz has called, in turn, for a split in the euro, with southern states disconnecting from the northern states to operate a 'soft euro', with more expansionist policies.[34] Alternative für Deutschland has taken up this idea with a particularly divisive call for a formal and binary split: one strong euro around Germany, one weak euro around France.

Yet the notion of a core Europe has been around for many years and has always met resistance. The main problem with the two-speed vision is that it would surely need to be forced on the states excluded from the self-selecting inner nucleus. Governments may welcome the principle, but recoil from any suggestion that *they* would be the ones resigned to an inferior status. As a result, it is a notion likely to unleash even more resentment across Europe and exacerbate the imbalances driving the poly-crisis. Those states in danger of being 'left behind' will in practice try to 'keep up' with the core, but do so very grudgingly and with little feeling of popular ownership – a dynamic likely to compound the EU's legitimacy shortfall.

In southern member states, citizens are clearly hostile to the notion of a two-speed Europe.[35] They fear forms of differentiation that leave them more vulnerable to the de facto dominance of an inner core. The turmoil of recent years has occurred precisely because there are no easy ways to downgrade eurozone members' degree of participation in existing integration commitments. The templates that have been forwarded for splitting the eurozone conspicuously fail to consider the real-life politics of how this is supposed to happen with any degree of harmony.[36]

Moreover, the notion of a core Europe does not run with the grain of current trends: much focus in 2017 has, of course, been on unease over deeper integration in parts of the supposed core, like the Netherlands and France. The Dutch are in the lead of states wanting a looser form of integration. Euro members themselves have different visions of the next steps towards political union. Even if member states signed up to the notion of an inner core, they would then disagree on which policies would require a complete buy-in from all countries and which would be pursued only by the vanguard group. In current debates, a two-speed Europe is presented in particular as a way of bypassing increasingly truculent central and Eastern European states; yet significant differences and reticence also exist among the supposedly core Western European states.

Moreover, proposals invariably advocate flexibility for future areas of new integration but not for *current* policies, and therefore do nothing to address the tensions and divergence that have arisen during the poly-crisis. Think of the importance now attached to activating the (already-existing, but so far unused) provision for 'permanent structured cooperation' in defence and security: while three or four states may usefully club together to buy certain types of military equipment or to participate in a training mission in Africa, this says nothing about how the EU should manage differences that currently exist over substantive security questions. When it comes to these kinds of issues, in practice member states usually still block others from adopting significant variations that don't match their own policy preferences – despite all their rhetorical support for flexibility.

A fiscal or economic union that included only a rich core of member states would negate much of the purpose of such deeper economic integration – even if its formation were politically possible. Conversely, if the new core were to include all states inside or signed up to the euro, this would hardly be a template for multiple levels of variation. This is because nearly all member states are either inside the eurozone or aspire to join the single currency. Positing the eurozone as a new vanguard for political union amounts to little more than potentially excluding Sweden and Denmark – not exactly a high degree of differentiation. So this most commonly suggested basis for 'flexibility' simply looks like a standard route to a fully federal Europe, not a way out of the current EU straitjacket.

These tensions and shortcomings infused debates around the Rome summit in March 2017. After the Commission's white paper and a summit of the French, German, Italian and Spanish leaders pushed the possibility of a two-speed EU to the top of the agenda, other member states and the Commission mobilised decisively against such a prospect. That meeting of the four largest member states simply sparked further recriminations and divisions, inciting the Benelux, Baltic and Visegrád states to call their own summit to counterbalance the influence of the bigger states.

After much bargaining, references to multi-speeds were dramatically watered down in the Rome Declaration. As of 2017, flexibility is now to be explored within existing treaty provisions. This brings the focus back to the relatively circumscribed enhanced cooperation mechanism that has so far been used for proposals on patents, a financial-transactions tax, divorce laws and a public prosecutor. Rather than unleashing a decisive breakthrough, the flurry of recent proposals for a two-speed Europe has in fact encouraged many politicians and analysts to insist that there be strict limits on flexibility and to argue that giving member states an ability to choose their preferred areas of cooperation would lead to disintegration.[37]

A final challenge relates to Brexit. Proposals for different-speed Europes have often been concerned with the singular problem of the UK. Brexit will, in this sense, add to the dilemma of giving coherent and clear substance to the broad principles of differentiation and flexibility.

A more radical model of flexibility may be necessary to allow the UK back into any kind of engaged relationship with the EU – and for the moment it seems that neither side in the Brexit negotiations has begun creatively to entertain any such far-reaching flexibility. This also means that Britain's departure will force other member states to clarify their ideas about flexibility as a notion that is about more than assuaging one difficult member state.

Pushing the idea of an inner–outer divide further, some have advocated an *associate*-member status. Such a status could be relevant both to neighbouring non-EU states and current member states wanting to escape the confines of full membership while maintaining a productive relationship with the Union. Again, this suggestion is not so much about rethinking the tenets of integration per se as about cooperating with those states not part of or wishing to leave the integration project. Moreover, after years of debate about this option, in practice it has not gained traction on policy agendas.

CLUSTERS

Some writers argue that the EU could become more like a 'club of clubs' organised around clusters of specifically defined cooperation. Under such a model, each area of cooperation would be allowed to find its appropriate form of policy-making, institutional structure and membership. There would be no single centre but rather lots of different forms and types of cooperation, separate from each other, in a polycentric Europe.[38] Resonating with such ideas, one survey of opinion in all 28 member states suggests there is support for a variegated and utilitarian 'Europe of projects'.[39]

Giandomenico Majone insists there should be no need for a heavy layer of institutions and rules that overarches functional spheres of cooperation. There should be less intrusive harmonisation and more pragmatic cooperation, with the EU refereeing this cooperation rather than pushing for its own vision of ever-deeper integration. This approach would allow states to find the optimal benefits from cooperation while avoiding the downsides of all-embracing integration.[40] It would also enable European integration to move away from legal centralism. It would be based on a spirit of healthy competition between EU member states. Proponents of the clusters approach insist that such competition will be better able to find the best solutions to problems, the best models of public policy and the optimal forms of economic policy.

The related argument is that the EU could learn from other regional initiatives around the world that are doing well on the basis of far looser modes of cooperation. These initiatives show that more flexible and informal types of resolving disputes can work well.[41] In line with this, Mark Mazower believes the key is to return to the beginnings of EU integration in the 1950s, when cooperation was largely technical and did not threaten national sovereignty or raise questions of democratic legitimacy.[42]

In one of the most thought-provoking accounts of recent years, Jan Zielonka also advocates a set of functional clusters of cooperation, operating without any single, strong institutional centre – cooperation based on 'task-oriented integrative networks'. He suggests that such 'neo-medieval polyphony' would involve a major downgrading of EU-wide law and existing institutions like the Commission, European Council and European Parliament. Functional clusters would be organised on varied bases, in accordance with the requirements of each area of cooperation – and could easily be run by sub-state actors such as cities, regions or NGOs as much as by national governments.[43]

Zielonka makes the point that the EU has, in a sense, done the job it was designed for: embedding peace between European states. We should not be afraid to acknowledge that it has served its purpose and that it is time to move on to a different form of cooperation more suited to today's challenges than those of 1945. Dismantling the heavily centralised and legalistic edifice of today's EU would not open the door to conflict between member states or precarious Westphalian power-balancing. Interdependence has progressed too far – economically, socially, functionally – for this to happen.[44] The EU's institutional logic was designed for an economy based on the control of resources; it sought to enforce a shared management of these resources to stop governments fighting to control them. But today's organising logic of an economy based on knowledge is entirely different, as knowledge sharing and co-generation proceed in a more naturally bottom-up and institution-lite fashion.

Others have even suggested that the disparate – and usually maligned – Holy Roman Empire could offer useful lessons. Charlemagne's creation embodied a system of loosely affiliated princedoms that endured from 800 to 1806. One historian argues that the longevity of this network of cooperation based on local autonomy suggests 'an alternative to the stark choice between the EU as a single, homogeneous super-state or fatally weakening Europe's global position by fragmenting it into a mosaic of national states'.[45]

The sentiment behind more task- and results-oriented cooperation is well grounded. And these accounts surely provide a valuable service in reminding us that the current EU institutional structures are a means, not an end in themselves: if integration can be better pursued in different forms, then the priority must be to explore such avenues rather than to preserve the institutions of the Union as an end goal in their own right.

Yet the clusters approach is not sufficient on its own and has an unduly apolitical feel to it. Overarching political issues cannot simply be excluded. The 'club of clubs' plan is often presented as a largely technocratic vision, based on a return to so-called output legitimacy – the EU simply getting things done and delivering results. As Zielonka warns, political accountability is the Achilles heel of functional visions of integration. This more flexible and pragmatic model must be made compatible with citizens' desire for stronger democratic control and participation. If it were pursued on a purely technocratic basis, offering citizens little input, it is likely to worsen the EU's crisis of legitimacy, not solve it.[46]

The challenge is to combine these models of flexible clusters with means of rebuilding bottom-up and democratic solidarity. This combination is the crucial political metric with which any successful model of flexibility must comply. Radical flexibility should not be about mere shapeless expediency. The European project needs a spine of common solidarity. The rationale for a better model of flexible integration should be about finding alternative ways of locating and fostering the factors that can help reconstruct this spine – given that the existing policies supposedly making up the EU's central pillars of solidarity have crumbled so badly during the poly-crisis years.

DEMOCRATIC FLEXIBILITY AND SOLIDARITY

This means that if a polycentric Europe is to play a role in setting European cooperation on a firmer footing then reforms must go further: integration must combine flexibility with democratic accountability and alternative measures of solidarity. There must be a link between the imperative of democratising the EU on the one hand, and the need to manage multi-divergence on the other. Flexibility must deepen democratic quality. This is clearly a challenge – requiring flexibility to be understood in a political and more controversial way than has typically been the case. But it also represents an opportunity: flexibility can be harnessed as a means of helping restore the EU's democratic legitimacy.

The key is that debates about democratising the EU and the trends in localism outlined in previous chapters should inform efforts to fashion a more flexible form of European integration. Traditionally, flexibility has been seen in terms of an enlightened elite deciding how policy-making dynamics should vary between different areas of policy and between different states. Differentiated integration is invariably equated with mind-bendingly complex ways of dividing formal legal competences. This hardly resonates with the need for citizens to be more engaged with the EU.

Flexibility must be understood in more political and democratic terms than is habitually the case if it is to work as a core component of a democratically transformed integration model. It should not simply be a device for ad hoc opt-outs from selected policies for particular member states. Differentiation as it exists today accentuates the democracy problem, because it worsens the disconnect between those who make decisions and those affected by them. Some noted experts believe the

Commission's March 2017 white paper was damaging in excluding all considerations of accountability from its concept of multiple speeds.[47]

Flexibility should be understood as democratic subsidiarity. A form of subsidiarity is needed that is carried out through particularly strong democratic input and weighs carefully which issues are amenable to a functional or practical logic of centralisation and which are not. This should not be defined in a technocratic way, and it should not rest on the assumption that there is an objectively correct division of competences between national and EU levels.

Instead of being a concept enabling technocratic elites to divide competences between European, national and local levels, flexibility must be a device for fostering democratic debate in issue areas where citizens wish to share responsibilities across borders. EU institutions have tended to present and understand flexibility as a kind of managerial slimming down of the EU, spending less and cutting red tape.[48] This dangerously takes away the necessary political components from the notion of a flexible Europe. The integration templates adopted by other regional organisations – in Africa, Asia or Latin America – are not a good model for the EU as they take the human and democracy dimensions even more damagingly out of the equation, which in the EU's case is simply not possible.

One example of this imbalance is seen in relation to the issue of free movement, where de facto flexibility is being introduced without open debate or accountability. While most governments insist they are categorically against flexibility on free movement, in practice they are resorting increasingly to regulatory requirements that make it more difficult for citizens of another member state to get a job.[49] And while governments insist absolute free movement is essential to the single market, they then block the latter's completion. President Macron wants to limit movement across borders by reducing companies' ability to offer lower wages to migrants.

Whatever one's own position on free movement, there must be a strong case for giving populations more ownership and flexible options over this issue. This might open ways of helping protect vulnerable communities from rapid increases in migration flows, without upending the core principle of cross-border interaction. While politicians fear this would open a Pandora's box of states erecting new barriers, recent Eurobarometer surveys show that citizens in most member states see free movement as the most positive of EU rules – implying that offering a degree of democratic choice in this field should not produce a massive backsliding.[50]

Democratic flexibility must also facilitate and reflect the spirit of empathy and *euro-civismo* discussed in the previous chapter. Critics of differentiated integration often raise the spectre of a merely à la carte spirit undercutting core principles of solidarity. However, through democratic oversight that embodies a degree of *euro-civismo*, this risk could be mitigated. Legitimate flexibility need not be interpreted as the inverse of solidarity. Radical flexibility should categorically not be seen as synonymous with dysfunctional expediency or a disempowerment of formal governance capabilities. A thicker web of democratic participation would veer an alternative Europe away from à la carte transactional or utilitarian minimalism.

The key is whether radical flexibility can be underpinned by the generation of more bottom-up and more firmly rooted forms of solidarity. As states and citizens are accorded greater flexibility to select those elements of integration they support, the quid pro quo will be to search for more informal and voluntary signals of solidarity. The crucial point is that a democratic rather than technocratic form of differentiation would be more likely to address the challenge of such bottom-up solidarity – and ensure that lines of mutual support bind together the newly variegated model of European integration.

Donald Tusk captured the necessary conjoining of flexibility with mutual responsibility in his letter to leaders before the September 2016 Bratislava summit, writing:

> The slogan 'less power for Brussels', which sounds attractive in political campaigns, should translate as more responsibility for the Union in national capitals. This responsibility for the Union is nothing other than a readiness to sacrifice part of one's own interests for the sake of the community.[51]

Exactly the same orientation would apply to sub-national actors, CSOs and citizens. An alternative EU will hinge around the mutually nourishing triumvirate of participation, flexibility and solidarity.

ALTERNATIVE FLEXIBILITY

To implement this kind of radical flexibility, an alternative Europe should be guided by six principles. These six tenets grow out of the analysis offered by the previous chapters to the extent that they propose new forms of differentiation that resonate with underlying social trends and transcend the shortcomings of existing understandings of flexible integration.

1. POLICY OPT-INS

The first guiding logic should be one of voluntary and flexible *opting in*. At present, there is a standard and uniform template for integration in different policy areas, with the onus on states having to justify any reticence about specific parts of the model. This should be inverted. There should be a menu of different areas of cooperation to which states should be invited to opt in. A state's selection of which policy areas to join would then represent a positive choice, not a passive obligation.

Agencies managing a series of policy communities would be created. These could be dispersed to different locations across Europe, to give tangible expression to the move away from one single supranational centre. For instance, an agency for the single market could be located in Copenhagen, one for monetary policy in The Hague, one for the environment in Stockholm, one for social questions in Madrid, one for industry in Toulouse, one for international and security strategy in Bonn, one for refugees and migration in Milan – along with any number of other possible agencies in other places, covering those policy areas in which there is sufficient demand for formally managed coordination.

The collection of policy communities could include new areas of cooperation that have not so far figured highly in EU affairs. The voluntary opt-in logic should not be seen as synonymous with a lesser degree of overall cooperation. On the contrary, it might well open up new avenues and possibilities for states working together – especially as governments would no longer feel obliged to slow others down for fear of being bludgeoned into unwanted commitments. An extension of the integration frontier might, for example, be likely in areas like industrial competitiveness, education, health, the low-carbon transition, identity and deradicalisation strategies and defence. Far from suffering a corrosion of governance capacities, the integration project's overall level of formal institutional power could increase.

States that are not full members of the current EU might be allowed to participate in some of the new policy communities, with decision-making powers. This would constitute a practically oriented expression of the long-discussed 'associate member' idea. While the associate-membership proposal has not progressed, allowing certain policy communities to incorporate the likes of the UK, Turkey or Ukraine might be deemed more politically feasible and a more operational way of rendering the EU's borders less absolute.

The flexible opting-in logic would undoubtedly make European cooperation messy, as there are linkages between different areas of policy. But it would be far worse to continue on the basis of states and citizens having no ability to separate out the aspects of integration they want from those they do not. Some core standards – such as on democratic rights and basic economic openness – would need to be retained across all states. Some kind of overarching coordinating forum would be needed to sit on top of the different policy communities, a political dimension beyond what is envisaged in the 'club of clubs' approach. These arrangements would safeguard the EU's core institutional integrity, operating with a light touch and as unobtrusively as possible. Thinning down the Brussels institutional architecture to some degree might help show that European cooperation does not need to be about an overreaching, distant and supranational centre.

2. POLICY ALTERNATIVES

Second, as there is such a wide variety of policy preferences across today's Europe, the EU should embrace a spirit of competition between different economic, social and political models. As a dramatically streamlined entity encasing an array of separate policy communities, the EU would set broad goals but not impose the details of how these aims are to be reached. Member states could then mould their own preferred routes towards meeting common goals. The most successful policy models will prosper by example, rather than through legal fiat.

This approach to ensuring democratic flexibility would offer member states the freedom to choose how to meet European objectives. Member states could sign up to common goals, but then select the routes to achieve those goals that enjoy strongest democratic legitimacy among their own citizens. The European level would become an umbrella framework for shared aspirations, rather than a set of detailed policy strictures. This might help combine solidarity with flexibility. Within the framework of shared integrative commitments, governments should be freer to choose their own policy mix – with the quid pro quo that they would also assume responsibility for the success or otherwise of their chosen routes.[52]

This route to flexibility would require a streamlining of formal, legal rules in each of the policy communities established. This would determine which centralised rules are absolutely essential to keep cooperation afloat; those that are not should be transformed into common aspirations that would allow states flexibility in how to go about securing their achievement. Such streamlining would need to go far beyond the Commission's current efforts to check if new legislation is necessary or not.

Of course, to a limited degree the EU has already deployed the method of setting broad targets, through the aforementioned open method of coordination. The effectiveness of such an approach has not been great. Most infamously, the Lisbon Agenda and its follow-up, the 'Europe 2020' strategy, set a range of targets for competitiveness that all but a small handful of member states have got nowhere near fulfilling.

The various targets that have been set on carbon emissions and energy efficiency have been taken more seriously but also leave the EU far from having an adequate climate-change policy. The open method of coordination has failed because it confuses flexibility with vagueness, as it is predicated on targets that have little concrete impact on government's day-to-day policy commitments and that lack any connection to democratic accountability.[53] In an alternative EU, flexibility would need to go much further. It should go beyond simply setting targets that reflect and express a basically uniform set of assumptions about socio-economic and political models. It would need to allow greater scope for competition between such models.

This logic could be applied most significantly to economic and monetary union. Management of the eurozone is one of the hardest cases for flexibility. During the crisis governments have struggled to find ways to allow national economies greater room to make their own economic choices without the euro unravelling. However, some scope for flexibility and differentiation surely exists within the parameters of economic and monetary union.

Christian Odendahl argues that national governments need to set their own fiscal and budget targets and live with the consequences. The European Central Bank would guard against serious slumps in demand and oversee certain aspects of financial regulation. Within this framework, decisions over fiscal policy would be taken nationally. National governments would coordinate on such decisions, but they would eschew the notion of a single, supranational economic policy.[54] Other prominent economists have similarly suggested that member states need more, not less, scope to mould their own fiscal policies and take their own decisions over deficit levels, with fiscal discipline being ensured by national governments having responsibility for their own sovereign-debt rescheduling procedure.[55]

In essence: those states that want to end austerity may not be able to convince creditor states to adopt pan-European Keynesianism, but they themselves could be allowed the chance to either succeed or fail in showing that pro-growth policies do indeed offer the better route to reducing debt levels. Without going as far as a politically damaging split between a 'hard euro' and 'soft euro', this would allow some space for models to compete – within a broadly common economic framework, this spirit of competition could be constructive rather than destructive.

3. DIVERSITY WITHIN STATES

A third key challenge is diversity *within* states. In almost every member state a breach has opened up between those happily signed up to the cosmopolitan and internationalist spirit of the EU project and those who feel marginalised by it. Little is to be gained from condescendingly bemoaning 'nativist ignorance'. An integration project incapable of taking on board doubters' concerns and that proceeds only by suppressing their democratic voice is hardly one worth defending. The question is whether the whole form of European cooperation can be rethought simultaneously to allow space for *both* groups – the globalists and the nativists. Is it, for example, possible to have different arrangements for Europe's multicultural, cosmopolitan cities than those that apply to the hinterlands?

This would not be easy in practice, of course, and within-state flexibility may well be feasible only in very select policy areas that do not threaten the EU's spine of common commitments. But it is here that at least some degree of innovative thinking is surely required. The EU could usefully tap into a rich vein of thinking on so-called legal pluralism, which explores how in very tightly defined areas different juridical and regulatory norms can coexist within a single political system. Many highly diverse societies around the world that struggle to deal with divergent identities among their populations – from India to Africa and parts of the Middle East – show that variability in formal, legal rules and institutional channels can make such pluralism workable.[56] Legal pluralism is a notion that might play a role in reviving European integration, however vocal and predictable the objections to such sub-state innovations.

For instance, slightly more liberal labour-market conditions for non-national workers might apply in Europe's big multicultural cities than in the hinterlands. One suggestion that has been floated in the UK context is for a 'London work visa' that draws from a model used in some Canadian cities.[57] Or some regions of a member state might want to adopt European cooperation initiatives that other regions of the same country oppose. Some areas of a state might be happy to make a financial contribution to be part of common European policy communities, while others might decide the cost is not worthwhile. Some communities might wish to contribute financially to benefit from EU citizenship rights, while others may not.[58]

It goes without saying that all such eventualities would be extremely difficult to manage. The principle of within-state flexibility would raise many practical questions related to how different parts of a single state could be effectively partitioned and allowed the kind of European cooperation they thought most desirable for their given local circumstances. Undoubtedly there would be limits to how far this could be taken. Nevertheless, the deepening of internal divisions in nearly all member states suggests that some efforts along these lines should at least be attempted.

4. REVERSIBILITY

A form of European cooperation is required that allows for fluid change – an essential element of democracy's signature ability to self-correct. Current structures assume agreement is reached between states on a given issue, and that then the issue is transferred to the EU level in perpetuity with little scope for fine-tuning. There needs to be a dynamic in which policies can move both ways – towards but also away from the centre. This principle must be central to an alternative EU.

Allowing decisions on whether or not to join a given policy community to have a degree of reversibility would help redress one of the most idiosyncratic and increasingly damaging features of European integration – namely, that governments may change, circumstances may alter utterly and popular preferences may undergo far-reaching shifts, but policy commitments at the EU level are irreversible and unbending.

Breaking integration down into its component parts through a collection of separate policy communities would help add a degree of reversibility. This is because a member state with a particularly serious set of new concerns may change its line on one area of policy without this sparking a major crisis for the whole integration project – as tends to happen at the moment. A state's shifting position on one issue does not need to be treated as a sin or affront to the overall spirit of European integration. Clearly, there would need to be a relatively strict set of conditions for states to withdraw from a given area of cooperation, so that policy changes do not become too ad hoc, unpredictable and unmanageable.

5. CITIZENS' OVERSIGHT

The mechanisms proposed in the previous chapter for civil society involvement should have a specific link to the question of flexibility. Sceptics and populists often assume that a flexible Europe means a Europe of Nations, handing governments the lead role. Even if flexible arrangements do involve competences residing at the national level, this is not the way that differentiation should be understood and engineered. Rather, citizens should be the arbiters of flexibility, and in a more regularised and participative fashion than current democratic channels allow for in European affairs. As a central pillar of the Compact of European Citizens, a dedicated 'Civic Forum for Flexible Integration' could be created to assess new legislation and to judge how to keep measures as close to the local level as possible.

National permutations of this forum should play a central role in states' decisions over which European policy communities to join. The forum should have a say over subsidiarity decisions – modifying the current subsidiarity assessment exercises that are conducted by the Commission with little visibility. It should also have the power and responsibility for preparing reports on the result of competition between different economic, social and political models. It might also consult with local communities on practical ideas for allowing flexibility within each member state, where this might help meet citizens' preferences. It would trigger deliberations where certain states or communities want to reverse a decision either to join or not to join a given policy community. Civil society input on all these important areas of a flexible, alternative Europe should be formalised, regularised and meaningful.

The basic aim would be to ensure that common policies are the result of bottom-up and proactive pressure, and come about after careful citizen deliberation on the right balance between healthy local ownership and diversity on the one hand and respect for necessarily common rules on the other. Of course, this balance will never be easy to strike and such a forum would hardly offer a magic panacea, but it would at least prompt governments and societies to frame the challenges of integration in this way – something that at present simply does not happen in EU debates, and certainly not with the active participation of European citizens.

6. FLEXIBLE SOLIDARITY

There should be practical efforts to ensure that flexibility is not simply about fewer rules but also about a thickening of mutual empathy or *euro-civismo*. There should be a process to assess how different policies contribute to common European objectives and deeper solidarity between states and societies. Governments would be obliged each year to explain how their policies are advancing the core of agreed objectives. There will be a need to show and measure exactly how differentiation enhances solidarity and reduces states' and societies' hostility to having measures they don't like imposed upon them.

The civic, democratic component would help ensure that 'flexibility' is not simply code for the negative unravelling of existing integration. Flexibility should not be about simply putting limits to cooperation but about citizens playing a positive role in suggesting new forms of cooperation that are likely to reflect their different preferences. This is certainly not to suggest that new routes to solidarity will be easy to locate or that they will emerge easily and spontaneously; but a more prominent democratic dimension will at least make the social aspects of flexible integration a central feature of debate to a far greater degree than the current technocratic, hyper-controlled approach to differentiation.

A well-structured civil society component could contribute positive ideas of how elements of flexibility and variation might help advance common objectives. It might provide a stronger force of binding peer pressure than the currently ad hoc and disorganised way in which many governments simply ignore those EU rules they dislike – whether on deficits or judicial independence – and escape sanction in a way that stirs up resentments across Europe. Citizens and governments should then seek alternative ideas to retain core solidarity, as they choose diverse policy options.

One example of flexible solidarity is currently being discussed as a way forward on migration policy. Apparently accepting that there may be downsides to imposing the 2015 relocation scheme on member states through a supranational EU policy, the Commission has proposed that states not willing to accept refugees make financial contributions to those that are. The Visegrád states say they are now funding refugees in other member states.

Critics remain unconvinced of this arrangement. It is certainly less than ideal, and one might strongly disagree with central and Eastern European states' hostility to refugees. Yet a significant upgrading and spread of such arrangements might be the only practical way forward – a means, albeit inelegant, of trying to square the circle of having flexibility with some solidarity, while preventing EU cooperation from breaking down altogether. In general, the solidarity component certainly needs to be strengthened far beyond the form it takes in this particular example. In some policy areas it might be possible for cautious governments to align themselves with central rules through informal measures of cooperation – retaining some degree of national control but without eviscerating all solidarity.

CONCLUSION

There is a sad irony in today's EU crisis. In historical terms, today's disagreements between European states are minor compared to centuries of wars and invasions. Yet because the model of integration aspires to squeeze states into a common mould, today's disagreements take on a greater magnitude than they need to. The overarching, structural issue for the EU integration model is how much further differentiation can and should go. Clearly, it is no longer simply a question of member states advancing towards a common goal at different speeds. Differentiation is not merely a matter of some states wanting to adopt new commitments while others do not; it also embraces debates about rolling back some areas of commitment. Flexibility cannot only be about existing 'enhanced cooperation' rules that allow a small group of member states to agree on a new area of integration. And even if it accords important roles to the nation state, neither can flexibility be reduced to the kind of purely nation-state-based model of integration now pushed by right-wing populists.

Many argue that extensive flexibility is either not feasible or would pander too much to ascendant Eurosceptics. But reformers should challenge the commonly made assumption that flexible integration necessarily equates to *less* integration. Under the flexible principles suggested in this chapter, those countries whose citizens desire a wide range of much deeper integration would have scope to pursue this – simply without obliging others to follow exactly the same path should they prefer other forms and degrees of cooperation. If flexibility is structured in the right way, over the longer term it could lead to more, not less, integration overall. It could enhance the degree of formal institutional power that can be mobilised to address European policy challenges; the flexibility options suggested in this chapter are certainly not aimed at disassembling effective governance capabilities – quite the reverse. An alternative EU needs to push back against the long-held assumption that solidarity is synonymous with the development of single-EU policies. Solidarity and singularity need to be delinked. A more pliable EU does not need to entail a more pinched and hunkered Europe, but can prompt a more positive and untethered form of cooperation.

CHAPTER SEVEN

A Secure Europe?

The events of recent years suggest that the existing model of integration has failed to provide European citizens with a sense of security. This problem involves a fusing together of internal and external policy challenges. It means that the international dimensions of the EU's poly-crisis loom ever larger. The prevailing model of EU integration has struggled to provide effective responses to the challenges crowding in on Europe from the outside world. The refugee influx and terrorist attacks have done as much as Brexit and the eurozone crisis to reveal the apparent inadequacy of existing policy recipes. While some might see this chapter's focus on security as separate from the internal issues discussed so far, I believe that a book on the EU's 'future directions' would be incomplete without an analysis of how the EU needs to reset its relations with the outside world.

The crisis has already had a profound impact on European foreign and security policies, widening differences but also driving a deepening of EU integration and cooperation over external borders and security. While in some ways this new impulse is positive, the EU's overall response to the international dimensions of the poly-crisis suffers from worrying shortfalls and imbalances. The response has been based on a combination of efforts to stiffen controls over EU borders and sporadic engagement in select conflicts. Taken together, these measures do not constitute a foreign policy capable of giving a major fillip to the beleaguered European project. The EU does not simply require more foreign-policy cooperation, but must fundamentally change the way it does external policy. This chapter maps out the international dimension to an alternative EU and, crucially, links this to the principles of flexibility and participation explored in previous chapters.

INTERNATIONAL SECURITY AND THE CRISIS

International issues have asked increasingly searching questions of the existing model of EU integration. As emphasised throughout this book, the general EU crisis is as much an external as an internal phenomenon. The heightened terrorist threat and the surge of refugees and migrants into Europe have taken on existential proportions. They have done as much to raise doubts about the EU's future and the viability of existing integration as any internal aspect of the Union's decade-long poly-crisis.

For several decades, EU foreign-policy cooperation has followed a familiar pattern. European governments have sought incremental development of the same basic policy template. They have aspired to a gradual strengthening of EU unity and a greater effort to extend EU engagement abroad. They have long assumed that this type of cooperation adds to the EU's value as a provider of security and that the current integration model protects harmony within Europe from divisive external influences.

The refugee influx and resurgent terrorism have disrupted the generally sanguine outlook on this incremental pattern of policy development. The increasingly brittle state of the liberal global order adds another layer of uncertainty and worry. EU approaches to foreign policy seem to have left citizens more exposed and vulnerable to events unfolding in the outside world. The EU's foreign-policy challenge is no longer simply 'out there', a remote question beyond the Union's borders. Rather, international issues today threaten to tear asunder the very foundations of the EU's own integration model. The links between the EU's internal crises and its external challenges are today tighter and more mutually conditioning than ever before. Some of the most respected analysts of EU affairs stress that foreign policy must work more directly to overcome the Union's internal crises.[1]

The fate of the whole European integration project is today inextricably tied up with the way that the EU and European governments act in the Middle East, in particular. Internally, many fear the rise of radical and illiberal Islam. This fear may be based on perceptions that are exaggerated or inaccurate, but it nonetheless exists as a potential driver of EU disintegration. Many ascendant populist parties have come to espouse counter-narratives that merge anti-EU and anti-Muslim positions. Illiberalism in some Islamist groups is breeding illiberalism in some European political parties. Radicalism within Europe stands at an unprecedented level and the participation of European fighters in violence in the Middle East is greater than that of any other region.[2]

External challenges have both integrative and disintegrative repercussions. On the one hand, they point to the need for deeper security cooperation. On the other hand, the same threats have made European governments look hard at the kind of cross-border openness that sits at the heart of the European integration project. For many, the threats to the EU model from outside require more nationally centred and defensive security, with national authorities needing to regain control over borders and security. Interdependencies now seem to be a source of vulnerability more than protection. The possibly systemic implications of Donald Trump's mercurial and unorthodox presidency compound this duality – on the one hand apparently menacing some tenets of the global liberal order, while on the other giving the EU more reason to lead on its own security.

In this vein, today's external problems raise a structural question of whether the EU requires not simply deeper cooperation on security issues but rather qualitatively different ways of carrying out foreign policy. While unity is increasingly needed to shore up the EU's flagging global power, flexibility is equally essential to catalyse effective action that may no longer always be possible among all EU member states. Many aspects of future foreign policies will require an agility and micro-adaptability that the traditional model of EU foreign policy does not always allow.

BORDERS, SECURITY, SURVIVAL

The poly-crisis has prompted European governments and EU institutions to change the way they view foreign policy – and indeed how they understand the whole relationship between the EU project and the wider world. The common line in response to the refugee crisis and terrorist attacks has been that the EU has to regain control of its borders and 'get serious' about security if it is to save itself. The dominant thinking is that the demarcation lines need to be far stronger between the European project and what lies beyond it.[3] Governments' response has combined measures to strengthen border controls and keep refugees from travelling into Europe, as well as beefing up internal surveillance – as reactions to the refugee and counter-terrorism challenges often overlap and confusingly blur into each other.

The refugee crisis has spurred an advance in integration, into the realm of external border and security control. Most leaders and diplomats argue that if the fundamental norms of free movement are to be retained within Europe, the EU requires stronger and more common efforts to control its common external frontier. Dutch prime minister Mark Rutte said in 2016 that if the EU did not strengthen the protection of its borders it would suffer the same fate as the Roman Empire. In October 2016, French prime minister Manuel Valls wrote: 'Reasserting our European identity also means coming to terms with the fact that there are borders – Europe starts and stops somewhere.'[4]

The idea of a 'Security Union' has risen to the top of the EU policy agenda. In June 2016, the EU's high representative for foreign and security policy, Federica Mogherini, presented a new EU Global Strategy that stresses that the EU's first priority must be to link external policy to internal security challenges and citizens' interests. It reiterates several times that security policy needs to move up a gear and be tailored to preserving the EU project itself.[5] In July 2016, the French and German foreign ministers proposed a European Security Compact to deal with 'the interaction between external threats and internal weaknesses' and in particular to bear down on radicalisation through enhanced judicial, intelligence and security cooperation.[6]

To this end, many policy developments now purport to strengthen a *protective perimeter* around the EU. This new level of commitment involves several elements: efforts to make borders more robust; resources to keep refugees and migrants in their own country or region; internal security cooperation; and security assistance and intervention in states outside Europe.

Borders. The EU has set up a European Border and Coastguard Agency and deployed Rapid Border Intervention Teams at its external frontiers. Tellingly, the new agency was created in the record time of under a year. Member states have pushed for full implementation of the border surveillance system, Eurosur, that was introduced in 2013. From mid-2016, the EU released several tranches of emergency aid to south-eastern member states, the bulk of which has been spent on strengthening border fences.[7] One of the priority focuses of the Global Strategy is the commitment to strengthen surveillance capacities.

Operations Sophia and Triton in the Mediterranean have been progressively beefed up to provide more extensive patrols. NATO has also deployed a Maritime Group to cut lines of trafficking and smuggling. An initiative called Joint Operational Team (JOT) Mare was launched in 2015 for information-sharing between member states on trafficking and migrant smuggling. In a strikingly hard-edged move, in November 2016 and again in early 2017 Germany proposed intercepting migrants and refugees at sea and returning them to North Africa to apply for asylum there; to speed readmissions further, Germany also opened a migration centre in Tunis.[8] More generally, overall EU defence spending increased in 2016 for the first time in a decade, driven in part by border-defence concerns.

Refugee funding. The EU has launched an Emergency Trust Fund of 2.5 billion euros to stem migration from Africa and the Middle East. EU member states promised an extra 200 million euros for multilateral agencies like the World Food Programme and the UN Refugee Agency to care for refugees within the Middle East. The EU's Madad Fund was set up specifically to channel emergency relief for Syrian refugees and provided with 1 billion euros – half of this from the European Commission, half from EU member states. Most high profile, of course, was the EU's awarding of 3 billion euros to the Turkish government to keep refugees in camps inside Turkey. The EU also introduced a European Investment Plan in November 2016, covering African and Mediterranean states, with the Commission providing 3.35 billion euros for guarantees designed to leverage private investment. Germany has also launched its own 'Marshall Plan for Africa', while President Macron has promised to reverse the cuts made to French development aid under his predecessor.

The EU has begun to tie external cooperation more tightly to readmission, partner countries receiving aid only if they agree to take back migrants from Europe. Under a first round of 'migration compacts' with Jordan, Lebanon, Niger, Nigeria, Senegal, Mali, Ethiopia, Tunisia and Libya, EU aid is being used explicitly to dissuade refugees and migrants from travelling to Europe. In October 2016, the Commission claimed that the EU had got these countries to agree to take back more migrants over the summer months of 2016 than in many previous years combined.[9] In the same month, the EU unveiled plans to repatriate Afghan asylum seekers in return for a new aid package to Afghanistan. In February 2017, European leaders agreed a new 200-million-euro initiative to train and equip the Libyan coastguard to intercept and turn back migrants embarked for Europe. Angela Merkel visited Cairo in March 2017 to suggest a deal similar to that struck with Turkey, under which the Egyptian regime would block migrants and refugees from travelling into the EU in exchange for economic aid and security cooperation.[10]

Internal security coordination. Cooperation between internal security forces has intensified, often overlapping with efforts to contain refugee and migrant flows. Europol opened a European Counter Terrorism Centre at the beginning of 2016. This new centre has dispatched experts into refugee arrival camps because of a perceived need to stop jihadis slipping into Europe as asylum seekers. Governments are pushing forward deeper cooperation between police forces and judicial sectors, through Europol and Eurojust. All but three member states have signed up to a reinforced intelligence-sharing arrangement managed through Europol. The EU has created a host of new institutional links between internal and external security policies. The EU's Internal Security Fund has been increased to 3.8 billion euros for 2014–20.[11] National governments have followed suit. The UK's counter-terrorism spending, for example, is now more than 2 billion pounds a year.[12]

External security engagement. Commitments in several areas of external security policy have been stepped up. Perhaps most visibly, a number of member states have intensified their actions against IS in Syria and Iraq. Belgium, Denmark, France, Germany, Italy, the Netherlands and the UK have provided hundreds of military trainers to Kurdish peshmerga fighters and Iraqi security forces since late 2014. France and the UK have stepped up training for Syrian rebels since 2015. In January 2017, the UK signed a 100-million-pound deal to help Turkey develop a new fighter jet.

In late 2015, Germany joined the anti-IS coalition, after having previously ruled this out. After the terrorist attack in Nice in July 2016, President Hollande promised increased French engagement against IS in Syria and Iraq. At the same time, the Paris attacks and the refugee crisis have made most European governments more willing to reach a negotiated settlement with the Assad regime in Syria – even after its horrific use of chemical weapons in April 2017.

France has dramatically beefed up its counter-terrorist efforts across five Sahel countries, in an undertaking known as Opération Barkhane – after his election, President Macron made an early trip to Mali to boost this initiative. The EU has opened security-training missions in Mali and Niger. It has also diverted more than 20 million euros to help Tunisia develop a national-security strategy; extended a Radicalisation Awareness Network centre of excellence to Tunisia; and begun a new dialogue with Tunisian authorities on counter-terrorism. Several EU governments have launched special-forces and intelligence operations inside Libya aimed at weakening IS.

In early 2016, a group of EU donors pushed the Organisation for Economic Co-operation and Development (OECD) to change its definition of 'aid' to include some military spending and funds for refugee camps. In a similar move, governments have sought to change the rules governing the Commission's financial instruments to allow development funds to be used for border controls and other measures to restrict migrant flows. In 2016, the EU introduced a new strategy to strengthen its cooperation with security actors in fragile contexts.[13] The UK has shifted more of its aid budget towards tempering instability, including through conflict initiatives and security training, specifically in the Middle East and North Africa.

RELUCTANT POWER, STILL

Taken together, these developments represent a notable effort to shore up the security dimensions of the European project. However, there are significant limits to this policy upgrade – and to how effective the EU's recalibrated strategic approach is likely to be.

Perhaps most obviously, despite all the security challenges now in play, European governments are still not inclined to engage in significant military intervention. Only five EU member states – Belgium, Denmark, France, the Netherlands and the UK – have participated in air strikes against IS in Iraq and Syria. Collectively, these states have contributed a small fraction of the level of air power provided by the United States. As of late 2016, the United States had carried out more than 5,000 air strikes inside Syria, EU states only about 100.[14]

No EU state has contemplated a large-scale military engagement involving ground troops. Moreover, in general they still refuse formally to supply the Syrian opposition with arms (even if it has been revealed that French and British special forces now provide covert support). European governments did not help opposition forces fight against Russia's bombing of Aleppo throughout 2016, which sent another wave of refugees fleeing from Syria and scuppered peace talks. It was the United States and not European governments that took action after President Assad's use of chemical weapons in April 2017.

The EU's engagement in Iraq remains strikingly limited. The EU has pressed for a more inclusive government in Baghdad and promised to support Iraqi prime minister Haider al-Abadi. The European Commission has funded initiatives in Iraq on religious tolerance, media freedom and human rights. Yet such support remains on an extremely modest scale. Shi'i militia are gaining power in Iraq as they battle IS and block political reforms pushed by Western powers. Little European support has been forthcoming to help the Iraqi army hold territory when it does make gains against IS. European help for the operation to retake Mosul from IS was limited.

One former security coordinator acknowledges that European states have in practice failed to link their domestic and international counter-terrorist policies. Most of the focus has been on procedural changes – most accounts list the ways in which different agencies within and between different member states need to be talking to each other – and much less on the actual substantive output of bigger-picture foreign-policy changes on the ground.[15]

Notwithstanding commitments to address the root causes of security risks threatening Europe, in practice EU initiatives backing modernising reforms in Arab states are becoming weaker rather than stronger. Much European aid has shifted to governments' security programmes as civil society is stifled across the Middle East. The UK, for example, has diverted half a billion pounds from its overseas development aid to help resettle refugees in the UK, dragging existing money away from the causes of instability in Syria and other places. Most European initiatives in Syria are being diluted into purely humanitarian operations as conditions worsen.[16]

Diplomats acknowledge that the Emergency Trust Fund is not nearly big enough to make any impact on the causes of migration over the 23 eligible recipient countries and is at best a small top-up to existing spending on development. Moreover, part of the new funding is being directed towards border controls and migration management in the recipient countries rather than 'root causes' development-related work.[17] Of all European donors, only the European Commission, Denmark, Germany, Sweden and the UK now give non-negligible amounts of governance and civil society aid. Few member states have significantly increased their aid to the region. French aid for reforms is extremely limited.[18] Most EU states have spent far more on enhancing domestic capabilities in surveillance, policing, border controls and intelligence than they direct at the external root causes of insecurity. The Commission's new Defence Fund risks the prospect of funds being taken away from such reform initiatives for military technology projects.

European security engagement sits increasingly uneasily alongside the promise to foster long-term growth and political change. Member-state arms sales have increased to states like Egypt, Algeria, Saudi Arabia and Jordan, which are all tightening repression. In Bahrain, the UK has started to build its first permanent naval base in the region in 40 years, even as the Bahraini regime intensifies repression against opposition forces. Tunisian activists feel that, in league with remnants of the former regime, the EU is walking their country backwards towards a soft version of a police state that draws its oxygen from the cross-Mediterranean counter-terrorism narrative.[19] The EU is now providing aid to Sudanese security bodies to control migration, despite having tried to take Sudan's president, Omar al-Bashir, to the International Criminal Court for many years. France's Opération Serval in Mali and other military ventures across the Sahel have had their mandates tightly drawn to steer clear of internal political issues in the region.

European involvement in Libya also remains limited. European states supported a rushed UN peace deal in late 2015 that was not balanced, fully inclusive or democratic because they primarily sought a governing partner to clamp down on migration and the export of terrorism from the country – without thinking through the requirements for longer-term stabilisation.[20] That UN deal has virtually collapsed. A renegade administration under the command of General Haftar in the city of Tobruk has refused to join the peace accord – and yet several European governments have cooperated with this very administration on pushing back against IS. In July 2017, President Macron mediated a ceasefire between the UN-recognised government and Haftar, giving the general further legitimacy – to the chagrin of other member states, such as Italy. Commission aid in Libya was a modest 8 million euros in 2016. Hardly any European projects have aimed at fostering a more inclusive political process or support reconciliation efforts at a local level, where tribes and other actors are trying to fashion deals to get community governance running.[21] The EU's engagement has certainly not been strong enough to negate Russia's support for Haftar to stay outside the unity accord.

SECURITY MISCONSTRUED?

Beyond these limits to new security commitments, it is unclear that the EU is approaching security in the most effective way. The emerging policy initiatives often reflect antiquated ways of thinking about security, alliances and borders in a context where strategic threats have undergone a qualitative shift, becoming more fluid, nebulous and less state-centred. While it is, of course, unquestionably the case that European frontier management needs fortifying, the EU risks leaning too heavily on border-strengthening as a means of supposedly protecting the Union from disintegration. The costs of erecting, policing and maintaining borders is extremely high relative to what such measures are able to achieve over the longer term. One policy-maker involved in drawing up the responses observes that they rely on a scale of resources – constantly to monitor borders, undertake deportations and pay off third countries – that European governments will in practice be unable to provide.[22]

Building fences has rarely worked as a primary means of managing refugee and migration flows. Border closures in Austria and the Balkans have simply forced refugees to search for other routes. Simply pushing the main refugee and migrant choke points further to the south, further away from the heart of the EU, is a precarious basis upon which to build a security strategy. The number of arrivals and deaths on the so-called central Mediterranean route increased significantly in 2017, showing that the deal with Turkey is simply compelling refugees to attempt more dangerous sea crossings from Egypt or Libya.[23] The EU has spent billions of euros simply to push asylum seekers from overt to covert routes – more dangerous for them and more difficult for the EU to police.[24]

Moreover, hardening borders may be necessary but does not sit easily with the aim of shoring up internal EU solidarity. The apparent goal of raising a protective perimeter against the external 'other' is not pulling the EU together but driving member states apart. The hard-border approach plays into the nativist narrative, counterproductively nourishing the very dynamics that menace the EU project internally. This security doctrine is part of what drives the EU poly-crisis, not its antidote.

The focus on external border controls has not reassured all member states enough to dissuade them from chipping away at internal free-movement provisions. If anything, the overly heavy focus on borders has reinforced member states' resort to beggar-thy-neighbour policies, pushing the burden of managing refugee and migrant inflows onto others. Member states have shown little solidarity with Italy and Greece to help get 'hotspot' processing centres for migrants up and running.[25] Persisting distrust means that member states have taken in only a small share of the 160,000 migrant relocations they signed up to in 2015.

Eventually, the EU will need a policy for the orderly and long-term management of migrant and refugee arrivals. Structural factors will drive an increase in migration regardless of what happens with the Syrian conflict and IS. In 2017, relatively few new arrivals have been from the Syrian or Libyan conflict zones, but come rather from sub-Saharan Africa and South Asia. While governments are justified in seeking more effective border management, reinforced fences and border controls will not stop people coming to Europe, and the distinction between migrants and refugees is not tenable indefinitely. Border controls are of only limited value as the vast majority of illegal migration is due to people entering legally and staying when their visas expire. The number of people returned under EU admission agreements is tiny, as this has proved a prohibitively difficult mechanism to implement.

The EU can only manage increasing migration flows by recognising that these reflect deep-seated changes in the global economic and political order, and by globalising migration management with the involvement of other powers.[26] Evidence shows that economic circumstances have to get a lot better for people to choose not to migrate and that a slight improvement in economic well-being can actually increase the outflow of migrants. This implies that the EU will need significantly upgraded external support mechanisms but also that its only realistic policy is also to put in place mechanisms to manage these flows more effectively.[27] Despite the European Commission proposing several such mechanisms since 2016, national governments still recoil from a proactive and long-term strategy that recognises the need to manage increased numbers of arrivals.[28]

Outsourcing control to poorer and authoritarian states cannot be a robust route to security in the long term. Forcing people back to their countries of origin is likely to add further to instability in those states and thus generate more pressure for migration. The EU is creating a vicious circle that rebounds negatively on its own security. Pushing the management of refugee flows onto poorer and more brittle states would hardly seem to be a recipe for regional stability – indeed, quite the contrary. Boosting unaccountable security forces and making land borders more impenetrable tends to add to regional instabilities and worsen the very conditions that push migrants towards Europe. Think what it means for the EU to be forcing record numbers of people back into the maelstroms of a new emergency law crackdown in Ethiopia, Boko Haram's rise in Nigeria, militant attacks in Mali and rising violence in Afghanistan. Brusquely throwing out asylum seekers in such circumstances is possibly the surest way to drive them angrily into the arms of anti-Western radicals.

In particular, the EU is likely to pay a heavy price for relying on its controversial deal with Turkey. While this has partially stemmed arrivals, thousands of refugees remain trapped on the Greek islands, as the rate of returns to Turkey has been slow. The EU complains that problems in Turkey are delaying much of the 3 billion euros of aid from being spent; for its part, the Turkish government is fighting for greater direct control over these funds for its own priorities. European leaders have done little to try to limit President Erdoğan's centralisation of power and assault on opposition leaders since the attempted coup against him in July 2016. France and Germany still pressed for more security cooperation with Turkey after the April 2017 referendum that opened the way for Erdoğan to assume even more unchecked, authoritarian power. By September 2017 European pressure had begun to mount as government repression intensified across Turkey, with new cooperation effectively stalling and several member states – including Germany – hinting at aid cuts. Yet for the moment the EU remains reluctant formally to suspend the accession process. While the EU needs Turkey's support in the battle against IS, the country's own internal fragility now represents a major strategic concern for European governments and it can hardly be defined as a reliable partner on refugee and conflict issues.[29] And if the premises of the Turkey deal are questionable, the EU's 2017 deal on migration control with Libya is even shakier, as it relies on a government that now has virtually no effective power. In August 2017, General Haftar moved to scupper Italy's plans to send its navy into Libyan waters to intercept traffickers' boats.

Neither is the EU's current focus on counter-terrorism and intelligence cooperation sufficient to make Europe significantly more secure. This cooperation cannot obviate underlying political and economic problems in the Middle East or elsewhere. Few incumbent regimes in the region make reliable or effective security partners. Egypt's current regime, for example, is not a stable autocracy, but one that presides over a dysfunctional state. Subject to brutal state violence, parts of the Muslim Brotherhood are now drifting towards a tactic of 'limited violence' or joining the ranks of jihadi groups. Far from helping EU aims, the country's president, Abdel Fattah el-Sisi, has ejected Syrians from Egypt, and his government actively colludes in people-smuggling.

While political change in Arab countries would not offer an automatic antidote to the EU's security concerns, the lack of democratic space in the region must be seen as the ultimate driver of the refugee, migrant and terrorist challenges – and yet this is still a secondary aspect of European strategy. This deficiency undermines the effectiveness of Europe's humanitarian efforts, its refugee and migration controls and its pursuit of counter-terrorism partnerships. Governance problems in Arab states are preventing much EU humanitarian aid from actually reaching refugee camps, and many of these funds have ended up feeding networks of criminal and illicit activity, which in turn nourish recruitment into jihadi groups.[30] The EU's new security sector strategy acknowledges that to date the EU has struggled to link security cooperation with partner states' core political pathologies.[31]

Underlying social and political conditions are so important because, however much it upgrades security engagement, the international community is unlikely to 'defeat' IS in any definitive sense. As al-Qaeda morphed into IS, so IS can simply morph into another form of radicalism or switch to attacks inside Europe. While the military and security dimensions of EU strategy are undoubtedly paramount, ultimately some form of political inclusion is needed for Islamist groups. Many European Muslims went to Syria to fight with IS out of frustration that the West was doing nothing to oust President Assad. People become radicalised due to political repression and then express this through Islam, rather than becoming Islamist and then being drawn into radical views.[32]

The value of additional intelligence cooperation may also have been oversold. Modern intelligence has achieved major successes, but in the vast amounts of material that signals intelligence now has to trawl through it can be no more than a precarious stopgap. The nature of today's threat means intelligence work has had to become increasingly predictive, intervening ahead of events to stop possible attacks. European intelligence agencies have struggled to penetrate jihadist groups.[33] Moreover, since the poly-crisis was generated in part by citizens' distance from decision-making, empowering such an intrinsically opaque area of policy is unlikely to do much to rescue the EU project.

A final and less tangible problem relates to the way that exclusionary and restrictive policies damage the EU's credibility as a supposedly liberal foreign-policy actor. When the EU talks about a 'shared neighbourhood' with a common set of aims to combat radicalisation, other states ask what kind of a common neighbourhood has huge wire fences running through it. It is difficult for the EU to be a good humanitarian abroad if governments are flouting basic humanitarian norms domestically. One key channel for EU humanitarian relief, Médecins Sans Frontières, was so incensed by the EU's approach of 'paying dictators' to make sure migrants and refugees are kept inside Africa and the Middle East that it decided to turn down aid worth 60 million euros a year from European donors.[34] One writer fears that ironclad external borders will make Europe 'not just a fortress but a tomb, where the best and noblest aspirations of the European Union are buried.'[35]

ALTERNATIVE APPROACHES TO GLOBAL ACTION

The new focus on securing Europe and addressing some of the continent's strategic frailties is necessary and long overdue – the EU integration model can no longer be engineered as a kind of hermetically
sealed Kantian paradise. However, the need for effective approaches
to foreign policy goes well beyond simply fortifying Europe's borders,
regulating refugees and stepping up international counter-terrorist operations. Alongside firm defence and hard power, a reset EU also needs
alternative forms of foreign and security policy action. Throughout the
book, I have argued for an integration model based on the principles
of legitimacy, diversity and flexibility. These principles also need to be
more fully developed within EU foreign policies.

The EU should contemplate three broad changes to its foreign
and security policy modus operandi. First, the Union needs more
far-reaching *flexibility* in its forms of foreign-policy engagement. The
emerging world order is not about neatly delineated poles of power, but
consists of myriad linkages and areas of international activity organised
on very different bases. In this context, the EU cannot relate to the
world beyond as an inflexible, monolithic block. European identities
are today so interwoven with social changes outside EU borders and
cross over these frontiers with such fluidity that it no longer makes
sense to think in terms of a single block standing in contradistinction
to the outside world.[36]

Changing patterns of economic and geopolitical dependence call
for updated modes of EU foreign-policy action.[37] European states need
more directly geostrategic forms of international engagement rather
than assuming that an extension outwards of the EU integration model
constitutes their best form of foreign policy. As one expert admonishes,
the EU's pressure for 'hard-law' alignment from third countries and
'functionalist hubris' has generally had a negative impact on other
states' stability, democratic potential and economic development.[38]
The EU integration project can no longer rely on its vaunted soft power
to protect itself in such a dangerous and tumultuous world; the power
of example can no longer give the EU the leverage it needs in global

affairs. If the integration model is suffering internally, neither can it be assumed to have such an exalted or venerated appeal outside Europe any more. Few now talk of the EU as a qualitatively superior form of superpower in the making.[39]

This implies that the EU cannot and should not rely so heavily in the future on the traditional forms of regional framework, like the European Neighbourhood Policy (ENP), the Eastern Partnership (EaP) and the Union for the Mediterranean (UfM). In private, EU officials despair that the situation in the southern Mediterranean has not improved in the last 20 years and that there is a need to think creatively beyond the ENP template. The EU model of regional security community is unlikely to work in regions like the Middle East, where cooperation will need to be more informal and adopt more flexible approaches to encouraging security architecture. It might also be useful to move away from free trade and economic integration being the leading edge of EU relations around the neighbourhood. The Union cannot assume that offers for non-EU countries to be included in parts of the integration project will suffice to make the EU more secure. Rather, European governments need to develop *multi-actor* forms of foreign-policy engagement.

Of course, to some extent, EU foreign policy is already an example of flexible, multi-actor cooperation. As the World Trade Organization Doha Round was killed off at the end of 2015, member states have begun to focus more on their national economic-diplomacy strategies. The new plans for defence cooperation described in Chapters 2 and 3 hinge on small groups of states progressing faster than others. The Global Strategy raises the need for flexibility, through the use of sub-groups of member states and governments using their particular areas of expertise. It acknowledges that the EU may not need a single voice on every international issue so much as a broadly common European message to the outside world.

However, these kinds of approaches now need to be taken much further and pursued on a more systematic basis. European foreign policy will need to be about more than EU foreign policy. Rather, EU member states will need to use other organisations like the OSCE and the Council of Europe, as well as NATO, far more actively and foster far better coordination between these bodies.

In particular, the UK's full participation in some kind of broader European security council will be a test of the EU's commitment to both flexibility and security. The UK's letter triggering Article 50 made a cursory mention of security cooperation and in March 2017 Britain and Germany agreed to work together on cyber-security, training and military patrols. Yet for now the UK and the EU have still to agree concrete plans for how British defence and security assets might be used to advance overarching European strategic priorities – whether through EU missions, UK involvement in bodies like the European Defence Agency and Europol, or broader British alignment with EU common foreign-policy positions and instruments like arms embargoes, controls on weapons exports, migration-management policies, security-oriented development aid and economic sanctions. In September 2017 the UK government published a paper indicating a general willingness to cooperate with EU external initiatives and security missions. This foreign policy dimension of the Brexit talks will need to be given much higher priority than it has received so far if innovative ideas for such cooperation are to prosper.[40]

In addition, new security threats call for more flexible, locally based measures. As IS quickly mobilised hundreds of operatives across Europe in 2016, EU bureaucracies were flat-footed. IS exploited the seams between member states. All of Europe was left open to increased danger because of the intelligence and security shortcomings of the weakest link in the chain – which appeared to be Belgium. EU cooperation seemed to increase vulnerabilities and leave counter-terrorism bogged down in slow and ineffective internal procedures. Member states sought quicker, action-oriented responses that they saw as more achievable in the short term at the national level.[41] The French government's deployment of soldiers inside France, through its so-called Opération Sentinelle, became larger than any of the army's overseas missions. One expert warns that 'a centralisation of counter-terrorist powers will not per se make the EU more effective – and may well make it less creative.'[42]

There are many deradicalisation initiatives across Europe, focusing especially on fighters returning from Syria and Iraq. These initiatives are of necessity very local in nature and tailored to the specifics of each member state and even city. The security threat requires very localised approaches – quite different from the standard aspiration of EU bloc unity against primarily state interlocutors. Today the adversary is very different from previous geostrategic eras and thus an updated approach to security is required, involving multiple levels of action at local and national as well as European and multilateral levels.

These trends have numerous implications for the practical design of EU foreign-policy frameworks. A radical move would be to wind up the failing ENP framework entirely and create a number of more agile, functional policies towards the states of the neighbourhood – policies not based on the export of the EU's governance models. Conditionality should be delinked from association (and other) agreements that seek to advance partner-country reforms specifically through the adoption of EU rules rather than more political tactics. Rather, national and sub-national actors should join forces, alongside EU-level coordination, around three or four core priorities in each outside country – with each actor then contributing in different ways to these broad objectives. In addition, security should be built from the ground up through connections between local deradicalisation- and information-sharing initiatives.

The kind of flexible models of integration proposed in the previous chapter could also be used positively for foreign policy. At the moment, the EU has taken its offers of cooperation with many states almost as far as it can without offering full membership – which most member states are unwilling to do with Ukraine, Georgia or Moldova, as well as Turkey or Morocco. The opening up of radical forms of internal flexibility would help move beyond this kind of sharp in-or-out dichotomy. Countries outside the EU might be offered some form of *graduated membership*, or involvement in a select number of dispersed policy communities. And this might give the EU more leverage over these states and a better platform from which to deal with their security challenges.

A second area of reform relates to the question of how the EU can improve the internal *legitimacy* of its external policies. So far, debates about the Union's flagging democratic legitimacy have been almost entirely disconnected from foreign-policy issues. The EU needs to tackle the external dimensions of its poly-crisis by imbuing its security policies with more participatory dynamics and democratic legitimacy. Once we acknowledge that the firm divide between domestic and foreign policy no longer stands, then the argument that foreign policy should somehow be exempt from domestic accountability also falls. The Global Strategy says nothing about the legitimacy problem of foreign and security policy and in that sense feels very disconnected from political events inside the EU; in fact, the strategy insists the EU must plough ahead with enlargement and military integration – issues that have raised popular concerns in many member states.

And yet the domain of foreign policy presents an immediate dilemma here: injecting greater democracy and flexibility in external questions might push the EU towards a kind of illiberal isolationism. Some polls suggest that citizens want less risky engagement in the outside world.[43] Despite the new security situation, the Danes, for example, voted to opt out of EU cooperation in these areas. Rising populists tend to push for less active foreign policies, less ambitious security commitment, aid cuts and protectionism.[44] In early 2017, as the EU reacted with alarm to Donald Trump's ban on people from several Muslim states entering the United States, a sobering Chatham House survey revealed that most citizens across ten European states wanted to see a similar block on any further migration from Muslim states.[45]

However, excluding popular engagement from major strategic issues runs counter to significant global trends. Today, international interests depend on dense networks of non-state, economic and civic actors beyond European borders, and not just on classical bloc-to-bloc diplomacy. In line with this, over the long term ways must be found to increase citizens' participation in foreign and security policies. Such engagement would help avoid the kind of knee-jerk populism likely to harm European strategic interests in the long run. Links between civil society actors can today be as important in attaining foreign-policy aims as classical diplomacy. Continuing to run foreign policy in an opaque way can only further feed the popular discontent that underlies the current state of public opinion. Although most Europeans want less openness, they do seem to want the EU to be more active and effective on international security issues.[46]

A number of concrete ideas could help implement these principles. The EU could work to embrace developments in democratic accountability within the foreign-policy sphere. For example, the EU could introduce participatory decision-making to a portion of its external aid budget, giving citizens the chance to have a say over how and where the EU spends its money internationally. The citizens' assemblies proposed in Chapter 5 could have a specific foreign-policy dimension. In addition, a group of national parliamentarians could meet once a year to review achievements in EU foreign policy over the previous 12 months.

A third qualitative change is that that the EU needs to become a *two-way liberal power*.[47] It needs to be a receptor and not only purveyor of influence. The internal–external link must be about European countries absorbing lessons and pressures from outside the continent. It is about the EU modifying its institutional structures and policies to absorb such influences in a systematic and effective way. So far, despite the ravages of the poly-crisis, neither EU institutions nor member states have opened themselves up to advice and help from outside Europe to any meaningful degree. In a reconfigured global order, the EU will need to get used to being shaped by others as much as it shapes developments beyond its own borders. It does not yet have either the conceptual orientation or the policy mechanisms to channel such outside influences to shore up cooperation and liberal values in Europe.

This is particularly worrying given the democratic deficiencies increasingly evident within Europe. The relative weakness of EU efforts to defend democratic norms in places like Hungary and Poland drains the credibility of its efforts to support reformers outside the Union. The EU could invite a group of non-Western democracies to write a strategy document for improving the EU's democratic quality. This group could evaluate the EU's efforts to restrain anti-democratic behaviour in its own member states. Why not invite democratic reformers whom the EU has supported in other regions to produce recommendations for how the Union should deal with autocrats like Viktor Orbán in its own ranks?

And other countries' CSOs should be invited and given the funding to prepare annual progress reports on the EU's internal-democracy efforts along the lines of those that the EU compiles on other countries.

Non-Western democracies like Brazil, India, Indonesia and South Africa have a wealth of experience that would be relevant to Europe's current problems. Latin American countries have a rich experience in trying to maintain democratic norms in the context of serious economic crisis and draconian structural adjustment. Other countries around the world have a much richer and more positive experience of dealing with diversity without resorting to nativist illiberalism. Several African countries, as well as India and Indonesia, offer interesting experiences of managing diversity in a democratic fashion. And non-Western expertise can shed light on how to combine the development of liberal rights with community values in a way that might help mitigate the kind of alienation and politics of fear that now drive European illiberalism. Asian democracies provide examples of countries that have grappled with this challenge.

It has become commonplace for European ministers and commissioners and the EU high representative to admit with repentant modesty that the EU model may no longer hold quite the same sway over other regions as it once did. But these words will increasingly ring false if they are not backed up by some substantive change that brings the EU into contact with the world as an importer, not merely an exporter, of liberal values.

CONCLUSION

External factors are today an integral pillar of the structural crisis facing European integration. The EU needs to avoid overreaction; but it does need to react. Analysts often admonish the EU for putting too much emphasis on short-term security. But the new context means that security does need to be made more of a priority and linked in a more purposive manner to the travails of the whole integration project. To some extent, the EU and member states have begun to show signs of greater strategic commitment. The refugee surge and rise of IS have served as alarm bells, a shrill alert that European governments cannot afford to look inwards as they grapple with the eurozone crisis and other difficulties of internal integration.

At the same time, the way in which most governments have reacted gives cause for concern. It must be recklessly simplistic to develop policies on the assumption that the EU project can be shored up by stricter border controls and foreign policies designed to push international instability as far away as possible. A fearful Europe is dangerously seduced by the siren notion of shutting out a turbulent world. Struggling in fretful decline to retain a standing among its neighbours, the EU brings to mind the famously wistful meditation from Timon of Athens: 'Men shut their doors against a setting sun.'[48]

In their search for a more robust protective perimeter, governments reason that the EU needs to ensure a sharper demarcation between itself and the outside world to safeguard the integration project. Precisely the opposite is the case. While more robust border management is certainly overdue, the EU risks securitising issues that cannot be solved primarily through security measures.[49] Some even believe the EU has slipped back into a colonial mindset of distinguishing itself, its own values and its own political project sharply from the rest of the world.[50] Paradoxically, the EU now acts as a physical and identity barrier against the outside world, while being castigated by nativist movements inside member states for being too open and multicultural. It has moved to indulge illiberalism abroad in the name of defeating illiberal populists at home – an inconsistency that is unlikely to be sustainable.

To some extent, flexibility and diversity have been allowed space in the foreign-policy realm, which lies outside the more rigid institutional procedures of many domestic policy spheres. However, European governments and EU institutions have made only limited steps towards a qualitatively different way of doing foreign policy. Without such a change, governments will struggle to link together fully the internal and external dimensions of the crisis. They will not be able to ensure that foreign and security policies play their part in a reimagined and more sustainable model of European integration.

CHAPTER EIGHT

The Long Road to Solidarity

While European leaders insist they are now leaving behind their decade of disquiet, the ravages of the poly-crisis have left the EU with a drained and sickly pallor. The multifaceted nature of the crisis has revealed problems that stem not only from individual issues like Brexit, the euro, insecurity or refugees, but from the very structure of how integration has been designed. At times in the last decade, Europe has got itself caught in a dangerously self-reflexive vortex, dissecting its own gloom yet unable to move forward to a new model of integration – slowly becoming 'the self-consumer of its own woes'.[1] It is telling that one of the most high-profile and intensely discussed novels of the crisis years has been Michel Houellebecq's *Submission* – a bleakly nihilistic prognosis for the demise of the whole secular-rational and liberal bases of the European order.[2]

If optimists are right that the EU is now in a position to embark towards a brighter horizon, then constructive ideas will be required that probe the frontiers of what innovative and distinctive forms of cooperation between states and societies are now possible. Even as a few fragile shoots of hopeful anticipation appear, especially in light of France's encouraging political turn, there is still an unmet need to think beyond the standard discussions about discrete areas of EU policy reform. It is unlikely that a handful of policy tweaks will suffice to re-energise the spirit of European cooperation. Integration needs to be refounded in a way that challenges received wisdom and inherited truths about what cooperation between nations and peoples looks like. As Lucretia's tragedy ushered in Rome's towering republic, the question is whether the poly-crisis might spur a wholesale renaissance of European integration.

ANALYSIS INTO ACTION

The EU's design flaws are well known and have been dissected and conceptualised for many years. But reforms that fully tackle these flaws remain elusive. The calls for flexibility and a more democratically rooted management of interdependence have been heard for some time. Yet European societies appear to wait passively for these changes to appear. Politicians have been calling for new ideas for many years, but there is little value in them continuing to do so if they show virtually no political will to carry forward radical innovations. As Loukas Tsoukalis writes of the crisis: 'Politicians from mainstream parties still find it difficult to think that this may be the end of an era; they find it even harder to think out of the box.'[3]

Afflicted with such a concertina of ordeals, Europe can no longer delay some genuinely inventive and creative reflection. And it needs not only to think but also to act outside the box. Waiting for formal EU institutions on their own to kick-start a fundamentally different process of integration is like asking turkeys not only to vote for Christmas but also to take charge of organising the festivities. So years of mapping out the conceptual problems of the EU integration model must give way to consideration of the *practical processes* of getting change started. Paraphrasing one famously frustrated intellectual: the point is not simply to interpret the EU, but to change it.[4]

I have couched this book in the spirit of such a practical agenda. It has not tried to map detailed policy in particular sectors or precise legal changes, but rather to suggest new guiding principles for European cooperation. Agreement and innovation are needed at this level of structural guidelines before the detail of individual policies is filled in. This is an equation I believe that the EU has got back to front in recent years: policy-makers focus on the nitty-gritty of resolving very specific policy crises, but without the anchor of a clear vision for the integration model into which these policies are supposed to fit over the longer term.

However, while I have kept the focus broad and on the structure of the integration model, rather than getting weighed down in discussion of one or more areas of policy or treaty provisions, I have also sought to flesh out in greater substance what some of these guidelines would entail in a practical sense. I have done this after reading countless articles, op-eds and books that suggest sound principles – that ordinary citizens need to have a greater role in the EU and that the Union needs to be less rigid and heavy-handed – but rarely take the next step of proposing a way to implement these injunctions beyond the standard set of existing institutional processes. This calls to mind the classically rooted lament: it is of little use to desire change but not the means to achieve it.

As they approach the end of the book, some readers may still question the feasibility of radical change. They may find themselves comfortable with the broad principles of democratic participation, diversity and flexibility, but also doubting whether it is practicable to let citizens have a say in continental affairs or to allow different parts of Europe to be subject to different kinds of rules and identities. It is because I disagree with these doubts that I have attempted to go beyond simply stating the case for a more democratic, flexible and secure Europe, and rather to sketch out concrete ideas for how these principles might be given substance. Certainly, this is no easy task and the detail it requires pushes at the boundaries of what is likely to be possible in terms of adjusting the European integration model. However, this strikes me as necessary in order to move the debate forward; it is perhaps important not only to find where the potential for a new kind of European project lies but also to discover where the limits to productive change are to be found.

In this vein, even if some readers may not agree with each of my ideas for EU reform, I hope to have shown that it is possible to think through different and workable ways of reorganising European integration and cooperation. I am conscious that by taking a step further than most accounts and mapping out specific ways of implementing new forms of integration, I am opening myself to objections over one or more of these very practical policy ideas. While it is invariably easier for the analyst to stick to very abstract principles, I believe it is possible to link new, overarching guidelines for the European project with tangible reforms, and with the reflections needed to specify what an alternative EU means in practice.

And if readers don't agree with all my policy suggestions, I hope the book will inspire them to propose their own concrete ideas and explain why these are better. Despite the momentous trials and tribulations of recent years, too many politicians and thinkers are highly dismissive of the case for far-reaching change to European integration and stridently incredulous that such change is at all viable. Predictably perhaps, many elites self-servingly support reforms that bolster their own influence, while finding ways to resist a dispersal of power among European citizens. Beyond its specific policy ideas, the book aims to convince readers that a spirit of analysis-into-action is the way forward in debates about Europe's future. This is surely more productive than a widespread, defeatist fatalism that holds the integration model to be impervious to major change. It is also more in tune with the times than EU defenders' stubborn insistence that any deviation from the inherited integration script is tantamount to Euro-blasphemy.

EUROPE RESET

The book has been animated by a focus on the core principles that I believe can and should form the backbone of a reset Europe: citizen-oriented agency, closely dovetailed to flexibility and diversity, along with a properly founded notion of security. An alternative model of integration should be made up of three pillars: a democratic Europe, a flexible Europe and a secure Europe.

My base assumption is that the EU's challenge is to conceive of more participative and flexible means of cooperation as a means of rebuilding solidarity – a form of solidarity that will have very different premises and principles from those that have borne the weight of European integration since the end of World War II. The EU requires more than modest institutional tweaks. Rather, it needs fundamentally new thinking on how to go back to basics and reconstruct Europe's badly damaged sense of partnership and solidarity.

The challenge is a broad one: an alternative EU must encourage more participative local-level debate, but also combine this with democratic processes within which people show better consideration of citizens' interests in other countries – what I have called *euro-civismo*. This is the fine and intricate balance upon which a genuinely European democratic project will depend. For the EU to succeed as a democratic project, active citizenship must be local, but not parochial. It must thrive at the national level without being nationalistic. It must be rooted in tangible citizen concerns, but also cosmopolitan mutual empathy. The EU must be about states and societies governing together, but not in uniformity.

Citizen-led change will not diminish the need for good EU leadership, institutions' formal processes of reform or stronger governance capacities. The need is for more active bottom-up influence and top-down change to complement each other in closer synchronicity than has been the case so far. I have focused on citizen participation in this book *not* because I see formal, top-down routes to change as any less important, but because these already tend to receive most policy and analytical attention – meaning that the balance of analysis needs shifting towards a focus on bottom-up, popular engagement.

Similarly, and crucially, I have advocated greater citizen involvement in redesigning European integration *not* because I believe this will engender instant consensus or provide a magic cure-all for the EU's current strains, but precisely because differences and tensions have become so profound that it is difficult to envisage a successful way forward *without* such engagement. Many tend disdainfully to dismiss the case for popular participation on the grounds that 'people have such divergent views', without realising that this is precisely why democratic involvement is needed. A more democratically participative EU is to be valued not as a means of immediately delivering particular common outcomes, but because an inclusive process for debating differences would give citizens a healthier sense of ownership over integration – and in this way smooth some of the frustrations and antipathies that have arisen against the Union in recent years.

European integration after World War II was the project of an enlightened elite. This elite cultivated creative ways to bind states and societies together in the name of preventing further conflict on the continent. The means were not democratic or participative, but the end goal justified the top-down approach. So much has changed since then – and yet the basic model of integration still stands. It has been fine-tuned at the margins, but not fundamentally revisited.

This paralysis cannot be sustainable. The EU has solved some problems, but has itself created others. History's cardinal lesson is that each advance sows the seeds of its own reversal. A fast-changing world requires a dramatic volte-face: the EU was set up to 'lock in' cooperation and *prevent* dramatic changes that might presage war; today the EU needs to *facilitate* change, as future trends are radically more uncertain and require from states and societies constant agile adaptation. The EU's challenge is so demanding because in effect it needs to make a 180-degree inversion, from limiting to multiplying citizens' options. The post-1945 logic is past its zenith and now often seems to hinder more than it enables. European cooperation does not have the same unquestioned, cosmic ideal to push it forward today. The crisis has had a chilling effect on what has stood as the core logic of Euro-idealism for many years.

Integration's future narrative has to be about the EU being a project to help citizens make autonomous choices, adapt and exert more effective influence over the issues that impact on their lives. The Compact of European Citizens that I mapped out in Chapter 5 would help achieve this reorientation. Under its rubric, a series of citizens' assemblies would mobilise debates and ideas, from the local to the national and onto the European level. The Compact would ensure citizens' voices count and that they are able to explore new and open-ended options in a proactive fashion – as opposed to simply having *ex post* scrutiny over the kind of conventional integration choices presented through formal institutional channels.

In Chapter 6 I outlined ideas for a radical form of flexibility in European integration – one that is capacious enough to encompass the widening diversity in policy preferences currently so evident across

Europe. Such radical flexibility would be predicated on dispersed policy communities that member states would choose whether or not to join. Crucially, the citizens' Compact would have important and defined roles in the process of deciding on more flexible forms of cooperation. And variation would also be explored within individual countries and not only between member states. An important element of radical flexibility is that governments' decisions to participate in certain areas of European cooperation must, under certain conditions, be reversible. A crucial lesson from the poly-crisis years is that the process of building solidarity might be smoother if citizens and authorities had at least some possibility of reversing direction or applying temporary brakes on certain commitments in times of trouble.

Finally, in Chapter 7 I proposed changes to EU security policy. These adjustments would form an integral part of and lock into the broader redesign of the European integration model. Many analysts lament that the EU has been focused too introspectively on its own economic woes and insufficiently attentive to the tectonic shifts under way in global politics. Ensnared in their internal crises, European governments have sometimes struggled to lift their collective gaze and realise that the EU's crisis is as much externally driven as internal – as the actions of Vladimir Putin, IS and Donald Trump have now made painfully clear.

European integration cannot be made more effective and legitimate if the EU does not also re-examine the way it does geopolitics. The increasing focus on fortified borders and surveillance is in some measure necessary but is currently imbalanced. A different model of foreign-policy cooperation is required, in line with the broader principles of an alternative EU. The EU should replace its existing modus operandi of basing foreign policy on the supposed allure of the Union's own model of cooperation with a more flexible, participative and multi-actor model of geopolitics. It will also need to start being a better receptor of useful international experiences. In its myopic self-assurance, the EU still does little to cast around for ideas from those outside who might have more successful integrative, economic and democratic lessons to share.

A broader issue cuts across the three pillars of participation, flexibility and security: these principles of an alternative EU have a bearing on the UK's future relationship with the integration project. If the EU were to become a radically different political entity, this would feed back into the debate about ensuring a positive British role in European affairs. It would open up all kinds of possibilities for UK re-engagement, as the core EU model the British people voted to leave would morph into a different kind of entity. As the Brexit talks proceed, these kind of constructive crossovers are urgently needed if the increasingly fractious divergence between the UK and the rest of Europe is to be stemmed.

CORRECTING COURSE

Many politicians, diplomats and analysts commonly assert that whole swathes of reform are already under way. They will invariably respond to criticism of the EU by pointing out that questions of democratic legitimacy and flexibility have been on the agenda for quite some time, and that policy changes are firmly tackling the need for new approaches to integration. They are likely to push back against the position I adopt in this book by insisting that the EU needs to refine its existing cooperation rather than entertain any adjustment to integration's core parameters.

I hope to have shown that this reaction is too sanguine and analytically complacent. Current deliberation about EU reform falls short of what is required, and in some instances risks pulling the Union in exactly the wrong direction. Measured in accordance with the principles of legitimacy, flexible diversity and reconstituted security, the claim that adequate rethinking is already bearing fruit is not convincing. It is true that concerns about legitimacy, flexibility and security have been on the agenda for several years, but that is precisely why the lack of any tangible progress in addressing such concerns is such an arresting failure. Promises of qualitative reform accumulate and fade, like 'prologues to an unwritten book'.[5] And this is why untried approaches are now warranted.

In the preceding chapters, I have charted how genuinely new ideas are failing to materialise and how most policy options now being brought forward replay rather stale notions of integration. Calls for change still follow well-trodden conceptual paths. We have seen throughout the book, across different policy areas and in relation to the varied challenges facing the EU, how very familiar ideas for reform are being recycled – in the form of proposals that in most cases have been kicked around in policy debates for many decades. In the apparently improved conditions of 2017, leaders seem to believe they can now advance on these kinds of select policy improvements without having to consider re-restructuring the integration model in any fundamental sense.

Contrary to many official government and EU claims, existing reform initiatives do little to bring citizens into the process of integration in ways that are genuinely empowering, agenda-setting or widely participative. Similarly, existing efforts to manage diversity and allow space for flexible integration are sanitised and managerial, and incapable of dealing with profound variations in what citizens and states want and expect from European cooperation. And the way that the EU's internal and external policies are changing is unlikely to create a more secure Europe, or ensure that foreign policy helps reconfigure the integration model.

Current reforms rarely target the underlying causes of the polycrisis. The EU has done little to offer more of a voice or protection for integration's losers, or to dissuade these citizens from turning back to the nation state and national identity in their quest for protective certainty. Useful changes in particular policy sectors have done little to improve the basic fairness of EU decision-making. What is perhaps most striking about the crisis is that nearly all states and all societies feel aggrieved that other states and societies are not respecting their concerns. This can be demonstrated with an anecdote: in July 2016, Jean-Claude Juncker quipped that France was getting its way in many internal debates and escaping economic sanctions, 'because it is France'. For many other nations, this off-the-cuff remark symbolised everything that is wrong with the EU's opaqueness and arbitrary political machinations.

Paradoxically, post-crisis reforms have been both overly harsh in the requirements they have imposed upon many European societies and insufficiently robust, as governments simply ignore EU rules with increasing frequency because they no longer judge them to be fair. A new Europe must mend the cracked link between authority and legitimacy. An EU that becomes a panopticon of constant surveillance and control is not the kind of alternative Europe likely to prosper or excite future generations. To date, the measures that governments have adopted to lighten the poly-crisis simply deepen the Union's underlying pathology. The EU often acts in a way that makes the crisis worse, not better. It recalls Richard III, brooding on his inexorable downward spiral: 'I am in so far [...] that sin will pluck on sin.'[6]

One reason for all this is that quantitative debate still prevails over qualitative reconsideration. Christopher Bickerton summarises this conceptual gridlock nicely, writing that there is a still-unmet need for 'recasting Europe as a new project of internationalism rather than as a tired one of integration or federalism.'[7] As the poly-crisis has deepened, so the Europhile versus Eurosceptic divide has become sharper and apparently even more all-defining. One side of this debate wants more Europe, the other wants less. Of course, it is impossible completely to get around this more-versus-less choice. But on its own it is not a way of framing the integration challenge that produces the kind of innovation that Europe needs. The pro-versus-anti, more-versus-less dynamic is so deep-rooted and apparently unshakeable that alternative ways of approaching integration are squeezed off the agenda.

Another powerful explanation for the EU's paralysis lies in the lack of osmosis between institutions and societies. A serious shortcoming is that most current reform templates do not dovetail well with – or grow organically out of – underlying structural trends in European societies. A point I have emphasised throughout the book is that both the 'more Europe' and 'less Europe' agendas lack a congruent theory of change. They are in effect seeking to put round pegs (their proposed changes to the EU) into square holes (the actual nature of evolving European societies, polities and economies). Many analysts have pointed out that the defining feature of modern society is that of fast-moving and unpredictable fluidity. Yet the EU's institutional set-up is notable for the very opposite: its essential lack of adaptability.

There is a glaring mismatch between the way that interstate cooperation is conceived through the prevailing practices, institutions and rules of the EU on the one hand, and evolving sociological dynamics on the other. Indeed, this is why so many apparently well-designed and well-meaning reforms seem to be floundering and failing to make a successful move from the drawing board to reality. The existing EU integration script is a dam blocking the flow of new ideas that faithfully mirror shifts in social reality. The EU's founding myths are so totemic that they militate against radically different conceptions of integration and cooperation that might be more attuned to the new contours of modern European societies. Europe's empowered social actors would benefit from a few long-reigning Euro-shibboleths being ripped down.

There has been much nervous talk about the old order being swept away by dangerous populists. This now-ubiquitous narrative gives the impression that the EU's main danger is one of chaos and disorder, requiring the steady hand of incumbent elites. Yet for all the focus on new parties, the old elite is in fact still the dominant political force, retaining its influence and privileges. Contrary to the impression given by much current commentary and discourse, Europe's main problem is not uncontrolled and insurgent people-driven chaos, but rather the unresponsive and opaque decision-making processes that persist at both the EU and national levels.

Hegel famously wrote about phases in history revealing their internal exhaustion after the fact and when a new phase is already set to begin. In one of the most famous metaphors of political philosophy, he described the epoch-heralding owl of Minerva taking flight and revealing the contours of a new order when the pillars of an existing order were already crumbling. This evocative image pinpoints precisely what is the EU's most worrying deficiency. Where is the herald of Europe's new historical phase? While Europe's old order crumbles, its owl of Minerva remains forlorn and flightless, weighed down by the crippled wings of EU integration orthodoxy.

EU OR NO EU?

The proposals that make up the three pillars of my alternative, reset Europe invite a provocative concluding thought: under a reimagined integration model, would the EU as such even need to exist any more? European cooperation might proceed without any single enveloping entity, or single treaty, or consolidated legal structure, or encompassing institutional umbrella. Might an alternative Europe be made up of a series of policy communities, in combination with the Compact of European Citizens – and have no need for a construct called 'the European Union'?

Disbanding the EU as a single entity would have the advantage of showing that European integration was certainly moving beyond business as usual. To disaffected citizens, it might represent an enlivening new start. It would help move away from a situation where there is one distant, heavy-handed and opaque supranational centre. In highlighting that the EU is not innately coterminous with workable and effective European solidarity, such a radical and controversial step might help clear away the grievances aimed at the EU that have accumulated over six decades. Indeed, some may believe that starting from a blank slate is now the only way to inject a meaningful reform dynamic into European integration.

I have not advocated or explored this route in the book. I have sought principally to identify the right bottom-up organising principles for a new Europe. Those principles that I have proposed could be advanced within the framework of the EU – and indeed I believe they would most productively be pursued through a rebooted Union. I have treated participation and legitimacy as means of improving EU powers and capacities, not of hollowing out the Union's institutional edifice. Too many would see closing down the EU as an acknowledgement of failure; such a step would be widely interpreted as a lowering of ambition and the beginning of a more fractured Europe. And, of course, the resistance to contemplating a completely fresh start would be considerable.

If the troubles afflicting Europe were to intensify even further and put in doubt the integrity of the EU's basic institutional framework, principles for a new beginning might then be needed. If the crisis were to return with even greater destructive vengeance at some point in the future, this book's ideas might still be relevant to thinking through how a post-EU integration process could be fashioned as a *modernised and upgraded* project, not a mere dilution of the current EU institutional framework. For now, it is thankfully unlikely that the poly-crisis will get anywhere near reaching this point. In 2017, amidst ubiquitous assertions that 'Europe is back', the EU's moment of most acute danger appears to have passed. But it might be no bad thing to have contingency alternatives ready to sustain productive European cooperation if the spectre of a major fracturing of the EU were to reappear.

Moreover, it should be pointed out that the more governments and EU institutions continue to stonewall on radical reform, the more citizens and other actors will feel themselves justified in exploring extra-official pathways to reform. As we saw in Chapters 4 and 5, many citizens' groups are already moving to create their own systems of social debate and interaction that are largely indifferent to official EU channels of influence. Some today intimate at campaigns of civil disobedience against Union rules. It might well be that an alternative Europe emerges in this way – by societies themselves chipping away at the EU's authority and bypassing its formal practices to establish new forms of cooperation and solidarity. Anyone thinking that such a scenario is ridiculously far-fetched might take a close look at the unprecedented intensity of social protest that has rocked Europe in recent years and how this reflects a growing popular disillusion with the EU's continually unmet promises to listen to and engage with citizens' concerns. It is not beyond the bounds of possibility that the EU as such will be simply left behind by social trends it has failed to grasp or take seriously.

Such forms of radical innovation would help rebut an often-heard riposte that is of broad and vital importance. Traditionalists tend to dismiss ideas for a flexible or alternative Europe as merely a *lesser* Europe. This does not need to be the case. It may measure as 'less' on some existing scales of integration, and yet entail more of other kinds of cooperation. There may be fewer formal rules and centralised laws, but more contact between citizens and more popular engagement beyond the relatively narrow sections of the population fully comfortable with the current EU labyrinth. There may be fewer single-template uniform policies, but more examples of informal networks of cities, citizen forums and select groups of states pushing cooperation into new areas.

FREE TO BE WHATEVER...

I finish with an important clarification and caveat: the book's template for an alternative Europe does not offer a quick fix, nor a firm road that is guaranteed to take the EU easily to a quiet and idyllic destination. It is not about returning to a prelapsarian, idealised European unity. If offers citizens the chance to remake integration in a way that more closely resonates with their interests, concerns and aspirations – it does not specify what the end points of that remake will be. Alternative Europe does not define a destination, but rather seeks to propel and aid a journey – towards whatever destinations European citizens deem appropriate. It points towards an EU that would rest a little less on Jean Monnet and more on the spirit of *A Clockwork Orange* – a novel whose moral suggests it is better to be free to err than to have goodness or correctness handed down from a higher authority.[8]

Of course, in the context of the poly-crisis, elites have expressed a fear that more popular participation, more flexibility, more diversity and risky innovation will simply amplify today's turbulence and sink the whole European project. But my premise is that more engaged debate could encourage citizens to build bridges, to shape productive coalitions and networks. The very process of airing differences and assessing what citizens really want from Europe might be what best enables a more common spirit of solidarity very gradually to take shape.

Europe has for centuries suffered periodic challenges to liberalism. Each of these has ended in ultra-aggressive nationalism, ethnic supremacism and chauvinistic authoritarianism in part because elites, technocrats and 'men of letters' fomented each backlash with little citizen participation. Each backlash ended up more elitist and damaging to ordinary citizens than the internationalist liberal rationalism its architects excoriated. The history of previous anti-liberal counter-projects provides sobering lessons for the EU's current crisis, as different sets of elites fight over alternative political projects with equally paternalistic disdain for citizen-led reform.[9]

Citizens need to discover ways towards such solidarity themselves; they will continue to resist it if such idealistic visions are dropped on them from above. Citizen participation and deliberative democracy will not generate perfect European harmony and understanding, but if citizens have some chance to put forward their opinions about the future of the EU and to argue these out, they are more likely to accept the eventual decisions taken at a European level – even if those decisions do not completely correspond to their own individual preferences but rather balance others' different interests.

Elites still use the standard template of integration as a crutch for a European citizenry that they assume is unready to bear the weight of responsibility for a shared future. Yet surely it is too pessimistic to believe that European populations stand eager to revert to mutually damaging hostility were the EU's existing institutional architecture to be modified. Rather, a better description of the current situation is that a broadly European spirit survives, but is encased in dangerously ossified institutional structures. While nationalist visions now claim attention, European states have not clamped shut and Brexit is for now an exception, not a model.

Much current thinking is back to front, and mistakes cause for effect. Populists have gained ground because citizens feel they lack a voice. European cooperation must make the journey back from the desocialisation of recent years to resocialisation, based on new avenues for trust. A longer historical view shows that the deepening of democracy has often gone hand in hand with the development of European-level cooperation – advances in popular participation routinely helped marshal support for alliances throughout the European state system.[10] Applying such lessons to today's predicaments, we might reasonably expect that getting democracy right could nourish cooperation between states rather than drain away integration's lifeblood, as elites seem to fear.

Democracy and flexibility will be about combining European solidarity with fostering the kind of subaltern participation and identities that are already taking root. Indeed, while it is important to be aware of the likely substantive outcomes of participative democracy, democratising the EU to some extent needs to be prioritised as an end in itself. When Eurosceptics talk of a more democratic EU they have in mind means to prevent European-level decisions. When EU elites talk of a more democratic EU they have in mind means to legitimise existing integration templates. But democracy should be neither simply spoiler nor co-option. Participation is to be valued on its own terms and not simply as a means to other, preset agendas. As they now optimistically explore policy initiatives to move the EU beyond its poly-crisis years, European leaders would be mistaken to continue dismissing the issues of participation and legitimacy as merely second-order expendables – desirable in principle, perhaps, but not really a priority.

The EU was built on weak civic foundations. Simply carrying on adding to the existing building in accordance with the original design plans will make the whole structure even more precarious. Europe first needs to strengthen the foundations upon which integration stands. And it must then look for lighter architectural designs so the integrity of the EU house is stronger, for longer. The question most commonly posed is: what must be done to save or strengthen the EU? But surely this is the wrong question. The EU is a means to an end, not an end in itself. The better question to probe is: what reasons and demands are there for designing a better form of European cooperation? What is the question that a new phase of European integration should really be seeking to answer?

This image of going back to rebuild Europe's foundations with stronger materials is not meant to put limits on the depth of integration. Rather, it is to suggest that cooperation must in the future grow more organically than it has been allowed to do in the last several decades. Only this can slowly reassemble the EU's distempered base of loyalty. The long road to an alternative Europe will not be smooth and the process will not be linear – the new integration model will be more workable precisely because it will move firmly away from such assumptions.

In sum, this book has suggested ways in which European integration needs to put down deeper roots before it can regain momentum. This will take time and involve much uncertainty. But it is possible if there is a willingness to reimagine the contours of European cooperation. And such patience and commitment to begin from the EU's core foundations can be made to pay off over the long term. The deeper river runs more smoothly.

Notes

PREFACE

1   The quote comes from a speech given by Suárez in the Spanish parliament on 6
     April 1978. The Spanish original reads slightly differently from Rivera's rendering:
     '*se nos pide que cambiemos las cañerías del agua, teniendo que dar agua todos los días.*'

INTRODUCTION

1   See 'The Rome Declaration', European Council [website] (25 March 2017).

1. CONFUSION'S MASTERPIECE: THE EUROPEAN POLY-CRISIS

1   B. Lippert and N. von Ondarza, *Brexiting into Uncharted Waters*, SWP Comments
     35 (Berlin: Stiftung Wissenschaft und Politik, July 2016).
2   *Special Eurobarometer 451: Future of Europe* (Brussels: European Commission,
     Directorate-General for Communication, December 2016).
3   E. Bonse, 'L'Europe après le Brexit: positions et perspectives allemandes', *Notes
     du Cerfa* 135 (2017).
4   J. Lanchester, 'Brexit blues', *London Review of Books* 38/15 (28 July 2016); M.
     Leonard, 'Europe seen from the outside – the British view', European Council
     on Foreign Relations [website] (4 August 2016).
5   J. Black et al., *Defence and Security after Brexit* (Cambridge: RAND Europe, 2017);
     P. Wilding, *What Next? Britain's Future in Europe* (London: I.B.Tauris, 2017),
     p. 81.
6   'Europe's desperate deal with Turkey on migrants', *Financial Times* (30 November
     2015).
7   A. Rettman, 'Denmark to rebel on EU free borders if need be', EUObserver
     [website] (17 May 2017).
8   *Back to Schengen – A Roadmap*, COM(2016)120 (Brussels: European Commission,
     4 March 2016).
9   N. Nielsen, 'Balkan states to introduce more anti-migrant controls', EUObserver
     [website] (9 February 2017).
10   G. Chazan, 'Backlash prompts tougher German approach to refugees', *Financial
     Times* (29 November 2016).
11   F. Tassinari, 'All for none, and none for all: life in a broken Europe', *Foreign Affairs*
     (13 January 2016).

12 N. Rush, 'Europeans' hardening stands following the migrant crisis', Center for Immigration Studies [website] (18 April 2016).

13 T. Nuttall, 'Looking for a home', *The Economist* (28 May 2016).

14 P. Vimont, 'Migration in Europe: bridging the solidarity gap', Carnegie Europe [website] (12 September 2016).

15 E. Zalan, 'Juncker: EU "not at risk" of disintegration', EUObserver [website] (14 September 2016).

16 P. Teffer, 'Merkel: euro and open borders "directly linked"', EUObserver [website] (12 January 2016).

17 R. Hilmer, *The European Union Facing Massive Challenges – What are Citizens' Expectations and Concerns?* (Berlin: International Policy Analysis, 2016).

18 P. Kingsley, *The New Odyssey: The Story of Europe's Refugee Crisis* (London: Faber, 2016), p. 7; T. Garton Ash, 'Europe's walls are going back up – it's like 1989 in reverse', *Guardian* (29 November 2015); W. Münchau, 'Europe enters the age of disintegration', *Financial Times* (28 February 2016); S. Lehne, 'How the refugee crisis will reshape the EU', Carnegie Europe [website] (2016); J.-M. Guéhenno, chapter 10, in A. Missiroli et al., *Towards an EU Global Strategy – Consulting the Experts* (Paris: European Union Institute for Security Studies, 2016); W. Streeck, *Exploding Europe: Germany, the Refugees and the British Vote to Leave*, Speri Paper no. 31 (Sheffield: Sheffield Political Economy Research Institute, September 2016).

19 'La sécurité', Elabe [website] (3 November 2016).

20 P. Neumann, *Radicalized: New Jihadists and the Threat to the West* (London: I.B.Tauris, 2016), p. 113.

21 R. Wike, B. Stokes and K. Simmons, 'Europeans fear wave of refugees will mean more terrorism, fewer jobs', Pew Research Center [website] (11 July 2016).

22 B. Weber, *Time for a Plan B: The European Refugee Crisis, the Balkan Route and the EU–Turkey Deal* (Berlin: Democratization Policy Council, September 2016).

23 L. Elliott and J. Treanor, 'Dutch PM says refugee crisis could shut down Europe's open borders for good', *Guardian* (21 January 2016).

24 D. Boffey, 'EU taskforce highlights security failings that facilitated terror attacks', *Guardian* (14 March 2017).

25 G. Kepel, *Terror in France: The Rise of Jihad in the West* (Princeton: Princeton University Press, 2016).

26 *Bratislava Declaration and Roadmap* (Bratislava: European Council, 16 September 2016).

27 Heads of state and government of the Republic of Cyprus, France, Greece, Italy, Malta, Portugal and Spain, 'Athens declaration of the 1st Mediterranean EU countries' summit' (9 September 2016). Available at http://www.topontiki.gr/sites/default/files/declaration_athens_summit.pdf.

28 F. Eder, 'The two-presidents Europe', Politico [website] (14 September 2016).

29 L. Tsoukalis, *In Defence of Europe: Can the European Project be Saved?* (New York: Oxford University Press, 2016), p. 93.

30 C. Bastasin, *Saving Europe: Anatomy of a Dream* (Washington DC: Brookings Institution Press, 2015).

31 Y. Varoufakis, *And the Weak Suffer What They Must? Europe, Austerity and the Threat to Global Stability* (London: Bodley Head, 2016), ch. 6.

32 *Financial Assistance Provided to Countries in Difficulties*, Special Report no. 18 (Luxembourg: European Court of Auditors, 2015).

33 D. Gros, 'The silent death of eurozone governance', Project Syndicate [website] (2016).

34 P. Wallace, *The Euro Experiment* (Cambridge: Cambridge University Press, 2016), ch. 9.

35 J.-C. Juncker et al., *Completing Europe's Economic and Monetary Union* (Brussels: European Commission, 2015).

36 *Reflection Paper on the Deepening of the Economic and Monetary Union*, COM(2017)291 (Brussels: European Commission, 31 May 2017).

37 J. Stiglitz, *Freefall: Free Markets and the Sinking of the Global Economy* (London: Penguin, 2010); A. Alesina and F. Giavazzi, *The Future of Europe: Reform or Decline* (Cambridge, MA: MIT Press, 2008).

38 *Country Report Spain 2017*, SWD(2017)74 (Brussels: European Commission, 22 February 2017).

39 *IMF Annual Report 2016: Finding Solutions Together* (Washington DC: International Monetary Fund, 2016).

40 Tsoukalis, *In Defence of Europe*, p. 171.

41 M. Copelovitch, J. Frieden and S. Walter, 'The political economy of the euro crisis', *Comparative Political Studies* 49/7 (2016).

42 N. Crafts, *Saving the Eurozone: Is a 'Real' Marshall Plan the Answer?*, CAGE–Chatham House Series no. 1 (London: Chatham House, June 2012); P. De Grauwe, G. Magnus, T. Mayer and H. Schmieding, *The Future of Europe's Economy: Disaster or Deliverance?* (London: Centre for European Reform, September 2013); G. Merritt, *Slippery Slope: Europe's Troubled Future* (New York: Oxford University Press, 2016).

43 P. Cerny, *Rethinking World Politics: A Theory of Transnational Neopluralism* (New York: Oxford University Press, 2010); R. Liddle, 'The political economy of the single market', in L. Tsoukalis and J. Emmanouilidis (eds), *The Delphic Oracle on Europe: Is There a Future for the European Union?* (New York: Oxford University Press, 2011).

44 T. Pappas, 'Distinguishing liberal democracy's challengers', *Journal of Democracy* 27/4 (2016).

45 F. Tassinari, 'Scandinavia's real lessons', *Foreign Affairs* [website] (27 October 2015).

46 For a flavour of this variation on the right, see A. L. P. Pirro and S. van Kessel, 'United in opposition? The populist radical right's EU-pessimism in times of crisis', *Journal of European Integration* 39/4 (2017).

47 H. van der Veer and S. Otjes, 'Can only Eurosceptics oppose austerity? How divisions over integration have replaced left/right divisions in the European Parliament', LSE Europp [blog] (24 March 2016).

48 B. Stokes, *Euroskepticism beyond Brexit* (Washington DC: Pew Research Center, 7 June 2016).

49 H. Grabbe and S. Lehne, 'Can the EU survive populism?', Carnegie Europe [website] (14 June 2016).

50 R. Inglehart and P. Norris, *Trump, Brexit, and the Rise of Populism: Economic Have-Nots and Cultural Backlash*, HKS working paper RWP16-026 (Harvard Kennedy School, August 2016).

51 C. Mudde, 'Europe's populist surge: a long time in the making', *Foreign Affairs* (November/December 2016).

52 M. Urban, 'A perfect storm of populism', BBC News [website] (26 December 2015).

53 L. Tsoukalis, 'The Delphic oracle on Europe', in L. Tsoukalis and J. Emmanouilidis (eds), *The Delphic Oracle on Europe: Is There a Future for the European Union?* (New York: Oxford University Press, 2011).

54 M. Mazower, 'Lessons from the past are key to Europe's survival', *Financial Times* (22 January 2016).

55 S. Fabbrini, 'The euro crisis and its constitutional implications', in S. Champeau, C. Closa, D. Innerarity and M. Poiares Maduro (eds), *The Future of Europe: Democracy, Legitimacy and Justice after the Euro Crisis* (London: Rowman & Littlefield International, 2015).

56 P. Morillas, 'Año de tránsito para la (de)construcción europea', *El País* (10 February 2016).

57 A. Möller, 'The end of Europakonsens?', European Council on Foreign Relations [website] (14 January 2016).

58 *Standard Eurobarometer 86* (Brussels: European Commission, Directorate-General for Communication, November 2016), p. 14.

59 A. Polyakova and N. Fligstein, 'Is European integration causing Europe to become more nationalist? Evidence from the 2007–9 financial crisis', *Journal of European Public Policy* 23/1 (2016).

60 *Special Eurobarometer 451; Major Trends in European Public Opinion with Regards to the European Union* [European Parliament document, 2015].

61 Ibid.

62 C. de Vries and I. Hoffmann, *Fear Not Values: Public Opinion and the Populist Vote in Europe*, EUpinions no. 2016/3 (Gütersloh: Bertelsmann Stiftung, November 2016).

63 S. Gaston, et al., *Nothing to Fear but Fear Itself?* (London: Demos, 2016).

64 C. de Vries and I. Hoffmann, *Supportive but Wary: How Europeans Feel about the EU 60 Years after the Treaty of Rome*, EUpinions no. 2017/1 (Gütersloh: Bertelsmann Stiftung, March 2017).

65 T. Raines, M. Goodwin and D. Cutts, *The Future of Europe: Comparing Public and Elite Attitudes* (London: Chatham House, June 2017).

66 B. Stokes, R. Wike and D. Manevich, 'Post-Brexit, Europeans more favorable toward EU', Pew Research Center [website] (15 June 2017).

67 J. A. Emmanouilidis and F. Zuleeg, *EU@60 – Countering a Regressive and Illiberal Europe* (Brussels: European Policy Centre, October 2016).

68 L. van Middelaar, 'Protect and survive', *Europe's World* (autumn 2016).

69 See the chapters on each Visegrád state in P. Morillas (ed.), *Illiberal Democracies in the EU: The Visegrád Group and the Risk of Disintegration* (Barcelona: CIDOB, 2017).

70 J. Peet and A. La Guardia, *Unhappy Union: How the Euro Crisis – and Europe – Can Be Fixed* (London: Economist/Profile Books, 2014).

71 J. Zielonka, *Is the EU Doomed?* (Cambridge: Polity Press, 2014).

72 I. Krastev, *After Europe* (Philadelphia: University of Pennsylvania Press, 2017), pp. 10, 81; I. Krastev, 'Eight visions for Europe' [video on Forum on European Culture website, 2016].

73 B. Simms, *Europe: The Struggle for Supremacy: 1453 to the Present* (London: Penguin, 2013).

74 F. Mogherini at World Economic Forum, 20 May 2017. Video available at https://www.weforum.org/events/world-economic-forum-on-the-middle-east-and-north-africa-2017/sessions/the-future-of-europe.

75 'Jean-Claude Juncker, upbeat and ready for a fight', Politico [website] (3 August 2017).

76 D. Phinnemore, 'Crisis-ridden, battered and bruised: time to give up on the EU?', *Journal of Common Market Studies* 53/S1 (2015); D. Ioannou, P. Leblond and A. Niemann, 'European integration and the crisis: practice and theory', *Journal of European Public Policy* 22/2 (2015); T. Risse, *A Community of Europeans? Transnational Identities and Public Spheres* (Ithaca, NY: Cornell University Press, 2010); J. McCormick, *Europeanism* (New York: Oxford University Press, 2010); A. Moravcsik, 'Europe after the crisis: how to sustain a common currency', *Foreign Affairs* (May/June 2012); S. Hutter, E. Grande and H. Kriesi (eds), *Politicising Europe: Integration and Mass Politics* (Cambridge: Cambridge University Press, 2016); K. McNamara, '*JCMS* annual review lecture: imagining Europe: the cultural foundations of EU governance', *Journal of Common Market Studies* 53/S1 (2015).

77 The term is paraphrased from *Macbeth*, act 2, scene 3 ("Confusion now hath made his masterpiece!").

2. FALSE SOLUTIONS

1 D. Rodrik, 'Rethinking democracy', Project Syndicate [website] (11 June 2014). For a critical discussion see B. Crum, 'Saving the euro at the cost of democracy?', *Journal of Common Market Studies* 51/4 (2013).

2 J.-C. Juncker et al., *Completing Europe's Economic and Monetary Union* (Brussels: European Commission, 2015). For an analysis, see N. Munin, 'The Five Presidents' Report: the dogs bark but the caravan moves on?', *European Politics and Society* 17/3 (2016).

3 One example of such a survey of views is E. Labeye and S. Smit, '"The Europe we want!": here's how Europe's policymakers should seize on their window of opportunity', *Europe's World* 31 (Autumn 2015).

4 'Para una nueva Europa', *El País* (9 May 2016).

5 J. M. García-Margallo, 'Pase lo que pase, más Europa', *El País* (23 June 2016).

6 J.-M. Ayrault and F.-W. Steinmeier, 'A strong Europe in a world of uncertainties', France Diplomatie [website] (28 June 2016).

7 *Launching the European Defence Fund*, COM(2017)295 (Brussels: European Commission, 7 June 2017).

8 Committee on Constitutional Affairs, 'Report on possible evolutions of and adjustments to the current institutional set-up of the European Union', European Parliament [website] (20 December 2016); Committee on Constitutional Affairs, 'Report on improving the functioning of the European Union building on the potential of the Lisbon Treaty', European Parliament [website] (9 January 2017).

9   *White Paper on the Future of Europe*, COM(2017)2025 (Brussels: European Commission, 1 March 2017).

10   J. A. Emmanouilidis et al., *The 2017 Elections across Europe: Facts, Expectations and Consequences* (Brussels: European Policy Centre, 14 March 2017).

11   B.-H. Lévy, 'SOS Europa', *El País* (7 March 2016).

12   J. A. Emmanouilidis (ed.), *Towards a New Pact for Europe* (Brussels: King Baudouin Foundation, the Bertelsmann Stiftung and the European Policy Centre, October 2014).

13   U. Guérot, *Warum Europa eine Republik werden muss!* (Bonn: Verlag J. H. W. Dietz Nachf., 2016).

14   S. Fabbrini, *Which European Union? Europe after the Euro Crisis* (Cambridge: Cambridge University Press, 2015). For an exploration of this perspective, see also S. Champeau, C. Closa, D. Innerarity and M. Poaires Maduro (eds), *The Future of Europe: Democracy, Legitimacy and Justice after the Euro Crisis* (London: Rowman & Littlefield International, 2015).

15   D. Tusk, Twitter post (30 May 2016).

16   J. R. Gillingham, *The EU: An Obituary* (New York: Verso, 2016), p. 191.

17   G. Delanty, 'Europe's nemesis? European integration and the contradictions of capitalism and democracy', in S. Champeau, C. Closa, D. Innerarity and M. Poaires Maduro (eds), *The Future of Europe: Democracy, Legitimacy and Justice after the Euro Crisis* (London: Rowman & Littlefield International, 2015), p. 143.

18   R. Rose and G. Borz, 'Aggregation and representation in European Parliament party groups', *West European Politics* 36/3 (2013).

19   I. Manners and R. Whitman, 'Another theory is possible: dissident voices in theorising Europe', *Journal of Common Market Studies* 54/1 (2016). See also the rest of the special edition that this article introduces.

20   S. Borg and T. Diez, 'Postmodern EU? Integration between alternative horizons and territorial angst', *Journal of Common Market Studies* 54/1 (2016).

21   B. Rosamond, 'Field of dreams: the discursive construction of EU studies, intellectual dissidence and the practice of "normal science"', *Journal of Common Market Studies* 54/1 (2016).

22   One example is T. Fazi, *The Battle for Europe: How an Elite Hijacked a Continent and How We Can Take It Back* (London: Pluto Press, 2014), p. 169.

23   G. Majone, *Rethinking the Union of Europe Post-Crisis: Has Integration Gone Too Far?* (Cambridge: Cambridge University Press, 2014), p. 214.

24   R. Hilmer, *The European Union Facing Massive Challenges – What are Citizens' Expectations and Concerns?* (Berlin: International Policy Analysis, 2016).

25   C. de Vries and I. Hoffmann, *Fear Not Values: Public Opinion and the Populist Vote in Europe*, EUpinions no. 2016/3 (Gütersloh: Bertelsmann Stiftung, November 2016).

26   A. Giddens, *Turbulent and Mighty Continent: What Future for Europe?* (Cambridge: Polity Press, 2014), ch. 3.

27   C. Booker and R. North, *The Great Deception: Can the European Union Survive?* (London: Bloomsbury, 2016).

28   Gillingham, *The EU: An Obituary*, ch. 6.

29 J. Grygiel, 'The return of Europe's nation-states', *Foreign Affairs* (September/ October 2016).

30 V. Pertusot (ed.), *The European Union in the Fog: Building Bridges between National Perspectives on the European Union* (Paris: Institut français des relations internationales, 2016).

31 See the chapters on each Visegrád state in P. Morillas (ed.), *Illiberal Democracies in the EU: The Visegrád Group and the Risk of Disintegration* (Barcelona: CIDOB, 2017).

32 Y. Varoufakis and A. Sakaris, '"One very simple, but radical, idea: to democratise Europe." An interview with Yanis Varoufakis', openDemocracy [website] (25 October 2015).

33 P. Manent, *Democracy without Nations: The Fate of Self-Government in Europe* (Wilmington, DE: ISI Books, 2013), p. 80.

34 Giddens, *Turbulent and Mighty Continent*, ch. 4.

35 R. Maxwell, 'Cultural diversity and its limits in Western Europe', *Current History* 115/779 (March 2016).

36 B. Rudloff and E. Schmieg, *European Disintegration: Too Much to Lose*, SWP Comments 21 (Berlin: Stiftung Wissenschaft und Politik, April 2016).

37 M. Leonard, 'The migration superpowers', Project Syndicate [website] (20 April 2016).

38 R. Rose and G. Borz, 'Static and dynamic views of European integration', *Journal of Common Market Studies* 54/2 (2016).

39 C. de Vries and I. Hoffmann, *What Do the People Want? Opinions, Moods and Preferences of European Citizens*, EUpinions no. 2015/1 (Gütersloh: Bertelsmann Stiftung, 2015).

3. THE DEMOCRACY PROBLEM

1   A. Mungiu-Pippidi, 'European trust: the perfect storm', openDemocracy [website] (15 October 2015).

2   S. Hix, *What's Wrong with the European Union and How to Fix It* (Cambridge: Polity Press, 2008).

3   C. Crouch, *The Strange Non-Death of Neo-Liberalism* (Cambridge: Polity Press, 2011).

4   V. Schmidt, *Democracy in Europe: The EU and National Politics* (New York: Oxford University Press, 2006).

5   Quoted in B. Carney, 'Britain's very European act', Politico [website] (29 June 2016).

6   J. Caporaso, M. Kim, W. Durrett and R. Wesley, 'Still a regulatory state? The European Union and the financial crisis', *Journal of European Public Policy* 22/7 (2015).

7   N. Nielsen, 'Secret EU law making takes over Brussels', EUObserver [website] (24 January 2017).

8   F. Schimmelfennig, 'What's the news in "new intergovernmentalism"? A critique of Bickerton, Hodson and Puetter', *Journal of Common Market Studies* 53/4 (2015).

9   R. Bellamy and D. Castiglione, 'Three models of democracy, political community and representation in the EU', *Journal of European Public Policy* 20/2 (2013).

10 C. Bickerton, *European Integration: From Nation-States to Member States* (Oxford: Oxford University Press, 2014).

11 S. Lehne, 'Are referenda blocking the EU's progress?', Carnegie Europe [website] (18 November 2015).

12 N. von Ondarza, *Blocked for Good by the Threat of Treaty Change? Perspectives for Reform in the European Union*, SWP Comments 50 (Berlin: Stiftung Wissenschaft und Politik, November 2015).

13 E. Jones, 'The euro: irreversible or conditional?', *Survival* 57/5 (2015).

14 A. Moravcsik, 'Europe after the crisis: how to sustain a common currency', *Foreign Affairs* (May/June 2012).

15 P. Morillas, *Shapes of a Union: From Ever Closer Union to Flexible Differentiation after Brexit* (Barcelona: CIDOB, 2017); V. Pertusot (ed.), *The European Union in the Fog: Building Bridges between National Perspectives on the European Union* (Paris: Institut français des relations internationales, 2016).

16 D. Herszenhorn, J. Barigazzi and G. Ariès, 'Europe confronts limitations at year-end summit', Politico [website] (16 December 2016).

17 B. Ramm, 'Are the people good enough?', openDemocracy [website] (16 January 2017).

18 A. Möller and D. Pardijs, *The Future Shape of Europe: How the EU Can Bend Without Breaking* (London: European Council on Foreign Relations, March 2016).

19 'Hollande quiere que España se sume a Francia, Alemania e Italia para liderar la UE', *El País* (20 February 2017).

20 *White Paper on the Future of Europe*, COM(2017)2025 (Brussels: European Commission, 1 March 2017).

21 J. Doward, 'EU member states may have to foot £3.5bn bill for military research', *Guardian* (23 October 2016).

22 'European Council conclusions', European Council [website] (23 June 2017). Available at http://www.consilium.europa.eu/en/press/press-releases/2017/06/23-euco-conclusions/.

23 C. Hobson, D. Hodson and U. Puetter, 'The new intergovernmentalism: European integration in the post-Maastricht era', *Journal of Common Market Studies* 53/4 (2015).

24 F. Schimmelfennig, 'Liberal intergovernmentalism and the euro area crisis', *Journal of European Public Policy* 22/2 (2015).

25 J. Peterson, 'Juncker's political European Commission and an EU in crisis', *Journal of Common Market Studies* 55/2 (2017).

26 S. Gaston et al., *Nothing to Fear but Fear Itself?* (London: Demos, 2016).

27 LSE Commission on the Future of Britain in Europe, *The UK's Democratic Moment on Europe?* (London: LSE European Institute, 2016).

28 K. Nicolaïdis, 'We, the peoples of Europe', *Foreign Affairs* (November/December 2004); K. Nicolaïdis, 'European democracy and its crisis', *Journal of Common Market Studies* 51/2 (2013); D. Innerarity, 'What must be democratized? The European Union as a complex democracy', in S. Champeau, C. Closa, D. Innerarity and M. Poaires Maduro (eds), *The Future of Europe: Democracy,*

Legitimacy and Justice after the Euro Crisis (London: Rowman & Littlefield International, 2015).

29 J. Hoeksma, *EU and EMU: Beyond the 2005–2014 Crises Decade*, DSF Policy Paper no. 51 (Amsterdam: Duisenberg School of Finance, April 2015), p. 4.

30 R. Bellamy, 'An ever closer union among the peoples of Europe: republican intergovernmentalism and demoicratic representation in the EU', *Journal of European Integration* 35/5 (April 2013).

31 F. Scharpf, 'Political legitimacy in a non-optimal currency area', in O. Cramme and S. Hobolt, *Democratic Politics in a European Union under Stress* (Oxford: Oxford University Press, 2015).

32 Economist Intelligence Unit, *Democracy Index 2016: Revenge of the 'Deplorables'* (London: The Economist, 2017), p. 7.

33 J. Dawson and S. Hanley, 'The fading mirage of the "liberal consensus"', *Journal of Democracy* 27/1 (2016).

34 *A New EU Framework to Strengthen the Rule of Law*, COM(2014)158 (Brussels: European Commission, 19 March 2014); *Annexes to the Communication: A New EU Framework to Strengthen the Rule of Law* (Brussels: European Commission, 11 March 2014); A. Magen, 'Cracks in the foundations: understanding the great rule of law debate in the EU', *Journal of Common Market Studies* 54/5 (2016).

35 P. Bárd, S. Carrera, E. Guild and D. Kochenov, *An EU Mechanism on Democracy, the Rule of Law and Fundamental Rights*, CEPS Papers in Liberty and Security in Europe no. 91 (Brussels: Centre for European Policy Studies, April 2016).

36 N. Nielsen, 'EU commission drops anti-corruption report', EUObserver [website] (2 February 2017).

37 R. D. Keleman, 'The EU's other democratic deficit: national authoritarianism in Europe's democratic union', *Government and Opposition* 52/2 (2017).

38 'El Consejo de Europa exige a España un Poder Judicial independiente', *El País* (10 October 2016).

39 Civicus and Civil Society Europe, 'Civic space in Europe survey', Civil Society Europe [website] (18 January 2016).

40 T. Abraham and M. Smith, 'Five findings from YouGov's European mega-survey', YouGov [website] (October 2016). Available at https://yougov.co.uk/news/2016/11/28/five-findings-yougovs-european-mega-survey/.

41 R. Foa and Y. Mounk, 'The democratic disconnect', *Journal of Democracy* 27/3 (2016). For the critique see P. Norris, *Is Western Democracy Backsliding? Diagnosing the Risks*, HKS working paper RWP17-012 (Harvard Kennedy School, March 2017).

42 Economist Intelligence Unit, *Democracy Index 2016*, p. 17.

43 N. Munin, 'The Five Presidents' Report: the dogs bark but the caravan moves on?', *European Politics and Society* 17/3 (2016).

44 T. Chopin, J.-F. Jamet and F.-X. Priollaud, *A Political Union for Europe*, Fondation Robert Schuman/European Issues no. 252 (Paris: Fondation Robert Schuman, 2012).

45 J. Bright, D. Garzia, J. Lacey and A. Trechsel, 'Europe's voting space and the problem of second-order elections: a transnational proposal', *European Union Politics* 17/1 (2016).

46   J. Fossum, *Democracy and Legitimacy in the EU: Challenges and Options*, IAI Working Papers 16/01 (Rome: Istituto Affari Internazionali, February 2016).

47   C. de Vries and I. Hoffmann, *What Do the People Want? Opinions, Moods and Preferences of European Citizens*, EUpinions no. 2015/1 (Gütersloh: Bertelsmann Stiftung, 2015).

48   T. Raunio, 'The role of national legislatures in EU politics', in O. Cramme and S. Hobolt, *Democratic Politics in a European Union under Stress* (Oxford: Oxford University Press, 2015).

49   R. Bellamy and A. Weale, 'Political legitimacy and European monetary union: contracts, constitutionalism and the normative logic of two-level games', *Journal of European Public Policy* 22/2 (2015).

50   A. Gostyńska-Jakubowska, *The Role of National Parliaments in the EU: Building or Stumbling Blocks?* (London: Centre for European Reform, June 2016).

51   J. Fossum, 'Democracy and differentiation in Europe', *Journal of European Public Policy* 22/6 (2015).

52   H. Grabbe and S. Lehne, 'Emotional intelligence for EU democracy', Carnegie Europe [website] (26 January 2015).

4. EUROPE AS A CITIZENS' PROJECT

1   M. Ferrin and H. Kriesi, *Europeans' Understandings and Evaluations of Democracy: Topline Results from Round 6 of the European Social Survey*, ESS Topline Results Series no. 4 (London: European Social Survey, 2014).

2   R. Hilmer, *The European Union Facing Massive Challenges – What are Citizens' Expectations and Concerns?* (Berlin: International Policy Analysis, 2016).

3   J. Habermas, *The Crisis of the European Union* (Cambridge: Polity Press, 2012); U. Beck and E. Grande, 'Cosmopolitanism: Europe's way out of crisis', *European Journal of Social Theory* 10/1 (2007); J. Dryzek, *Global Deliberative Politics* (Cambridge: Polity Press, 2006); L. Siedentop, *Democracy in Europe* (London: Penguin, 2000); T. Judt, *A Grand Illusion? An Essay on Europe* (New York: New York University Press, 2011); K. Nicolaïdis, '*JCMS* annual review lecture: sustainable integration: towards EU 2.0?', *Journal of Common Market Studies* 48 (2010); F. Schimmelfennig, 'The normative origins of democracy in the European Union: toward a transformationalist theory of democratization', *European Political Science Review* 2/2 (2010); B. Simms, 'Towards a mighty union: how to create a democratic European superpower', *International Affairs* 88/1 (2012); O. Parker, *Cosmopolitan Government in Europe* (London: Routledge, 2012).

4   G. Majone, *Rethinking the Union of Europe Post-Crisis: Has Integration Gone Too Far?* (Cambridge: Cambridge University Press, 2014), p. 189.

5   E. Isin and M. Saward, *Enacting European Citizenship* (Cambridge: Cambridge University Press, 2013).

6   J. B. Judis, 'Us v them: the birth of populism', *Guardian* (13 October 2016).

7   See many of the contributions to S. Champeau, C. Closa, D. Innerarity and M. Poaires Maduro (eds), *The Future of Europe: Democracy, Legitimacy and Justice after the Euro Crisis* (London: Rowman & Littlefield International, 2015).

8   S. Hix, 'Democratizing a macroeconomic union in Europe', in O. Cramme and S. Hobolt, *Democratic Politics in a European Union under Stress* (Oxford: Oxford University Press, 2015).

9   M. Mazower, 'What remains: on the European Union', *The Nation* (5 September 2012).

10 D. della Porta, *Mobilizing for Democracy: Comparing 1989 and 2011* (Oxford: Oxford University Press, 2014).

11 D. della Porta, *Can Democracy Be Saved?* (Cambridge: Polity Press, 2013), p. 57.

12 Z. Bauman, *Liquid Times: Living in an Age of Uncertainty* (Cambridge: Polity Press, 2006).

13 S. Tormey, *The End of Representative Politics* (Cambridge: Polity Press, 2015), chs 5 and 6.

14 D. Held and G. Schott, *Models of Democracy* (Palo Alto, CA: Stanford University Press, 1996), ch. 9.

15 J. Bohman, *Democracy across Borders: From Dêmos to Dêmoi* (Cambridge, MA: MIT Press, 2010); Dryzek, *Global Deliberative Politics*.

16 J. Keane, *The Life and Death of Democracy* (New York: Simon & Schuster, 2009), p. 691.

17 E. Fries-Tersch, T. Tugran and H. Bradley, *2016 Annual Report on Intra-EU Labour Mobility* (Brussels: European Commission, 2016); S. Parker, *Taking Power Back: Putting People in Charge of Politics* (Bristol: Policy Press, 2015).

18 G. Monbiot, 'This is how people can truly take back control: from the bottom up', *Guardian* (8 February 2017).

19 'Portugal has announced the world's first nationwide participatory budget: plans for voting via ATM machines to massively boost turnout', Apolitical [website] (27 October 2016).

20 Parker, *Taking Power Back*.

21 C. Chwalisz, *The Populist Signal: Why Politics and Democracy Need to Change* (London: Rowman & Littlefield International, 2015).

22 One of the best of the more critical takes is I. Krastev, *Democracy Disrupted: The Politics of Global Protest* (Philadelphia: University of Pennsylvania Press, 2014). See also M. Saward, *Democracy* (Cambridge: Polity Press, 2003); P. Ginsborg, *Democracy: Crisis and Renewal* (London: Profile Books, 2008); P. Rosanvallon, *Counter-Democracy: Politics in an Age of Distrust* (New York: Cambridge University Press, 2008).

23 N. Bolleyer and C. Reh, 'EU legitimacy revisited: the normative foundations of a multilevel polity', *Journal of European Public Policy* 19/4 (2012).

24 M. Kaldor, S. Selchow, S. Deel and T. Murray-Leach, *The 'Bubbling Up' of Subterranean Politics in Europe* (London: Civil Society and Human Security Research Unit, London School of Economics and Political Science, 2012); C. Bee and R. Guerrina, 'Framing civic engagement, political participation and active citizenship in Europe', *Journal of Civil Society* 10/1 (2014).

25 L. Bherer, P. Dufour and F. Montambeault, 'The participatory democracy turn: an introduction', *Journal of Civil Society* 12/3 (2016); F. Polletta, 'Participatory enthusiasms: a recent history of citizen engagement initiatives', *Journal of Civil Society* 12/3 (2016).

26 S. Žižek, *The Year of Dreaming Dangerously* (London: Verso, 2012), p. 11.

27 The lack of connection between vibrant city-level activism and EU reforms is evident for example, in D. Büllesbach et al. (eds), *Shifting Baselines of Europe* (Bielefeld: Transcript, 2017).

28 T. Pappas, 'Distinguishing liberal democracy's challengers', *Journal of Democracy* 27/4 (2016); J.-W. Müller, *What Is Populism?* (Philadelphia: University of Pennsylvania Press, 2016); J. B. Judis, *The Populist Explosion: How the Great Recession Transformed American and European Politics* (New York: Columbia Global Reports, 2016).

29 D. Albertazzi and S. Mueller, 'Populism and liberal democracy: populists in government in Austria, Italy, Poland and Switzerland', *Government and Opposition* 48/3 (2013).

30 P. Taggart and C. Rovira Kaltwasser, 'Dealing with populists in government: some comparative conclusions', *Democratization* 23/2 (2016).

31 D. Altman, *Direct Democracy Worldwide* (New York: Cambridge University Press, 2011).

32 D. Innerarity, 'Transnational self-determination: resetting self-government in the age of interdependence', *Journal of Common Market Studies* 53/5 (2015).

33 K. Nicolaïdis, 'European demoicracy and its crisis', *Journal of Common Market Studies* 51/2 (2013); K. Nicolaïdis, 'Demoicratic theory and Europe's institutional architecture in times of crisis', in S. Piattoni (ed.), *The European Union: Democratic Principles and Institutional Architectures in Times of Crisis* (Oxford: Oxford University Press, 2015); F. Cheneval and K. Nicolaïdis, 'The social construction of demoicracy in the European Union', *European Journal of Political Theory* 16/2 (2016). See also J. Hoeksma, *From Common Market to Common Democracy: A Theory of Democratic Integration* (Oisterwijk: Wolf Legal Publishers, 2016).

34 Ferrin and Kriesi, *Europeans' Understandings and Evaluations of Democracy*.

35 J. Janning (ed.), *Keeping Europeans Together: Assessing the State of EU Cohesion* (London: European Council on Foreign Relations, 2016).

36 K. Nicolaïdis and R. Youngs, 'Europe's democracy trilemma', *International Affairs* 90/6 (November 2014).

5. A COMPACT OF EUROPEAN CITIZENS

1 *Better Regulation and Transparency* (Brussels: European Commission, 2016).

2 The so-called Plato project. See http://www.plato.uio.no/research/index.html.

3 H. Grabbe and S. Lehne, 'Can the EU survive populism?', Carnegie Europe [website] (14 June 2016).

4 L. Bouza Garcia, *Participatory Democracy and Civil Society in the European Union* (London: Palgrave Macmillan, 2015).

5 R. Sanchez Salgado, *Europeanizing Civil Society: How the EU Shapes Civil Society Organizations* (London: Palgrave Macmillan, 2014).

6 R. Bellamy, 'The inevitability of a democratic deficit', in H. Zimmermann and A. Dür (eds), *Controversies in European Integration* (London: Palgrave Macmillan, 2012).

7   S. Gherghina and A. Groh, 'A poor sales pitch? The European citizens' initiative and attitudes toward the EU in Germany and the UK', *European Politics and Society* 17/3 (2016).

8   *Better Regulation and Transparency*.

9   J. Brunsden, 'EU gatekeeper toughens test for new proposals', *Financial Times* (22 February 2017).

10 *EU Citizenship Report 2017*, COM(2017) 30 (Brussels: European Commission, 31 January 2017).

11 S. Hix, *What's Wrong with the European Union and How to Fix It* (Cambridge: Polity Press, 2008), chapters 7 and 8.

12 H. Sicakkan, 'The role of EU policies in the making of a European public sphere', in H. Sicakkan (ed.), *Integration, Diversity and the Making of a European Public Sphere* (Cheltenham: Edward Elgar, 2016).

13 European Parliament Budgetary Committee, *Democratic Accountability and Budgetary Control of Non-Governmental Organisations Funded by the EU Budget* (Brussels: European Union, 2016).

14 En Marche! programme. Available at at https://en-marche.fr/emmanuel-macron/le-programme/europe.

15 *Plan C pour l'Europe* (Paris: European Civic Forum, 2014); V. Dupouey, A. Najmowicz and J. Oldfield, *A State of Democracy: Towards Citizen Rights Protection in the EU* (Paris: European Civic Forum, 2015).

16 *Activenship* 2 [online publication of the European Civic Forum] (2016).

17 L. Marsili and B. Spinelli, 'Reclaiming Europe from the powers that be: an interview with Barbara Spinelli MEP', openDemocracy [website] (3 August 2016).

18 See the European Association for Local Democracy website. Available at http://www.alda-europe.eu/newSite/project.php.

19 *DEmocratic Compact: Improving Democracy in Europe* (European Association for Local Democracy, 2015).

20 'Democracy in practice', European Students' Forum [website]. Available at http://www.aegee.org/projects/democracy-in-practice.

21 *Reviving Democracy for a Citizens-Led Europe* (Brussels: FutureLab Europe, 2016); *Bring Back the Citizens! How to Revive Democracy for a Citizens-Led Europe* (Brussels: FutureLab Europe, April 2016).

22 'Reframing democracy' [European Movement International internal document, 2016].

23 *Resolution on the Transnationalisation of European Democracy and the Innovation of the European Political System* (Rome: European Movement International, 2014).

24 See the Our New Europe website. Available at http://www.our-new-europe.eu/english/.

25 See the Civico Europa website. Available at www.civico.eu.

26 European Youth Press, *Shaping Europe: 50 Ideas for a Better Future* [report of the European Youth Event, Strasbourg, 2016].

27 See the ECIT website. Available at www.ecit-foundation.eu.

28 See the ECAS website. Available at www.ecas.org.

29 See the Pulse of Europe website. Available at www.pulseofeurope.eu.

30   See the Our Europe website. Available at http://www.lanostraeuropa.org/appello-la-nostra-europa/nuestra-europa-unida-democratica-solidaria/.

31   L. Abraham et al., *Europe. Think. Again* (Zurich: Foraus, March 2017).

32   See 'Manifesto', ¡Democracia real YA! [website] (2017). Available at http://www.democraciarealya.es/manifiesto-comun/manifiesto-english/.

33   Y. Varoufakis, 'Why we must save the EU', *Guardian* (5 April 2016).

34   Y. Varoufakis (interviewed by Michel Feher), 'Europe and the specter of democracy', *Near Futures Online* 1 (March 2016).

35   *European New Deal* (DiEM25, 2017).

36   N. Papastergiadis, 'Transversal cultural spheres and the future of Europe', openDemocracy [website] (22 February 2016).

37   A. Wilkinson, M. Mayer and V. Ringler, 'Collaborative futures: integrating foresight with design in large scale innovation processes – seeing and seeding the futures of Europe', *Journal of Future Studies* 18/4 (2014).

38   J. Keane, *The Life and Death of Democracy* (New York: Simon & Schuster, 2009), p. 691.

39   M. Neblo, *Deliberative Democracy between Theory and Practice* (Cambridge: Cambridge University Press, 2015).

40   C. Chwalisz, 'Can liberal democracy be rescued?', *Renewal* [website] (15 June 2016).

41   D. Van Reybrouck, *Against Elections: The Case for Democracy* (London: Bodley Head, 2016).

42   See S. Villines, 'Using majority vote to create autocracies', Sociocracy [website] (15 March 2017). Available at www.sociocracy.info.

43   Neblo, *Deliberative Democracy*.

44   *Democratic Participation in a Citizens' Europe: What Next for the EU?* [conference report, University of Liverpool, 5 May 2016].

45   E. Isin and M. Saward, *Enacting European Citizenship* (Cambridge: Cambridge University Press, 2013).

6. DIVERGENT EUROPE: TOWARDS RADICAL FLEXIBILITY

1   J. A. Emmanouilidis (ed.), *Towards a New Pact for Europe* (Brussels: King Baudouin Foundation, the Bertelsmann Stiftung and the European Policy Centre, October 2014).

2   D. Marsh, *Europe's Deadlock: How the Euro Crisis Could Be Solved – And Why It Still Won't Happen* (New Haven, CT: Yale University Press, 2016); P. Legrain, 'The disintegration of Europe', Project Syndicate [website] (19 October 2015).

3   Y. Varoufakis, *And the Weak Suffer What They Must? Europe, Austerity and the Threat to Global Stability* (London: Bodley Head, 2016).

4   G. Daniele and B. Geys, 'Public support for European fiscal integration in times of crisis', *Journal of European Public Policy* 22/5 (2015).

5   M. Scherer, 'United by reformation: British and northern European Euroscepticism is rooted in religious history', LSE British Politics and Policy [blog] (9 October 2015).

6   C. de Vries and I. Hoffmann, *What Do the People Want? Opinions, Moods and*

Preferences of European Citizens, EUpinions no. 2015/1 (Gütersloh: Bertelsmann Stiftung, 2015).

7   F. Schimmelfennig, 'Differentiated integration before and after the crisis', in O. Cramme and S. Hobolt, *Democratic Politics in a European Union under Stress* (Oxford: Oxford University Press, 2015).

8   M. Busemeyer and T. Tober, 'European integration and the political economy of inequality, *European Union Politics* 16/4 (2015).

9   P. A. Hall, 'The euro crisis and the future of European integration', in BBVA, *The Search of Europe: Contrasting Approaches* (Madrid: BBVA, 2016).

10 G. Jackson and R. Deeg, 'The long-term trajectories of institutional change in European capitalism', *Journal of European Public Policy* 19/8 (2012).

11 J.-W. Müller, 'Rule-breaking', *London Review of Books* 37/16 (August 2015).

12 M. Otero-Iglesias, 'Still waiting for Paris: Germany's reluctant hegemony in pursuing political union in the euro area', *Journal of European Integration* 39/3 (2017).

13 B. Leruth, 'Operationalizing national preferences on Europe and differentiated integration', *Journal of European Public Policy* 22/6 (2015).

14 V. Pertusot (ed.), *The European Union in the Fog: Building Bridges between National Perspectives on the European Union* (Paris: Institut français des relations internationales, 2016).

15 J.-W. Müller, 'The EU's democratic deficit and the public sphere', *Current History* 115/779 (March 2016).

16 H. Kundnani, *The Paradox of German Power* (New York: Oxford University Press, 2014).

17 G. Hellmann, 'Germany's world: power and followership in a crisis-ridden Europe', *Global Affairs* 2/1 (2016).

18 J. Zielonka, *Is the EU Doomed?* (Cambridge: Polity Press, 2014), p. 22.

19 I. Manners and P. Murray, 'The end of a noble narrative? European integration narratives after the Nobel Peace Prize', *Journal of Common Market Studies* 54/1 (2016).

20 Such interpretations of liberalism were put forward some time ago, for example in R. Nozick, *Anarchy, State, and Utopia* (New York: Basic Books, 1974).

21 H. Kissinger, *World Order* (London: Penguin, 2014), pp. 93, 95.

22 B. Simms, *Europe: The Struggle for Supremacy: 1453 to the Present* (London: Penguin, 2013).

23 F. Schimmelfennig, D. Leuffen and B. Rittberger, 'The European Union as a system of differentiated integration: interdependence, politicization and differentiation', *Journal of European Public Policy* 22/6 (2015); D. Leuffen, B. Rittberger and F. Schimmelfennig, *Differentiated Integration: Explaining Variation in the European Union* (London: Palgrave Macmillan, 2012).

24 N. Koenig, *A Differentiated View of Differentiated Integration* (Berlin: Jacques Delors Institute, 23 July 2015).

25 P. Genschel and M. Jachtenfuchs, 'More integration, less federation: the European integration of core state powers', *Journal of European Public Policy* 23/1 (2016).

26 J. Fossum, 'Democracy and differentiation in Europe', *Journal of European Public Policy* 22/6 (2015).

27   G. Martinico, *A Multi-Speed EU? An Institutional and Legal Assessment*, IAI Working Papers 15/48 (Rome: Istituto Affari Internazionali, December 2015).

28   A. Möller and D. Pardijs, *The Future Shape of Europe: How the EU Can Bend Without Breaking* (London: European Council on Foreign Relations, March 2016).

29   T. Palmeri, 'Ministers of "core" Europe plan EU's future', Politico [website] (8 February 2016).

30   *White Paper on the Future of Europe*, COM(2017)2025 (Brussels: European Commission, 1 March 2017).

31   J. C. Piris, *The Future of Europe: Towards a Two-speed EU?* (New York: Cambridge University Press, 2012).

32   'Creaking at 60: the future of the European Union', *The Economist* (25 March 2017).

33   S. Fabbrini, *Which European Union? Europe after the Euro Crisis* (Cambridge: Cambridge University Press, 2015).

34   J. Stiglitz, 'A split euro is the solution for the single currency', *Financial Times* (17 August 2016).

35   G. Merritt, *Slippery Slope: Europe's Troubled Future* (New York: Oxford University Press, 2016), p. 177.

36   This is particularly true of the influential J. Stiglitz, *The Euro and Its Threat to the Future of Europe* (London: Allen Lane, 2017).

37   For one example, see B. Laffan, 'Birthday wishes to the European Union', EUObserver [website] (24 March 2017).

38   J. Zielonka, 'Legitimacy in a neomedieval (postcrisis) Europe', in S. Champeau, C. Closa, D. Innerarity and M. Poaires Maduro (eds), *The Future of Europe: Democracy, Legitimacy and Justice after the Euro Crisis* (London: Rowman & Littlefield International, 2015).

39   See Pertusot (ed.), *The European Union in the Fog*.

40   G. Majone, *Rethinking the Union of Europe Post-Crisis: Has Integration Gone Too Far?* (Cambridge: Cambridge University Press, 2014).

41   Ibid., pp. 3–15.

42   M. Mazower, 'Lessons from the past are key to Europe's survival', *Financial Times* (22 January 2016).

43   Zielonka, *Is the EU Doomed?*, ch. 4.

44   Ibid., p. 77.

45   P. Wilson, 'The Holy Roman Empire can help inspire a different European Union', *Financial Times* (20 January 2016).

46   Zielonka, *Is the EU Doomed?*, pp. 111–12.

47   V. Schmidt and M. Wood, "The EU's new white paper underlines why Europe needs to be more open to its citizens', LSE Europp [blog] (10 Match 2017).

48   L. Andor, 'Europe between deconstruction and reconstruction', Hertie School of Governance [website] (6 January 2016).

49   C. Mortera-Martinez and C. Odendahl, *What Free Movement Means to Europe and Why It Matters for Britain* (London: Centre for European Reform, January 2017).

50   *Standard Eurobarometer 86* (Brussels: European Commission, Directorate-General for Communication, November 2016).

51   D. Tusk, 'Letter from President Donald Tusk before the Bratislava summit', European Council press release 511/16 (13 September 2016).

52   J. Peet and A. La Guardia, *Unhappy Union: How the Euro Crisis – and Europe – Can Be Fixed* (London: Economist/Profile Books, 2014).

53   C. Schweiger, *Exploring the EU's Legitimacy Crisis* (Cheltenham: Edward Elgar, 2016), p. 162.

54   C. Odendahl, *We Don't Need No Federation: What a Devolved Eurozone Should Look Like* (London: Centre for European Reform, December 2015).

55   L. Garicano, 'Europe inches closer to a plan for fixing its financial flaws', *The Economist* (2 June 2017).

56   R. Youngs, *The Puzzle of Non-Western Democracy* (Washington DC: Carnegie Endowment for International Peace, 2015).

57   S. Jenkins, 'London's MPs have the power to change the course of Brexit', *Guardian* (16 June 2017).

58   M. Maduro, presentation at the State of the Union conference, European University Institute, Florence, 5 May 2017.

7. A SECURE EUROPE?

1   S. Biscop, *Global and Operational: A New Strategy for EU Foreign and Security Policy*, IAI Working Papers 15/27 (Rome: Istituto Affari Internazionali, July 2015); M. Leonard, chapter 8, and S. Ulgen, chapter 17, in A. Missiroli et al., *Towards an EU Global Strategy – Consulting the Experts* (Paris: European Union Institute for Security Studies, 2016).

2   F. Reinares, 'Prevenir la radicalización yihadista: un fracaso europeo', Elcano Blog [website] (14 April 2016).

3   One recent example of the many works arguing that European security has been weakened primarily by being too open to immigration and refugees is D. Murray, *The Strange Death of Europe* (London: Bloomsbury, 2017).

4   M. Valls, 'The Brexit vote pushes EU to refine itself', *Financial Times* (12 October 2016).

5   *Shared Vision, Common Action: A Stronger Europe: A Global Strategy for the European Union's Foreign and Security Policy* (Brussels: European External Action Service, June 2016).

6   J.-M. Ayrault and F.-W. Steinmeier, 'A strong Europe in a world of uncertainties', France Diplomatie [website] (28 June 2016).

7   'EU funds for Bulgaria target border security', EUObserver [website] (28 September 2016).

8   'German ministry wants migrants stopped at sea', EUObserver [website] (8 November 2016).

9   *First Progress Report on the Partnership Framework with Third Countries under the European Agenda on Migration*, COM(2016)700 (Brussels: European Commission, 18 October 2016).

10   D. Alghoul, 'Merkel under fire for "uncritical engagement" with Egypt during visit', Middle East Eye [website] (2 March 2017).

11   *Towards a 'Security Union': Bolstering the EU's Counter-Terrorism Response*, EPSC
     Strategic Notes no. 12 (Brussels: European Political Strategy Centre, 20 April 2016).

12   J. Black et al., *Defence and Security after Brexit* (Cambridge: RAND Europe, 2017),
     p. 31.

13   European Commission and High Representative for Foreign Affairs and Security
     Policy, *Elements for an EU-Wide Strategic Framework to Support Security Sector
     Reform*, JOIN(2016)31 (Strasbourg: European Commission, 5 July 2016).

14   A. Dworkin, *Europe's New Counter-Terror Wars* (London: European Council on
     Foreign Relations, October 2016).

15   D. Omand, 'Keeping Europe safe: counterterrorism for the continent', *Foreign
     Affairs* (September/October 2016).

16   D. Boffey, 'Gaziantep: home to Isis killers, sex traders… and a quest to rebuild
     Syria', *Guardian* (8 May 2016).

17   C. Castillejo, *The European Union Trust Fund for Africa: A Glimpse of the Future
     for EU Development Cooperation* (Bonn: German Development Institute, 2016).

18   For updated aid figures, see http://www.oecd.org/dac/financing-sustainable-
     development/development-finance-data/.

19   F. Aliriza, 'Between democracy and police state: Tunisia's troubled transition',
     in I. Fakir (ed.), *The Middle East Unbalanced: Analysis from a Region in Turmoil*
     (Washington DC: Carnegie Endowment for International Peace, 2016).

20   'The Libyan political agreement: time for a reset', International Crisis Group
     [website] (4 November 2016).

21   M. Toaldo, *Intervening Better: Europe's Second Chance in Libya* (London: European
     Council on Foreign Relations, 13 May 2016).

22   P. Vimont, 'Migration in Europe: bridging the solidarity gap', Carnegie Europe
     [website] (12 September 2016).

23   See the regular updated figures posted on the website of the International
     Organization for Migration. Available at https://www.iom.int/news/
     mediterranean-migrant-arrivals-approach-43000-2017-deaths-962.

24   J. Cosgrave, *Europe's Refugees and Migrants* (London: Overseas Development
     Institute, September 2016).

25   House of Commons Home Affairs Committee, *Migration Crisis: Seventh Report
     of Session 2016–17*, HC 24 (3 August 2016).

26   R. Parkes, *People on the Move: The New Global (Dis)order*, Chaillot Papers no. 138
     (Paris: European Union Institute for Security Studies, June 2016).

27   P. Kingsley, *The New Odyssey: The Story of Europe's Refugee Crisis* (London: Faber,
     2016).

28   M. Mayer and M. Mehregani, 'Beyond crisis management: the path towards an
     effective, pro-active and fair European refugee policy', in *Vision Europe Summit:
     Improving the Responses to the Migration and Refugee Crisis in Europe* (Lisbon:
     Vision Europe/Bertelsmann Stiftung, November 2016).

29   B. Weber, *Time for a Plan B: The European Refugee Crisis, the Balkan Route and the
     EU–Turkey Deal* (Berlin: Democratization Policy Council, September 2016).

30   R. Smits, F. Molenaar, F. El-Kamouni-Janssen and N. Grinstead, *Cultivating Conflict
     and Violence? A Conflict Perspective on the EU Approach to the Syrian Refugee Crisis*
     (The Hague: Clingendael Conflict Research Unit, August 2016).

31 European Commission and High Representative for Foreign Affairs and Security Policy, *Elements for an EU-Wide Strategic Framework to Support Security Sector Reform*, JOIN(2016)31 (Strasbourg: European Commission, 5 July 2016).

32 O. Roy, *Jihad and Death: The Global Appeal of Islamic State* (Oxford: Oxford University Press, 2017).

33 S. Grey, *The New Spymasters* (London: Penguin, 2016), pp. 255, 282.

34 'MSF rejects aid in protest at EU refugee deal', *Guardian* (18 June 2016).

35 M. Carr, *Fortress Europe: Inside the War against Immigration* (London: Hurst, 2015), p. 287.

36 A. Giddens, *Turbulent and Mighty Continent: What Future for Europe?* (Cambridge: Polity Press, 2014), p. 15 and ch. 4.

37 H. Kundnani, *How Economic Dependence Could Undermine Europe's Foreign Policy Coherence* (Washington DC: German Marshall Fund, January 2016).

38 S. Lavenex, 'On the fringes of the European peace project: the neighbourhood policy's functionalist hubris and political myopia', *British Journal of Politics and International Relations* 19/1 (2016).

39 One contrarian exception is A. Moravcsik, 'Europe is still a superpower', *Foreign Affairs* (March/April 2017).

40 Black et al., *Defence and Security after Brexit*; P. Wintour, 'UK offers to maintain defence and security cooperation with EU', *Guardian* (12 September 2017).

41 C. Watts, 'The Islamic State in Europe: terrorists without borders, counterterrorists with all borders', War on the Rocks [website] (29 March 2016).

42 R. Parkes, *The EU as a Terrorist Target: Why, Where and How*, ISS Brief no. 16 (Paris: European Union Institute for Security Studies, May 2016), p. 3.

43 C. de Vries, and I. Hoffmann, *Border Protection and Freedom of Movement: What People Expect of European Asylum and Migration Policies*, EUpinions no. 2016/1 (Gütersloh: Bertelsmann Stiftung, 2016).

44 R. Balfour (ed.), *Europe's Troublemakers: The Populist Challenge to Foreign Policy* (Brussels: European Policy Centre, February 2016).

45 M. Goodwin, T. Raines and D. Cotts, 'What do Europeans think about Muslim immigration?', Chatham House [website] (2017).

46 B. Stokes, R. Wike and J. Poushter, *Europeans Face the World Divided* (Washington DC: Pew Research Center, 13 June 2016).

47 This section borrows from R. Youngs, 'European liberal power as a two-way street', Carnegie Europe [website] (17 May 2016).

48 Shakespeare, *Timon of Athens*, act 1, scene 2.

49 S. Biscop, *Geopolitics with European Characteristics: An Essay on Pragmatic Idealism, Equality, and Strategy*, Egmont Paper 82 (Brussels: Egmont Institute, March 2016).

50 C. Kinnvall, 'The postcolonial has moved into Europe: bordering, security and ethno-cultural belonging', *Journal of Common Market Studies* 54/1 (2016).

8. THE LONG ROAD TO SOLIDARITY

1 From 'I Am' by the English poet John Clare (1793–1864).

2 M. Houellebecq, *Soumission* (Paris: Flammarion, 2015).

3   L. Tsoukalis, *In Defence of Europe: Can the European Project be Saved?* (New York: Oxford University Press, 2016), p. 175.

4   Paraphrased from Karl Marx, *Eleven Theses on Feuerbach*.

5   The phrase is from F. Pessoa, *The Book of Disquiet* (London: Profile Books, 1991), p. 8.

6   Shakespeare, *Richard III*, act 4, scene 2.

7   C. Bickerton, *The European Union: A Citizen's Guide* (London: Penguin, 2016), p. 230.

8   A. Burgess, *A Clockwork Orange* (London: Heinemann, 1962).

9   P. Mishra, *The Age of Anger: A History of the Present* (London: Allen Lane, 2017), p. 358.

10   B. Simms, *Europe: The Struggle for Supremacy: 1453 to the Present* (London: Penguin, 2013), p. xxviii and ch. 3.

Bibliography

Abraham, L., et al., *Europe. Think. Again* (Zurich: Foraus, March 2017).

Albertazzi, D., and S. Mueller, 'Populism and liberal democracy: populists in government in Austria, Italy, Poland and Switzerland', *Government and Opposition* 48/3 (2013).

Alesina, A. and F. Giavazzi, *The Future of Europe: Reform or Decline* (Cambridge, MA: MIT Press, 2008).

Alghoul, D., 'Merkel under fire for "uncritical engagement" with Egypt during visit', Middle East Eye [website] (2 March 2017).

Aliriza, F., 'Between democracy and police state: Tunisia's troubled transition', in I. Fakir (ed.), *The Middle East Unbalanced: Analysis from a Region in Turmoil* (Washington DC: Carnegie Endowment for International Peace, 2016).

Altman, D., *Direct Democracy Worldwide* (New York: Cambridge University Press, 2011).

Andor, L., 'Europe between deconstruction and reconstruction', Hertie School of Governance [website] (6 January 2016).

Ayrault, J.-M., and F.-W. Steinmeier, 'A strong Europe in a world of uncertainties', France Diplomatie [website] (28 June 2016).

Balfour, R. (ed.), *Europe's Troublemakers: The Populist Challenge to Foreign Policy* (Brussels: European Policy Centre, February 2016).

Bárd, P., S. Carrera, E. Guild and D. Kochenov, *An EU Mechanism on Democracy, the Rule of Law and Fundamental Rights*, CEPS Papers in Liberty and Security in Europe no. 91 (Brussels: Centre for European Policy Studies, April 2016).

Bastasin, C., *Saving Europe: Anatomy of a Dream* (Washington DC: Brookings Institution Press, 2015).

Bauman, Z., *Liquid Times: Living in an Age of Uncertainty* (Cambridge: Polity Press, 2006).

Beck, U., and E. Grande, 'Cosmopolitanism: Europe's way out of crisis', *European Journal of Social Theory* 10/1 (2007).

Bee, C., and R. Guerrina, 'Framing civic engagement, political participation and active citizenship in Europe', *Journal of Civil Society* 10/1 (2014).

Bellamy, R., 'The inevitability of a democratic deficit', in H. Zimmermann and A. Dür (eds), *Controversies in European Integration* (London: Palgrave Macmillan, 2012).
———— 'An ever closer union among the peoples of Europe: republican intergovernmentalism and demoicratic representation in the EU', *Journal of European Integration* 35/5 (April 2013).

Bellamy, R., and A. Weale, 'Political legitimacy and European monetary union: contracts, constitutionalism and the normative logic of two-level games', *Journal of European Public Policy* 22/2 (2015).

Bellamy, R., and D. Castiglione, 'Three models of democracy, political community and representation in the EU', *Journal of European Public Policy* 20/2 (2013).

Bherer, L., P. Dufour and F. Montambeault, 'The participatory democracy turn: an introduction', *Journal of Civil Society* 12/3 (2016).

Bickerton, C., *European Integration: From Nation-States to Member States* (Oxford: Oxford University Press, 2014).

—— *The European Union: A Citizen's Guide* (London: Penguin, 2016).

Biscop, S., *Global and Operational: A New Strategy for EU Foreign and Security Policy*, IAI Working Papers 15/27 (Rome: Istituto Affari Internazionali, July 2015).

—— *Geopolitics with European Characteristics: An Essay on Pragmatic Idealism, Equality, and Strategy*, Egmont Paper 82 (Brussels: Egmont Institute, March 2016).

Black, J., et al., *Defence and Security after Brexit* (Cambridge: RAND Europe, 2017).

Boffey, D., 'Gaziantep: home to Isis killers, sex traders… and a quest to rebuild Syria', *Guardian* (8 May 2016).

—— 'EU taskforce highlights security failings that facilitated terror attacks', *Guardian* (14 March 2017).

Bohman, J., *Democracy across Borders: From Dêmos to Dêmoi* (Cambridge, MA: MIT Press, 2010).

Bolleyer, N., and C. Reh, 'EU legitimacy revisited: the normative foundations of a multilevel polity', *Journal of European Public Policy* 19/4 (2012).

Bonse, E., 'L'Europe après le Brexit: positions et perspectives allemandes', *Notes du Cerfa* 135 (2017).

Booker, C., and R. North, *The Great Deception: Can the European Union Survive?* (London: Bloomsbury, 2016).

Borg, S., and T. Diez, 'Postmodern EU? Integration between alternative horizons and territorial angst', *Journal of Common Market Studies* 54/1 (2016).

Bouza Garcia, L., *Participatory Democracy and Civil Society in the European Union* (London: Palgrave Macmillan, 2015).

Bright, J., D. Garzia, J. Lacey and A. Trechsel, 'Europe's voting space and the problem of second-order elections: a transnational proposal', *European Union Politics* 17/1 (2016).

Büllesbach, D., et al. (eds), *Shifting Baselines of Europe* (Bielefeld: Transcript, 2017).

Busemeyer, M., and T. Tober, 'European integration and the political economy of inequality', *European Union Politics* 16/4 (2015).

Caporaso, J., M. Kim, W. Durrett and R. Wesley, 'Still a regulatory state? The European Union and the financial crisis', *Journal of European Public Policy* 22/7 (2015).

Carney, B., 'Britain's very European act', *Politico* [website] (29 June 2016).

Carr, M., *Fortress Europe: Inside the War against Immigration* (London: Hurst, 2015).

Castillejo, C., *The European Union Trust Fund for Africa: A Glimpse of the Future for EU Development Cooperation* (Bonn: German Development Institute, 2016).

Cerny, P., *Rethinking World Politics: A Theory of Transnational Neopluralism* (New York: Oxford University Press, 2010).

Champeau, S., C. Closa, D. Innerarity and M. Poaires Maduro (eds), *The Future of Europe: Democracy, Legitimacy and Justice after the Euro Crisis* (London: Rowman & Littlefield International, 2015).

Chazan, G., 'Backlash prompts tougher German approach to refugees', *Financial Times* (29 November 2016).

Cheneval, F., and K. Nicolaïdis, 'The social construction of demoicracy in the European Union', *European Journal of Political Theory* 16/2 (2016).

Chopin, T., J.-F. Jamet and F.-X. Priollaud, *A Political Union for Europe*, Fondation Robert Schuman/European Issues no. 252 (Paris: Fondation Robert Schuman, 2012).

Chwalisz, C., *The Populist Signal: Why Politics and Democracy Need to Change* (London: Rowman & Littlefield International, 2015).

———— 'Can liberal democracy be rescued?', *Renewal* [website] (15 June 2016).

Civicus and Civil Society Europe, 'Civic space in Europe survey', Civil Society Europe [website] (18 January 2016).

Clare, J., 'I am', *Bedford Times* (1848).

Committee on Constitutional Affairs, 'Report on possible evolutions of and adjustments to the current institutional set-up of the European Union', European Parliament [website] (20 December 2016).

———— 'Report on improving the functioning of the European Union building on the potential of the Lisbon Treaty', European Parliament [website] (9 January 2017).

Copelovitch, M., J. Frieden and S. Walter, 'The political economy of the euro crisis', *Comparative Political Studies* 49/7 (2016).

Cosgrave, J., *Europe's Refugees and Migrants* (London: Overseas Development Institute, September 2016).

Crafts, N., *Saving the Eurozone: Is a 'Real' Marshall Plan the Answer?*, CAGE–Chatham House Series no. 1 (London: Chatham House, June 2012).

'Creaking at 60: the future of the European Union', *The Economist* (25 March 2017).

Crouch, C., *The Strange Non-Death of Neo-Liberalism* (Cambridge: Polity Press, 2011).

Crum, B., 'Saving the euro at the cost of democracy?', *Journal of Common Market Studies* 51/4 (2013).

Daniele, G., and B. Geys, 'Public support for European fiscal integration in times of crisis', *Journal of European Public Policy* 22/5 (2015).

Dawson, J., and S. Hanley, 'The fading mirage of the "liberal consensus"', *Journal of Democracy* 27/1 (2016).

De Grauwe, P., G. Magnus, T. Mayer and H. Schmieding, *The Future of Europe's Economy: Disaster or Deliverance?* (London: Centre for European Reform, September 2013).

de Vries, C., and I. Hoffmann, *What Do the People Want? Opinions, Moods and Preferences of European Citizens*, EUpinions no. 2015/1 (Gütersloh: Bertelsmann Stiftung, 2015).

———— *Border Protection and Freedom of Movement: What People Expect of European Asylum and Migration Policies*, EUpinions no. 2016/1 (Gütersloh: Bertelsmann Stiftung, 2016).

———— *Fear Not Values: Public Opinion and the Populist Vote in Europe*, EUpinions no. 2016/3 (Gütersloh: Bertelsmann Stiftung, November 2016).

———— *Supportive but Wary: How Europeans Feel about the EU 60 Years after the Treaty of Rome*, EUpinions no. 2017/1 (Gütersloh: Bertelsmann Stiftung, March 2017).

Delanty, G., 'Europe's nemesis? European integration and the contradictions of capitalism and democracy', in S. Champeau, C. Closa, D. Innerarity and M.

Poaires Maduro (eds), *The Future of Europe: Democracy, Legitimacy and Justice after the Euro Crisis* (London: Rowman & Littlefield International, 2015).

della Porta, D., *Can Democracy Be Saved?* (Cambridge: Polity Press, 2013).

—— *Mobilizing for Democracy: Comparing 1989 and 2011* (Oxford: Oxford University Press, 2014).

¡Democracia real YA!, 'Manifesto', ¡Democracia real YA! [website] (2017).

Democratic Participation in a Citizens' Europe: What Next for the EU? [conference report, University of Liverpool, 5 May 2016].

DiEM25, *European New Deal* (DiEM25, 2017).

Dryzek, J., *Global Deliberative Politics* (Cambridge: Polity Press, 2006).

Dupouey, V., A. Najmowicz and J. Oldfield, *A State of Democracy: Towards Citizen Rights Protection in the EU* (Paris: European Civic Forum, 2015).

Dworkin, A., *Europe's New Counter-Terror Wars* (London: European Council on Foreign Relations, October 2016).

Eder, F., 'The two-presidents Europe', Politico [website] (14 September 2016).

Elliott, L., and J. Treanor, 'Dutch PM says refugee crisis could shut down Europe's open borders for good', *Guardian* (21 January 2016).

Emmanouilidis, J. A. (ed.), *Towards a New Pact for Europe* (Brussels: King Baudouin Foundation, the Bertelsmann Stiftung and the European Policy Centre, October 2014).

Emmanouilidis, J. A., and F. Zuleeg, *EU@60 – Countering a Regressive and Illiberal Europe* (Brussels: European Policy Centre, October 2016).

Emmanouilidis, J. A., et al., *The 2017 Elections across Europe: Facts, Expectations and Consequences* (Brussels: European Policy Centre, 14 March 2017).

'Europe's desperate deal with Turkey on migrants', *Financial Times* (30 November 2015).

European Association for Local Democracy, *DEmocratic Compact: Improving Democracy in Europe* (European Association for Local Democracy, 2015).

European Civic Forum, *Plan C pour l'Europe* (Paris: European Civic Forum, 2014).

European Commission, *A New EU Framework to Strengthen the Rule of Law*, COM(2014)158 (Brussels: European Commission, 19 March 2014).

—— *Better Regulation and Transparency* (Brussels: European Commission, 2016).

—— *Back to Schengen – A Roadmap*, COM(2016)120 (Brussels: European Commission, 4 March 2016).

—— *First Progress Report on the Partnership Framework with Third Countries under the European Agenda on Migration*, COM(2016)700 (Brussels: European Commission, 18 October 2016).

—— *Special Eurobarometer 451: Future of Europe* (Brussels: European Commission, Directorate-General for Communication, December 2016).

—— *EU Citizenship Report 2017* (Luxembourg: Publications Office of the European Union, 2017).

—— *Country Report Spain 2017*, SWD(2017)74 (Brussels: European Commission, 22 February 2017).

—— *White Paper on the Future of Europe*, COM(2017)2025 (Brussels: European Commission, 1 March 2017).

—— *Reflection Paper on the Deepening of the Economic and Monetary Union*, COM(2017)291 (Brussels: European Commission, 31 May 2017).

——— *Launching the European Defence Fund*, COM(2017)295 (Brussels: European Commission, 7 June 2017).

European Commission and High Representative for Foreign Affairs and Security Policy, *Elements for an EU-Wide Strategic Framework to Support Security Sector Reform*, JOIN(2016)31 (Strasbourg: European Commission, 5 July 2016).

European Council, *Bratislava Declaration and Roadmap* (Bratislava: European Council, 16 September 2016).

——— 'The Rome Declaration', European Council [website] (25 March 2017).

European Court of Auditors, *Financial Assistance Provided to Countries in Difficulties*, Special Report no. 18 (Luxembourg: European Court of Auditors, 2015).

European External Action Service, *Shared Vision, Common Action: A Stronger Europe: A Global Strategy for the European Union's Foreign and Security Policy* (Brussels: European External Action Service, June 2016).

European Movement International, *Resolution on the Transnationalisation of European Democracy and the Innovation of the European Political System* (Rome: European Movement International, 2014).

European Parliament Budgetary Committee, *Democratic Accountability and Budgetary Control of Non-Governmental Organisations Funded by the EU Budget* (Brussels: European Union, 2016).

European Parliament, *Major Trends in European Public Opinion with Regards to the European Union* [European Parliament document, 2015].

European Political Strategy Centre (EPSC), *Towards a 'Security Union': Bolstering the EU's Counter-Terrorism Response*, EPSC Strategic Notes no. 12 (Brussels: European Political Strategy Centre, 20 April 2016).

European Youth Press, *Shaping Europe: 50 Ideas for a Better Future* [report of the European Youth Event, Strasbourg, 2016].

Fabbrini, S., 'The euro crisis and its constitutional implications', in S. Champeau, C. Closa, D. Innerarity and M. Poaires Maduro (eds), *The Future of Europe: Democracy, Legitimacy and Justice after the Euro Crisis* (London: Rowman & Littlefield International, 2015).

——— *Which European Union? Europe after the Euro Crisis* (Cambridge: Cambridge University Press, 2015).

Fazi, T., *The Battle for Europe: How an Elite Hijacked a Continent and How We Can Take It Back* (London: Pluto Press, 2014).

Ferrin, M., and H. Kriesi, *Europeans' Understandings and Evaluations of Democracy: Topline Results from Round 6 of the European Social Survey*, ESS Topline Results Series no. 4 (London: European Social Survey, 2014).

Foa, R., and Y. Mounk, 'The democratic disconnect', *Journal of Democracy* 27/3 (2016).

Fossum, J., 'Democracy and differentiation in Europe', *Journal of European Public Policy* 22/6 (2015).

——— *Democracy and Legitimacy in the EU: Challenges and Options*, IAI Working Papers 16/01 (Rome: Istituto Affari Internazionali, February 2016).

Fries-Tersch, E., T. Tugran and H. Bradley, *2016 Annual Report on Intra-EU Labour Mobility* (Brussels: European Commission, 2016).

FutureLab Europe, *Bring Back the Citizens! How to Revive Democracy for a Citizens-Led Europe* (Brussels: FutureLab Europe, April 2016).

———— *Reviving Democracy for a Citizens-Led Europe* (Brussels: FutureLab Europe, 2016).

García-Margallo, J. M., 'Pase lo que pase, más Europa', *El País* (23 June 2016).

Garicano, L., 'Europe inches closer to a plan for fixing its financial flaws', *The Economist* (2 June 2017).

Garton Ash, T., 'Europe's walls are going back up – it's like 1989 in reverse', *Guardian* (29 November 2015).

Gaston, S., et al., *Nothing to Fear but Fear Itself?* (London: Demos, 2016).

Genschel, P., and M. Jachtenfuchs, 'More integration, less federation: the European integration of core state powers', *Journal of European Public Policy* 23/1 (2016).

Gherghina, S., and A. Groh, 'A poor sales pitch? The European citizens' initiative and attitudes toward the EU in Germany and the UK', *European Politics and Society* 17/3 (2016).

Giddens, A., *Turbulent and Mighty Continent: What Future for Europe?* (Cambridge: Polity Press, 2014).

Gillingham, J. R., *The EU: An Obituary* (New York: Verso, 2016).

Ginsborg, P., *Democracy: Crisis and Renewal* (London: Profile Books, 2008).

Goodwin, M., T. Raines and D. Cotts, 'What do Europeans think about Muslim immigration?', Chatham House [website] (2017).

Gostyńska-Jakubowska, A., *The Role of National Parliaments in the EU: Building or Stumbling Blocks?* (London: Centre for European Reform, June 2016).

Grabbe, H., and S. Lehne, 'Emotional intelligence for EU democracy', Carnegie Europe [website] (26 January 2015).

———— 'Can the EU survive populism?', Carnegie Europe [website] (14 June 2016).

Grey, S., *The New Spymasters* (London: Penguin, 2016).

Gros, D., 'The silent death of eurozone governance', Project Syndicate [website] (2016).

Grygiel, J., 'The return of Europe's nation-states', *Foreign Affairs* (September/October 2016).

Guéhenno, J.-M., chapter 10, in A. Missiroli et al., *Towards an EU Global Strategy – Consulting the Experts* (Paris: European Union Institute for Security Studies, 2016).

Guérot, U., *Warum Europa eine Republik werden muss!* (Bonn: Verlag J. H. W. Dietz Nachf., 2016).

Habermas, J., *The Crisis of the European Union* (Cambridge: Polity Press, 2012).

Hall, P. A., 'The euro crisis and the future of European integration', in BBVA, *The Search of Europe: Contrasting Approaches* (Madrid: BBVA, 2016).

Heads of state and government of the Republic of Cyprus, France, Greece, Italy, Malta, Portugal and Spain, 'Athens declaration of the 1st Mediterranean EU countries' summit' (9 September 2016). Available at http://www.topontiki.gr/sites/default/files/declaration_athens_summit.pdf.

Held, D., and G. Schott, *Models of Democracy* (Palo Alto, CA: Stanford University Press, 1996).

Hellmann, G., 'Germany's world: power and followership in a crisis-ridden Europe', *Global Affairs* 2/1 (2016).

Herszenhorn, D., J. Barigazzi and G. Ariès, 'Europe confronts limitations at year-end summit', Politico [website] (16 December 2016).

Hilmer, R., *The European Union Facing Massive Challenges – What are Citizens' Expectations and Concerns?* (Berlin: International Policy Analysis, 2016).

Hix, S., *What's Wrong with the European Union and How to Fix It* (Cambridge: Polity Press, 2008).

―――― 'Democratizing a macroeconomic union in Europe', in O. Cramme and S. Hobolt, *Democratic Politics in a European Union under Stress* (Oxford: Oxford University Press, 2015).

Hobson, C., D. Hodson and U. Puetter, 'The new intergovernmentalism: European integration in the post-Maastricht era', *Journal of Common Market Studies* 53/4 (2015).

Hoeksma, J., *EU and EMU: Beyond the 2005–2014 Crises Decade*, DSF Policy Paper no. 51 (Amsterdam: Duisenberg School of Finance, April 2015).

―――― *From Common Market to Common Democracy: A Theory of Democratic Integration* (Oisterwijk: Wolf Legal Publishers, 2016).

Houellebecq, M., *Soumission* (Paris: Flammarion, 2015).

House of Commons Home Affairs Committee, *Migration Crisis: Seventh Report of Session 2016–17*, HC 24 (3 August 2016).

Hutter, S., E. Grande and H. Kriesi (eds), *Politicising Europe: Integration and Mass Politics* (Cambridge: Cambridge University Press, 2016).

Inglehart, R., and P. Norris, *Trump, Brexit, and the Rise of Populism: Economic Have-Nots and Cultural Backlash*, HKS working paper RWP16-026 (Harvard Kennedy School, August 2016).

Innerarity, D., 'Transnational self-determination: resetting self-government in the age of interdependence', *Journal of Common Market Studies* 53/5 (2015).

―――― 'What must be democratized? The European Union as a complex democracy', in S. Champeau, C. Closa, D. Innerarity and M. Poaires Maduro (eds), *The Future of Europe: Democracy, Legitimacy and Justice after the Euro Crisis* (London: Rowman & Littlefield International, 2015).

International Crisis Group, 'The Libyan political agreement: time for a reset', International Crisis Group [website] (4 November 2016).

International Monetary Fund, *IMF Annual Report 2016: Finding Solutions Together* (Washington DC: International Monetary Fund, 2016).

Ioannou, D., P. Leblond and A. Niemann, 'European integration and the crisis: practice and theory', *Journal of European Public Policy* 22/2 (2015).

Isin, E., and M. Saward, *Enacting European Citizenship* (Cambridge: Cambridge University Press, 2013).

Jackson, G., and R. Deeg, 'The long-term trajectories of institutional change in European capitalism', *Journal of European Public Policy* 19/8 (2012).

Janning, J. (ed.), *Keeping Europeans Together: Assessing the State of EU Cohesion* (London: European Council on Foreign Relations, 2016).

Jenkins, S., 'London's MPs have the power to change the course of Brexit', *Guardian* (16 June 2017).

Jones, E., 'The euro: irreversible or conditional?', *Survival* 57/5 (2015).

Judis, J. B., 'Us v them: the birth of populism', *Guardian* (13 October 2016).

―――― *The Populist Explosion: How the Great Recession Transformed American and European Politics* (New York: Columbia Global Reports, 2016).

Judt, T., *A Grand Illusion? An Essay on Europe* (New York: New York University Press, 2011).

Juncker, J.-C., et al., *Completing Europe's Economic and Monetary Union* (Brussels: European Commission, 2015).

Kaldor, M., S. Selchow, S. Deel and T. Murray-Leach, *The 'Bubbling Up' of Subterranean Politics in Europe* (London: Civil Society and Human Security Research Unit, London School of Economics and Political Science, 2012).

Keane, J., *The Life and Death of Democracy* (New York: Simon & Schuster, 2009).

Keleman, R. D., 'The EU's other democratic deficit: national authoritarianism in Europe's democratic union', *Government and Opposition* 52/2 (2017).

Kepel, G., *Terror in France: The Rise of Jihad in the West* (Princeton: Princeton University Press, 2016).

Khanna, A., 'Seeing citizen action through an "unruly" lens', *Development* 55/2 (2012).

Kingsley, P., *The New Odyssey: The Story of Europe's Refugee Crisis* (London: Faber, 2016).

Kinnvall, C., 'The postcolonial has moved into Europe: bordering, security and ethno-cultural belonging', *Journal of Common Market Studies* 54/1 (2016).

Kissinger, H., *World Order* (London: Penguin, 2014)/

Koenig, N., *A Differentiated View of Differentiated Integration* (Berlin: Jacques Delors Institute, 23 July 2015).

Krastev, I., *Democracy Disrupted: The Politics of Global Protest* (Philadelphia: University of Pennsylvania Press, 2014).

—— 'Eight visions for Europe' [video on Forum on European Culture website, 2016].

——*After Europe* (Philadelphia: University of Pennsylvania Press, 2017).

Kundnani, H., *The Paradox of German Power* (New York: Oxford University Press, 2014).

——*How Economic Dependence Could Undermine Europe's Foreign Policy Coherence* (Washington DC: German Marshall Fund, January 2016).

'La sécurité', Elabe [website] (3 November 2016).

Labeye, E., and S. Smit, '"The Europe we want!": here's how Europe's policymakers should seize on their window of opportunity', *Europe's World* 31 (Autumn 2015).

Laffan, B., 'Birthday wishes to the European Union', EUObserver [website] (24 March 2017).

Lanchester, J., 'Brexit blues', *London Review of Books* 38/15 (28 July 2016).

Lavenex, S., 'On the fringes of the European peace project: the neighbourhood policy's functionalist hubris and political myopia', *British Journal of Politics and International Relations* 19/1 (2016).

Legrain, P., 'The disintegration of Europe', Project Syndicate [website] (19 October 2015).

Lehne, S., 'Are referenda blocking the EU's progress?', Carnegie Europe [website] (18 November 2015).

—— 'How the refugee crisis will reshape the EU', Carnegie Europe [website] (2016).

Leonard, M., chapter 8, in A. Missiroli et al., *Towards an EU Global Strategy – Consulting the Experts* (Paris: European Union Institute for Security Studies, 2016).

—— 'The migration superpowers', Project Syndicate [website] (20 April 2016).

——— 'Europe seen from the outside – the British view', European Council on Foreign Relations [website] (4 August 2016).

Leruth, B., 'Operationalizing national preferences on Europe and differentiated integration', *Journal of European Public Policy* 22/6 (2015).

Leuffen, D., B. Rittberger and F. Schimmelfennig, *Differentiated Integration: Explaining Variation in the European Union* (London: Palgrave Macmillan, 2012).

Lévy, B.-H., 'SOS Europa', *El País* (7 March 2016).

Liddle, R., 'The political economy of the single market', in L. Tsoukalis and J. Emmanouilidis (eds), *The Delphic Oracle on Europe: Is There a Future for the European Union?* (New York: Oxford University Press, 2011).

Lippert, B., and N. von Ondarza, *Brexiting into Uncharted Waters*, SWP Comments 35 (Berlin: Stiftung Wissenschaft und Politik, July 2016).

LSE Commission on the Future of Britain in Europe, *The UK's Democratic Moment on Europe?* (London: LSE European Institute, 2016).

McCormick, J., *Europeanism* (New York: Oxford University Press, 2010).

McNamara, K., '*JCMS* annual review lecture: imagining Europe: the cultural foundations of EU governance', *Journal of Common Market Studies* 53/S1 (2015).

Magen, A., 'Cracks in the foundations: understanding the great rule of law debate in the EU', *Journal of Common Market Studies* 54/5 (2016).

Majone, G., *Rethinking the Union of Europe Post-Crisis: Has Integration Gone Too Far?* (Cambridge: Cambridge University Press, 2014).

Manent, P., *Democracy without Nations: The Fate of Self-Government in Europe* (Wilmington, DE: ISI Books, 2013).

Manners, I., and P. Murray, 'The end of a noble narrative? European integration narratives after the Nobel Peace Prize', *Journal of Common Market Studies* 54/1 (2016).

Manners, I., and R. Whitman, 'Another theory is possible: dissident voices in theorising Europe', *Journal of Common Market Studies* 54/1 (2016).

Marsh, D., *Europe's Deadlock: How the Euro Crisis Could Be Solved – And Why It Still Won't Happen* (New Haven, CT: Yale University Press, 2016).

Marsili, L., and B. Spinelli, 'Reclaiming Europe from the powers that be: an interview with Barbara Spinelli MEP', openDemocracy [website] (3 August 2016).

Martinico, G., *A Multi-Speed EU? An Institutional and Legal Assessment*, IAI Working Papers 15/48 (Rome: Istituto Affari Internazionali, December 2015).

Maxwell, R., 'Cultural diversity and its limits in Western Europe', *Current History* 115/779 (March 2016).

Mayer, M., and M. Mehregani, 'Beyond crisis management: the path towards an effective, pro-active and fair European refugee policy', in *Vision Europe Summit: Improving the Responses to the Migration and Refugee Crisis in Europe* (Lisbon: Vision Europe/Bertelsmann Stiftung, November 2016).

Mazower, M., 'What remains: on the European Union', *The Nation* (5 September 2012).
——— 'Lessons from the past are key to Europe's survival', *Financial Times* (22 January 2016).

Merritt, G., *Slippery Slope: Europe's Troubled Future* (New York: Oxford University Press, 2016).

Mishra, P., *The Age of Anger: A History of the Present* (London: Allen Lane, 2017).

Möller, A., 'The end of Europakonsens?', European Council on Foreign Relations [website] (14 January 2016).

Möller, A., and D. Pardijs, *The Future Shape of Europe: How the EU Can Bend Without Breaking* (London: European Council on Foreign Relations, March 2016).

Monbiot, G., 'This is how people can truly take back control: from the bottom up', *Guardian* (8 February 2017).

Moravcsik, A., 'Europe after the crisis: how to sustain a common currency', *Foreign Affairs* (May/June 2012).

———— 'Europe is still a superpower', *Foreign Affairs* (March/April 2017).

Morillas, P., 'Año de tránsito para la (de)construcción europea', *El País* (10 February 2016).

———— *Shapes of a Union: From Ever Closer Union to Flexible Differentiation after Brexit* (Barcelona: CIDOB, 2017).

———— (ed.), *Illiberal Democracies in the EU: The Visegrad Group and the Risk of Disintegration* (Barcelona: CIDOB, 2017).

Mortera-Martinez, C., and C. Odendahl, *What Free Movement Means to Europe and Why It Matters for Britain* (London: Centre for European Reform, January 2017).

Mudde, C., 'Europe's populist surge: a long time in the making', *Foreign Affairs* (November/December 2016).

Müller, J.-W., 'Rule-breaking', *London Review of Books* 37/16 (August 2015).

———— 'The EU's democratic deficit and the public sphere', *Current History* 115/779 (March 2016).

———— *What Is Populism?* (Philadelphia: University of Pennsylvania Press, 2016).

Münchau, W., 'Europe enters the age of disintegration', *Financial Times* (28 February 2016).

Mungiu-Pippidi, A., 'European trust: the perfect storm', openDemocracy [website] (15 October 2015).

Munin, N., 'The Five Presidents' Report: the dogs bark but the caravan moves on?', *European Politics and Society* 17/3 (2016).

Murray, D., *The Strange Death of Europe* (London: Bloomsbury, 2017).

Neblo, M., *Deliberative Democracy between Theory and Practice* (Cambridge: Cambridge University Press, 2015).

Neumann, P., *Radicalized: New Jihadists and the Threat to the West* (London: I.B.Tauris, 2016).

Nicolaïdis, K., 'We, the peoples of Europe', *Foreign Affairs* (November/December 2004).

———— '*JCMS* annual review lecture: sustainable integration: towards EU 2.0?', *Journal of Common Market Studies* 48 (2010).

———— 'European demoicracy and its crisis', *Journal of Common Market Studies* 51/2 (2013).

———— 'Demoicratic theory and Europe's institutional architecture in times of crisis', in S. Piattoni (ed.), *The European Union: Democratic Principles and Institutional Architectures in Times of Crisis* (Oxford: Oxford University Press, 2015).

Nicolaïdis, K., and R. Youngs, 'Europe's democracy trilemma', *International Affairs* 90/6 (November 2014).

Nielsen, N., 'Balkan states to introduce more anti-migrant controls', EUObserver [website] (9 February 2017).

Norris, P., *Is Western Democracy Backsliding? Diagnosing the Risks*, HKS working paper RWP17-012 (Harvard Kennedy School, March 2017).

Nozick, R., *Anarchy, State, and Utopia* (New York: Basic Books, 1974).

Nuttall, T., 'Looking for a home', *The Economist* (28 May 2016).

Odendahl, C., *We Don't Need No Federation: What a Devolved Eurozone Should Look Like* (London: Centre for European Reform, December 2015).

Omand, D., 'Keeping Europe safe: counterterrorism for the continent', *Foreign Affairs* (September/October 2016).

Otero-Iglesias, M., 'Still waiting for Paris: Germany's reluctant hegemony in pursuing political union in the euro area', *Journal of European Integration* 39/3 (2017).

Palmeri, T., 'Ministers of "core" Europe plan EU's future', Politico [website] (8 February 2016).

Papastergiadis, N., 'Transversal cultural spheres and the future of Europe', openDemocracy [website] (22 February 2016).

Pappas, T., 'Distinguishing liberal democracy's challengers', *Journal of Democracy* 27/4 (2016).

'Para una nueva Europa', *El País* (9 May 2016).

Parker, O., *Cosmopolitan Government in Europe* (London: Routledge, 2012).

Parker, S., *Taking Power Back: Putting People in Charge of Politics* (Bristol: Policy Press, 2015).

Parkes, R., *The EU as a Terrorist Target: Why, Where and How*, ISS Brief no. 16 (Paris: European Union Institute for Security Studies, May 2016).

——— *People on the Move: The New Global (Dis)order*, Chaillot Papers no. 138 (Paris: European Union Institute for Security Studies, June 2016).

Peet, J., and A. La Guardia, *Unhappy Union: How the Euro Crisis – and Europe – Can Be Fixed* (London: Economist/Profile Books, 2014).

Pertusot, V. (ed.), *The European Union in the Fog: Building Bridges between National Perspectives on the European Union* (Paris: Institut français des relations internationales, 2016).

Pessoa, F., *The Book of Disquiet* (London: Profile Books, 1991).

Peterson, J., 'Juncker's political European Commission and an EU in crisis', *Journal of Common Market Studies* 55/2 (2017).

Phinnemore, D., 'Crisis-ridden, battered and bruised: time to give up on the EU?', *Journal of Common Market Studies* 53/S1 (2015).

Piris, J. C., *The Future of Europe: Towards a Two-speed EU?* (New York: Cambridge University Press, 2012).

Pirro, A. L. P., and S. van Kessel, 'United in opposition? The populist radical right's EU-pessimism in times of crisis', *Journal of European Integration* 39/4 (2017).

Polletta, F., 'Participatory enthusiasms: a recent history of citizen engagement initiatives', *Journal of Civil Society* 12/3 (2016).

Polyakova, A., and N. Fligstein, 'Is European integration causing Europe to become more nationalist? Evidence from the 2007–9 financial crisis', *Journal of European Public Policy* 23/1 (2016).

'Portugal has announced the world's first nationwide participatory budget: plans for voting via ATM machines to massively boost turnout', Apolitical [website] (27 October 2016).

Raines, T., M. Goodwin and D. Cutts, *The Future of Europe: Comparing Public and Elite Attitudes* (London: Chatham House, June 2017).

Ramm, B., 'Are the people good enough?', openDemocracy [website] (16 January 2017).

Raunio, T., 'The role of national legislatures in EU politics', in O. Cramme and S. Hobolt, *Democratic Politics in a European Union under Stress* (Oxford: Oxford University Press, 2015).

Reinares, F., 'Prevenir la radicalización yihadista: un fracaso europeo', Elcano Blog [website] (14 April 2016).

Risse, T., *A Community of Europeans? Transnational Identities and Public Spheres* (Ithaca, NY: Cornell University Press, 2010).

Rodrik, D., 'Rethinking democracy', Project Syndicate [website] (11 June 2014).

Rosamond, B., 'Field of dreams: the discursive construction of EU studies, intellectual dissidence and the practice of "normal science"', *Journal of Common Market Studies* 54/1 (2016).

Rosanvallon, P., *Counter-Democracy: Politics in an Age of Distrust* (New York: Cambridge University Press, 2008).

Rose, R., and G. Borz, 'Aggregation and representation in European Parliament party groups', *West European Politics* 36/3 (2013).

—— 'Static and dynamic views of European integration', *Journal of Common Market Studies* 54/2 (2016).

Roy, O., *Jihad and Death: The Global Appeal of Islamic State* (Oxford: Oxford University Press, 2017).

Rudloff, B., and E. Schmieg, *European Disintegration: Too Much to Lose*, SWP Comments 21 (Berlin: Stiftung Wissenschaft und Politik, April 2016).

Rush, N., 'Europeans' hardening stands following the migrant crisis', Center for Immigration Studies [website] (18 April 2016).

Sanchez Salgado, R., *Europeanizing Civil Society: How the EU Shapes Civil Society Organizations* (London: Palgrave Macmillan, 2014).

Saward, M., *Democracy* (Cambridge: Polity Press, 2003).

Scharpf, F., 'Political legitimacy in a non-optimal currency area', in O. Cramme and S. Hobolt, *Democratic Politics in a European Union under Stress* (Oxford: Oxford University Press, 2015).

Scherer, M., 'United by reformation: British and northern European Euroscepticism is rooted in religious history', LSE British Politics and Policy [blog] (9 October 2015).

Schimmelfennig, F., 'The normative origins of democracy in the European Union: toward a transformationalist theory of democratization', *European Political Science Review* 2/2 (2010).

—— 'Differentiated integration before and after the crisis', in O. Cramme and S. Hobolt, *Democratic Politics in a European Union under Stress* (Oxford: Oxford University Press, 2015).

—— 'Liberal intergovernmentalism and the euro area crisis', *Journal of European Public Policy* 22/2 (2015).

—— 'What's the news in "new intergovernmentalism"? A critique of Bickerton, Hodson and Puetter', *Journal of Common Market Studies* 53/4 (2015).

Schimmelfennig, F., D. Leuffen and B. Rittberger, 'The European Union as a system of differentiated integration: interdependence, politicization and differentiation', *Journal of European Public Policy* 22/6 (2015).

Schmidt, V., *Democracy in Europe: The EU and National Politics* (New York: Oxford University Press, 2006).

Schmidt, V., and M. Wood, 'The EU's new white paper underlines why Europe needs to be more open to its citizens', LSE Europp [blog] (10 Match 2017).

Schweiger, C., *Exploring the EU's Legitimacy Crisis* (Cheltenham: Edward Elgar, 2016).

Sicakkan, H., 'The role of EU policies in the making of a European public sphere', in H. Sicakkan (ed.), *Integration, Diversity and the Making of a European Public Sphere* (Cheltenham: Edward Elgar, 2016).

Siedentop, L., *Democracy in Europe* (London: Penguin, 2000).

Simms, B., 'Towards a mighty union: how to create a democratic European superpower', *International Affairs* 88/1 (2012).

––––––– *Europe: The Struggle for Supremacy: 1453 to the Present* (London: Penguin, 2013).

Smits, R., F. Molenaar, F. El-Kamouni-Janssen and N. Grinstead, *Cultivating Conflict and Violence? A Conflict Perspective on the EU Approach to the Syrian Refugee Crisis* (The Hague: Clingendael Conflict Research Unit, August 2016).

Stiglitz, J., *Freefall: Free Markets and the Sinking of the Global Economy* (London: Penguin, 2010).

––––––– 'A split euro is the solution for the single currency', *Financial Times* (17 August 2016).

––––––– *The Euro and Its Threat to the Future of Europe* (London: Allen Lane, 2017).

Stokes, B., *Euroskepticism beyond Brexit* (Washington DC: Pew Research Center, 7 June 2016).

Stokes, B., R. Wike and D. Manevich, 'Post-Brexit, Europeans more favorable toward EU', Pew Research Center [website] (15 June 2017).

Stokes, B., R. Wike and J. Poushter, *Europeans Face the World Divided* (Washington DC: Pew Research Center, 13 June 2016).

Streeck, W., *Exploding Europe: Germany, the Refugees and the British Vote to Leave*, Speri Paper no. 31 (Sheffield: Sheffield Political Economy Research Institute, September 2016).

Taggart, P., and C. Rovira Kaltwasser, 'Dealing with populists in government: some comparative conclusions', *Democratization* 23/2 (2016).

Tassinari, F., 'Scandinavia's real lessons', *Foreign Affairs* [website] (27 October 2015).

––––––– 'All for none, and none for all: life in a broken Europe', *Foreign Affairs* (13 January 2016).

Teffer, P., 'Merkel: euro and open borders "directly linked"', EUObserver [website] (12 January 2016).

Toaldo, M., *Intervening Better: Europe's Second Chance in Libya* (London: European Council on Foreign Relations, 13 May 2016).

Tormey, S., *The End of Representative Politics* (Cambridge: Polity Press, 2015).

Tsoukalis, L., 'The Delphic oracle on Europe', in L. Tsoukalis and J. Emmanouilidis (eds), *The Delphic Oracle on Europe: Is There a Future for the European Union?* (New York: Oxford University Press, 2011).

───── *In Defence of Europe: Can the European Project be Saved?* (New York: Oxford University Press, 2016).

Tusk, D., 'Letter from President Donald Tusk before the Bratislava summit', European Council press release 511/16 (13 September 2016).

Ulgen, S., chapter 17, in A. Missiroli et al., *Towards an EU Global Strategy – Consulting the Experts* (Paris: European Union Institute for Security Studies, 2016).

Urban, M., 'A perfect storm of populism', BBC News [website] (26 December 2015).

Valls, M., 'The Brexit vote pushes EU to refine itself', *Financial Times* (12 October 2016).

van der Veer, H., and S. Otjes, 'Can only Eurosceptics oppose austerity? How divisions over integration have replaced left/right divisions in the European Parliament', LSE Europp [blog] (24 March 2016).

van Middelaar, L., 'Protect and survive', *Europe's World* (autumn 2016).

Van Reybrouck, D., *Against Elections: The Case for Democracy* (London: Bodley Head, 2016).

Varoufakis, Y., *And the Weak Suffer What They Must? Europe, Austerity and the Threat to Global Stability* (London: Bodley Head, 2016).

───── (interviewed by Michel Feher), 'Europe and the specter of democracy', *Near Futures Online* 1 (March 2016).

───── 'Why we must save the EU', *Guardian* (5 April 2016).

Varoufakis, Y., and A. Sakaris, '"One very simple, but radical, idea: to democratise Europe." An interview with Yanis Varoufakis', openDemocracy [website] (25 October 2015).

Vimont, P., 'Migration in Europe: bridging the solidarity gap', Carnegie Europe [website] (12 September 2016).

von Ondarza, N., *Blocked for Good by the Threat of Treaty Change? Perspectives for Reform in the European Union*, SWP Comments 50 (Berlin: Stiftung Wissenschaft und Politik, November 2015).

Wallace, P., *The Euro Experiment* (Cambridge: Cambridge University Press, 2016).

Watts, C., 'The Islamic State in Europe: terrorists without borders, counterterrorists with all borders', War on the Rocks [website] (29 March 2016).

Weber, B., *Time for a Plan B: The European Refugee Crisis, the Balkan Route and the EU–Turkey Deal* (Berlin: Democratization Policy Council, September 2016).

Wike, R., B. Stokes and K. Simmons, 'Europeans fear wave of refugees will mean more terrorism, fewer jobs', Pew Research Center [website] (11 July 2016).

Wilding, P., *What Next? Britain's Future in Europe* (London: I.B.Tauris, 2017).

Wilkinson, A., M. Mayer and V. Ringler, 'Collaborative futures: integrating foresight with design in large scale innovation processes – seeing and seeding the futures of Europe', *Journal of Future Studies* 18/4 (2014).

Wilson, P., 'The Holy Roman Empire can help inspire a different European Union', *Financial Times* (20 January 2016).

Youngs, R., 'European liberal power as a two-way street', Carnegie Europe [website] (17 May 2016).

Zalan, E., 'EU leaders to define new priorities in Bratislava', EUObserver [website] (6 September 2016).

───── 'Juncker: EU "not at risk" of disintegration', EUObserver [website] (14 September 2016).

Zielonka, J., *Is the EU Doomed?* (Cambridge: Polity Press, 2014).

——— 'Legitimacy in a neomedieval (postcrisis) Europe', in S. Champeau, C. Closa, D. Innerarity and M. Poaires Maduro (eds), *The Future of Europe: Democracy, Legitimacy and Justice after the Euro Crisis* (London: Rowman & Littlefield International, 2015).

Žižek, S., *The Year of Dreaming Dangerously* (London: Verso, 2012).

Index